M

Understanding Emerson

Understanding Emerson

"THE AMERICAN SCHOLAR" AND HIS
STRUGGLE FOR SELF-RELIANCE

Kenneth S. Sacks

PRINCETON UNIVERSITY PRESS

PRINCETON AND OXFORD

Copyright © 2003 by Princeton University Press
Published by Princeton University Press, 41 William Street,
Princeton, New Jersey 08540
In the United Kingdom: Princeton University Press,
3 Market Place, Woodstock, Oxfordshire OX20 1SY

The text of "The American Scholar" reprinted in the appendix is taken from
Transcendentalism: A Reader, edited by Joel Myerson, copyright © Oxford University
Press, 2000, and is reprinted by permission granted by Oxford University Press, Inc.

Sacks, Kenneth.
Understanding Emerson: "The American scholar" and his struggle for self-reliance /
Kenneth S. Sacks.
p.cm.
Includes bibliographical references and index.
ISBN 0-691-09982-0 (cl.: alk. paper)
1. Emerson, Ralph Waldo, 1803–1882. American scholar. 2. Emerson, Ralph Waldo,
1803–1882—Knowledge and learning. 3. United States—Intellectual life—19th century.
4. Learning and scholarship in literature. 5. Self-reliance. I. Title.
PS1615.A84 S23 2003
814'.dc21   2002075963

British Library Cataloging-in-Publication Data is available

This book has been composed in Sabon and Woodtype Ornament

Printed on acid-free paper. ∞

www.pupress.princeton.edu

Printed in the United States of America

1 3 5 7 9 10 8 6 4 2

If the light come to our eyes, we see; else not. And if truth come to our mind, we suddenly expand to its dimensions, as if we grew to worlds. We are as lawgivers; we speak for Nature; we prophesy and divine. This insight throws us on the party and interest of the Universe, against all and sundry; against ourselves, as much as others.
—*Ralph Waldo Emerson, "Fate"*

CONTENTS

LIST OF ILLUSTRATIONS

I FIRST WAS DRAWN TO "THE AMERICAN SCHOLAR"—IN THE
spirit of an old academic joke—because, after discussing the talk with Phi
Beta Kappa initiates, I decided I had better read it again. And when I
did, I found Emerson's words both personally inspiring and hauntingly
appropriate to contemporary higher education. As a classical historian, I
also began to appreciate the significance of Transcendentalism, a modern
interpretation of Stoic and Neoplatonic thought, not only to me, but to
students. What could be better in challenging young adults who struggle
with conformity and individuality? But it was a sense that there was more
to his life than appears in Emerson's essays and speeches that led me to
follow the trail of Transcendentalism into the archives.

Once there, I became amazed at the depth and richness of the documentary record. Individuals came alive in their correspondence and journals,
revealing themselves more honestly than we, in our tell-all, though tell-
nothing-of-importance world, can fully appreciate. "Cut these words &
they would bleed," Emerson wrote in his diary. Bleed they do, with an
unstemmable passion for expressing life. Though awed by the exuberance,
I soon began to see that Emerson was after all only human. His essays and
orations may have been seminal events in the intellectual life of antebellum
America. But behind the inspiring vision stood an individual who struggled
mightily to live the ideals he espoused. In an age which debunks and denies
heroes, I believe it is essential to appreciate that heroism often lies precisely
in that struggle. When he delivered "The American Scholar," Emerson
tried to live up to himself. In the year in which we celebrate the bicentennial of his birth, that is a tale especially worth telling.

Working outside my field of training was like walking a tightrope: it was
exhilarating so long as I focused on the perch across the way, but I dared

not look down. Many friends and colleagues helped me complete the walk and even assured me that there was a net below. Professors Alfred L. Brophy, Phyllis Cole, Robert Milder, Anne Rose, Nancy Craig Simmons, and Michael Vorenberg generously responded to queries and offered their expertise freely. Knight Edwards and the Brown University chapter of Phi Beta Kappa invited me to talk on my preliminary research, which, in fact, showed me how much I still had to do. Peter Hocking, a fellow Emersonian and Director of the Howard R. Swearer Center for Public Service at Brown, was a constant conversationalist on the project. Professors Paul Boyer, Len Gougeon, Louis Menand, and Joel Myerson carefully worked through the manuscript at various stages. To them, I am especially grateful for suggestions and encouragement. They have saved me from many mistakes of fact, interpretation, and expression; those remaining are mine alone. Joel Myerson not only encouraged my research; far more importantly, by his prodigious scholarship and support of others, he is transforming the study of Transcendentalism. My work could not have been done without his and that of the many colleagues he's inspired, and my admiration for his many contributions is what others have more eloquently expressed elsewhere.[1] That Oxford University Press generously allowed me to reproduce his text of "The American Scholar" only adds to my debt. For assistance and for their extraordinary knowledge of the source material, I am also beholden to the librarians and archivists at the John Hay Library at Brown University, the Houghton Library at Harvard University, the Arthur and Elizabeth Schlesinger Library on the History of Women in America at the Radcliffe Institute for Advanced Study, the Andover-Harvard Theological Library at Harvard University, the Harvard University Archives, the Massachusetts Historical Society, the American Antiquarian Society, the Concord Free Public Library, and the Boston Public Library. Permission to use materials in their collections is also here gratefully acknowledged. Thomas LeBien, formerly of Princeton University Press, was enthusiastic from the moment I approached him, and to him and the entire Press I am deeply grateful for wise counsel and a firm belief in the project. Most importantly, as always, there is Jane. She listened to my rant for three years, encouraged me to take the risk, and read it all—several times—even claiming to like it. Together, we dedicate this book to our parents and our children.

Understanding Emerson

Introduction

WHEN, IN 1932, THE GOVERNING BODY OF PHI BETA KAPPA established a journal, there was little doubt what it would be called. The society named it after the most celebrated academic talk in American history—Ralph Waldo Emerson's Phi Beta Kappa oration, delivered at Harvard ninety-five years earlier. And when that journal, *The American Scholar*, recently adopted a motto, it came just as inevitably from the same Emersonian speech. But readers who enthusiastically endorse the assertion "Life is our dictionary" might be surprised to learn that, only a few months earlier and in a quieter state of mind, Emerson had proposed in his diary, "My garden is my dictionary."[1]

Nature was long Emerson's preoccupation: he had even published an essay of that title the previous year. Yet as the summer of 1837 progressed and as he faced the prospect of delivering his address on the last day of August, Emerson's gaze reluctantly turned from nature to humanity. His closest friends felt under attack by the institution where he was to talk, and he knew they expected him to defend their common beliefs. But despite having high-minded principles, Emerson agonized when putting them into practice. Struggling to maintain his self-reliance while rebuking himself for remaining unengaged, in the end he chose to speak boldly. Life, at that moment, had to be his dictionary.

Misunderstanding and hostility, far more than applause, greeted the talk. After "The American Scholar" and the Divinity School address the following year, it was nearly three decades before Emerson was again invited to speak at Harvard. In the interim, Emerson went from being castigated as a dangerous thinker to being acclaimed as the central figure in American literature and thought. At Harvard, he was to be honored with a Doctorate of Letters, a second invitation to address Phi Beta Kappa, and an appointment as overseer. The university's greatest president, Charles William Eliot, called Emerson the inspiration for his curricular reforms, and its first building devoted to philosophy was named for him and dedicated on the centenary of his birth. "He had not grown more orthodox," explained a close friend, "but opinion had been advancing in his direction." Although both sides of that judgment are only partly true, "The American Scholar" was to become this country's most revered expression of intellectual integrity. In our own time, Harold Bloom has called Emerson "Mr. America," while Alfred Kazin considered him "the father of us all" and wondered, "Where would Emerson find his scholar now?" That has remained, since 1837, a worthy question.[2]

Just as worthy a question, however, is how Emerson came to create his scholar. Among the fine intellectual biographies of Emerson, none examines what turned out to be his difficult and risky decision to deliver the oration. Proclaiming to the world his own journey toward self-reliance, Emerson's essays and speeches convey emotional certainty and lofty ideals. That apparent confidence makes it all too easy to consider these public statements also representative of his innermost thoughts. His private writings, however, suggest something more complex. Along with some four thousand pages of correspondence, the eight thousand pages of his journals, only recently published in full, provide essential insight into the development of his public voice. These personal expressions show Emerson in turmoil at the time of "The American Scholar." They reveal the hesitation and ultimate courage of an insecure intellectual trying to become simultaneously self-reliant and famous.[3]

Emerson is, of course, universally portrayed as the central figure of Transcendentalism—this country's most romanticized religious, philosophical, and literary movement. But in assessing his true place among his peers, their opinions ought to count, too. In recent decades, a trove of letters and diaries has been brought to light. Considered here, along with much that remains unpublished, this testimony indicates that in 1837 Emerson, hardly their leader, was still struggling for his place among Transcendentalists.

The public text that frames Emerson's struggle is "The American Scholar" (the speech is reprinted in the appendix). Despite its extraordinary idealism, the oration speaks directly to humanity. Emerson's audience that day consisted of some two hundred of Boston's elite and therefore, in early-nineteenth-century America, the nation's elite. Most he had known all his life, and he wrote the talk specifically with them in mind. David Robinson has observed of Emerson that "no writer ever needed an audience more, nor assumed an audience more completely." Yet here, in front of lifelong friends, he chastised and intentionally shocked the assembly. The passion the usually soft-spoken Emerson brought to his oration suggests it was precisely that audience at that time that drove him on. The summer following "The American Scholar," at Dartmouth and far away from his Cambridge community, he delivered a similar address. Who has since heard of it?[4]

Beyond an expression of individual idealism, Emerson's remarkable oration represents perhaps the first instance in America of academic debate intended also for public consideration. Founded in support of confessional faith, colleges played the role of churches when they used formal ritual to confirm community values. Emerson held Harvard, the nation's oldest and richest college, not to the standard of confirming values, but to that of investigating them. He was uncompromising in treating the university—despite the strict social conventions of the moment—as an institution that must reject pretense and easy conformity. He demanded that Harvard live up to itself, and he made that demand in front of everyone who counted.

Yet if in taking a stand for friends and principles Emerson believed that he was moving toward greater self-reliance, he was wrong. Despite proclamations of personal freedom, Emerson was beset with anxiety and self-doubt, depending on others and concerned with what they thought of him. And in confronting his own college and community, he was in effect bowing to his own patrimony.

But the tension in those attachments provided much of the fire in the talk and propelled him to greater heights of social awareness. A few months later, and as a result of his oration, he began his long and erratic public struggle against slavery, following soon with a defense of Native American rights and his great attack on organized religion at the Harvard Divinity School. After that, Emerson had to wait twenty-seven years for another invitation to speak at his alma mater. Then, at commencement on July 21, 1865, he was asked to salute the conclusion of the Civil War and the victory of abolitionism, an issue with which he had become increasingly identified (despite the heckling of Harvard students in 1851 as he spoke against slavery in Cambridge). "The American Scholar" was the fountainhead of his engagement with humanity.[5]

The oration also gave him legitimacy of sorts among peers, not in proving that his views were right—for his ideals were too extreme even for most American Transcendentalists—but, much more, in demonstrating that he could finally stand up for his beliefs. It certainly strengthened the admiration of Thomas Carlyle, who rejoiced at reading the speech (Jane Carlyle said that she knew nothing like it "since Schiller went silent"). And that, in turn, led directly to Emerson's great popularity in Europe.[6]

"The American Scholar," then, accounts for much of how Emerson succeeded. The early chapters of this book explain the revolutionary intent of the oration, as Emerson turned his back on tradition and offered an entirely new understanding of what it meant to be an American scholar.

Breaking with the materialism in which he was raised, Emerson proposed an extreme vision of the intellectual who transcends all convention, including the institutions of one's own country, to speak the truth that emerges from within. Colleges, if they are to serve humanity faithfully, must nurture the individual voice. Appearing in one of the most controlled of all academic environments, Emerson challenged its constraints and anticipated by a half-century curricular and pedagogical reforms. The distinguished authority Lawrence A. Cremin believed that "no single figure was more influential in the education of nineteenth-century Americans" than Emerson. But "The American Scholar" ought not be tethered to its historical context. As today's reform becomes tomorrow's convention, we would all do well to ponder the spirit and courage of his eternal vision.[7]

In the end, however, because he labored to become the very scholar he proposed to his audience, the oration is mainly about Emerson himself. In summoning the courage to defy tradition, Emerson overcame, though he could not extinguish, his almost pedestrian feelings of inadequacy. For, having renounced his pulpit largely in pursuit of greater intellectual freedom, Emerson found that as lyceum speaker he continued to compromise his desire to express himself with complete candor. Then, aware that he was failing his friends, Emerson felt compelled to surrender something of his self-reliance and fight a battle others had begun. "The American Scholar," far more direct and forceful than his essays, succeeds so well because its idealism arose out of historical circumstances. And that is the part of the story that merits most attention.

Yet however one interprets "The American Scholar," the fact is, the oration does not make for easy reading. Exhibiting many of Emerson's most notorious quirks (or, to put it kindly, his rhetorical strategies), the talk rambles, rapidly shifts styles, and delights in obscurities. In fact, referred to today with reverence, "The American Scholar" is, I suspect, not well understood. In a world beset by ironic detachment, that is our loss. To approach the talk sympathetically, with a knowledge of Emerson's trials, is to feel his commitment to people and principles, to ideals that matter. What makes the oration great—what ultimately makes Emerson great—is the passion, intensity, and towering integrity. Moments such as that at Harvard in 1837 come rarely to anyone. Confronting so many forces in his life, Emerson triumphed over himself and in that instant set course to become America's scholar.

Chapter One

"THE AMERICAN SCHOLAR"

WHEN EMERSON DELIVERED THE ANNUAL PHI BETA KAPPA address at Harvard, the First Parish Meetinghouse, larger than any campus lecture hall of its day, could barely accommodate the guests. And what important guests they were. The event, according to a contemporary, was "attended generally by a large assembly of the most accomplished and intelligent portions of our community, and not infrequently by distinguished visitors from different parts of the country." That observer might have added that not infrequently it was also attended by distinguished international visitors, for it was a high point of Harvard's commencement. Among the presiding alumni on August 31, 1837, were two of the nation's most prominent public figures, Massachusetts governor Edward Everett and U.S. Supreme Court justice Joseph Story. As was expected of distinguished graduates, both had in previous years delivered their own orations, and they were the powers within the chapter. Famed Unitarian leader William Ellery Channing, who years earlier had modestly declined to speak, understood that addressing Phi Beta Kappa was a singular honor, a *rite de passage*, in the intellectual society of Cambridge and Boston.[1]

Yet Emerson's own speech, the most famous in American academic history, was somewhat of an accident. He had long considered writing on "the Duty and Discipline of a Scholar," but had done nothing on it. Then, a mere two months before the event, he was asked to give the Phi Beta Kappa address in place of Jonathan Mayhew Wainwright, who, for now unknown reasons, could not.[2]

The thirty-four-year-old Waldo Emerson, as he called himself, did not yet own the reputation of most previous Phi Beta Kappa orators. Wain-

Figure 1. First Parish Meetinghouse, where Emerson delivered "The American Scholar." Lithograph by James Kidder, c. 1830. Courtesy of the Boston Athenaeum.

wright, for example, had taught at Harvard and was rector of Trinity Church, Boston, and trustee of Columbia University. But Emerson was well-enough known around Cambridge, belonging to a family that Oliver Wendell Holmes, Sr., called one of New England's "Academic Races." With several relatives, including his father and three brothers, also alumni, Harvard was his patrimony. As an undergraduate, Waldo, like his brothers, respected authority—no small consideration then. But unlike them, he did not place high in his class. Recollected Charles William Eliot: "He was an omnivorous reader, and an observant and reflective wanderer in the woods and by-ways. He worked on the things that interested him, with companions of his choice, and college duties obstructed him hardly at all."[3]

Since graduating in 1821 at the then-customary age of eighteen, Emerson conscientiously kept in touch with fellow alums (there were sixty in his class), attended commencement, and helped organize annual reunions. It must have been at one of these that he proved himself a good chum, rising to offer these verses to the president of Harvard:

To jolly old Kirkland we'll fill the first glass
Whom the bottle did ne'er with impunity pass,
Let us pray to the gods to keep him from harm,
And find him a wife to tuck him up warm.[4]

Like his late father before him, Emerson was popular with classmates. After graduation, he also followed in his father's footsteps by first working as a teacher and then returning to Harvard for divinity training. And, again like his father, he became a minister of a liberal theology that had just recently taken the name of Unitarianism. But in a crisis of belief and perhaps of life, Emerson soon departed from family tradition. At twenty-nine years old, with the death of his first wife, Ellen, whom during their seventeen months together he loved with poetic abandon, and concerned that he could not longer administer the sacraments with sincere faith, he gave up his pulpit at Boston's Second Church (in earlier days home to Increase and Cotton Mather). After spending a year abroad, he came to settle in the ancestral village of Concord, which his family, seven generations earlier, had helped found. From there, he began to carve out a speaking career on the newly formed lyceum circuit. Although not yet publishing any of his lectures, he did, in 1836, produce an extensive essay. *Nature* at least at first sold well, and his talks were just beginning to attract the large audiences he would eventually enjoy. They helped establish him with a group of what became known as Transcendentalists.[5]

It was the year before his Phi Beta Kappa address, on the evening of Harvard's bicentennial celebration, that the Transcendental Club was formed. Its members shared the belief that the current state of theology and philosophy was "very unsatisfactory." Over the next four years, until its final meeting in September, 1840, the club met some thirty times at private homes—often Emerson's—to discuss topics usually of philosophical or religious interest. Its founding members were Frederic Henry Hedge, George Putnam, George Ripley, and Emerson, and they timed their gatherings to coincide with Hedge's visits from Maine. Along the way, a number of individuals dropped in once or twice, but, of the score or so who attended more regularly, these are the names that will appear here frequently: Hedge, Ripley, Emerson, Bronson Alcott, Margaret Fuller, Orestes Brownson, James Freeman Clarke, Convers Francis, Theodore Parker, Caleb Stetson, Samuel Osgood, John Sullivan Dwight, and William Henry Channing. Almost all were young, Harvard-trained Unitarian ministers.[6]

The club's chief organizer, Henry Hedge—son of Levi Hedge, the Alford Professor of Natural Religion, Moral Philosophy, and Civil Polity at Harvard—was moved by what he believed to be "a rigid, cautious, circumspect, conservative *tang* in the very air of Cambridge which no one, who has resided there for any considerable time, can escape." Hedge merely expressed more candidly what he and George Ripley had long been suggesting in print. The object of their impatience was the Unitarian culture in which they had been raised.[7]

Breaking free at the beginning of the nineteenth century from Trinitarian theology and Calvinist notions of original sin and determinism, Unitarians held to a benevolent, if distant, god, a demonstrably rational world, and the possibility of moral perfection—all validated by a thriving materialistic culture. Many philosophies, especially Scottish Common Sense, contributed to their outlook. But it is in particular John Locke's notion of the mind as a blank tablet, a *tabula rasa*, in which consciousness is largely shaped by external experience (though not quite so completely as *tabula rasa* might suggest), that had the greatest influence on Unitarian beliefs. With the quiet fervor of those who know they are right, Boston clerical, commercial, and academic elite—related to each other by birth or marriage to a degree they made famous—followed British empirical philosophy in defining human thought as directly dependent on the material world.

Within just a few decades, however, their own offspring rebelled against what they saw as a smug certitude, espousing with equal conviction a romantic idealism that favored individual instinct, self-knowledge, and a belief in transcendent, eternal ideas. In his *Critique of Pure Reason* of 1781, Immanuel Kant had observed that metaphysicians such as Locke were unable to show precisely how external objects shape human perception. And so Kant proposed to do the opposite: "We must therefore make trial whether we may not have more success in the task of metaphysics, if we suppose that objects must conform to our knowledge." When Kant called his assertion a "Copernican Revolution," he wasn't being immodest. European thought since the Enlightenment had depended on the belief that the external world was knowable and predictable. Kant maintained that if the material world appears knowable and predictable, it is largely because the human mind makes it so. The categories of understanding that are intuitive to us all determine the way we perceive what we call reality. Epistemology, recollected James Freeman Clarke, was suddenly turned on its head:

> The books of Locke, Priestley, Hartley, and Belsham were in my grandfather Freeman's library, and the polemic of Locke against innate ideas was one of my earliest philosophical lessons. But something within me revolted at all such attempts to explain soul out of sense, deducing mind from matter. . . . So I concluded I had no taste for metaphysics and gave it up, until Coleridge showed me from Kant that though knowledge begins *with* experience it does not come *from* experience. Then I discovered that I was born a transcendentalist.[8]

Although the difference between Lockean acquired and Kantian innate knowledge is somewhat a matter of emphasis, Unitarians and Transcendentalists, as Clarke testified, considered the philosophies incompatible. It is no exaggeration to say in fact that, had they believed in the devil, each would have seen Satan's hand in the other's thinking. That was especially so when it came to applying German idealism to religion. Despite being labeled an atheist for his assertion that the human mind determined what it perceived, Kant argued mightily for an ultimately unknowable, though omnipresent, god. But it was British poet Samuel Taylor Coleridge, in his 1825 work *Aids to Reflection*, who conveyed to American Transcendentalists the spiritual side of Kant's system that proved most influential to them. Coleridge somewhat misleadingly reduced Kant's theory of human cognition to a sharp dichotomy between Reason, which is common to all humanity and contains intuition and the inherent moral faculties, and Understanding, which evaluates the material world and thus varies among individuals. Because we can never be certain of transient external perceptions, the innate and eternal moral sentiments provided by Reason transcend (hence: Transcendentalism) what we learn through Understanding. A pious Anglican, Coleridge argued that Reason—which separates us from all other living things—reveals to humanity the mysteries of Christian faith.[9]

American Transcendentalists followed Coleridge in seeing the reflection of God within human Reason. Many of them also continued to believe in Jesus's divine nature, while some, especially Emerson, Alcott, and Parker, considered his ministry simply representative of the best of humanity. But all believed that the miracles he performed were perceived through human Understanding and thus susceptible to misinterpretation. His physical deeds, therefore, could not be the measure of his accomplishments. Rather, it was how his words awakened sentiments residing in human Reason that gave Jesus's message its eternal value. Trusting that all important knowledge is self-knowledge, Transcendentalists argued against the significance of historically based miracles. Not coincidentally, at precisely the same moment empirically minded Unitarians, armed with new methods of evaluating the Bible (originating, ironically, in Germany), were busy insisting on the centrality of Jesus's miracles to Christian theology.

During the next decade, the Transcendentalist challenge to Unitarianism and its chief secular institution, Harvard, would turn increasingly bitter. By the nineteenth century, philosophy had established a secure place alongside and in support of theology. Just as today the relative truths in the literary canon are debated in public (for which Emerson is largely responsible), philosophical disputes were then considered of great and pressing moment by the general populace. The so-called miracles controversy, for example, was fought not only in professional books and journals, but in daily newspapers, with lay readers, clergy, and academics alike contributing letters and articles. When the Harvard-Unitarian establishment proclaimed Transcendentalism "the new heresy," public diatribes and spiteful accusations were hurled from all sides. Before being overshadowed by the great cause of abolitionism, the conflict transformed what it meant to be an American intellectual. Beginning with "The American Scholar," Emerson placed himself at the center of the new vision and yet to the side of most of the conflict.[10]

But much of this lay in the future, for the young rebels were still developing their beliefs and determining how theirs differed from those of their teachers. Despite existing tensions, the Transcendental Club was probably not formed in direct opposition to Harvard. The alma mater was not even a formal topic of discussion until three years later, and by then the situation had changed dramatically. Hedge's initial proposal to Emerson in 1836 was that friends should meet at least once a year, when they gathered for Harvard's commencement. After some hesitation, Emerson agreed, so long as there was no defining agenda: "The rule suggested by the club," Emerson affirmed, "was this, that no man should be admitted whose presence excluded any one topic."[11]

Although affiliation with the Transcendental Club might have been viewed suspiciously by members of Phi Beta Kappa, as a substitute orator Emerson had some appeal. Elected in 1828 as one of the first graduate initiates, he participated actively, even enjoying the administrative and political aspects of the society. Sentiment was on Emerson's side, for two of his brothers, both of whom had achieved brilliantly as undergraduates and had been elected to the chapter, had recently met premature deaths (Edward in 1834 and Charles in 1836).[12]

Yet, a young Transcendentalist had to have more than mere sentiment to recommend his selection as speaker. We don't know for certain what happened when Jonathan Mayhew Wainwright suddenly informed the society that he could not give the Phi Beta Kappa oration. But although no one has since thought to ask, it's easy to guess. The chapter's by-laws of 1825 stipulated that a seven-person Committee on Appointments select the annual orator. In 1837, the vice president of the society happened to be Nathaniel Langdon Frothingham, Harvard overseer and brother-in-law of Governor Everett. Succeeding Emerson's late father as minister of the First Church, he had deep and abiding affection for the Emerson family, especially for Waldo. Frothingham had already proved himself sufficiently independent-minded that Transcendentalists had invited him to join their club. Although he demurred, he soon began sounding like one of their own. Frothingham wrote Emerson a note that August: "Good luck for Commencement & the day after!—particularly the latter, say I" (meaning of course the Phi Beta Kappa oration). As the senior-most member of the Committee on Appointments and almost certainly its chair, he would have had the most influence in determining the orator. The committee also included George Bradford, Emerson's lifelong friend and a member of the Transcendental Club, as well as James Walker, who did not attend but had been invited to join the club. Even C. C. Felton who, as the society's corresponding secretary, also sat on the committee, contributed to George Ripley's Transcendentalist-inspired series *Specimens of Foreign Standard Literature*. The initial choice of Wainwright was unexceptional. But when it became possible to introduce a new voice, perhaps on the sly, as the decision was made in summer when few would pay attention, Frothingham and friends made the most of the opportunity.[13]

His selection had to surprise Emerson, and the first question that must have occurred to him was: what type of oration should he deliver? The appointments committee was composed of moderate men. If they desired to hear a new voice, it should stimulate but not offend. Other Transcendentalists, such as Ripley and Hedge, were more accomplished than Emerson and might have merited consideration as speaker. But they had publicly attacked Harvard and Unitarian belief, while Emerson always appeared circumspect and soft-spoken. Three years previously, in fact, he had delivered the Phi Beta Kappa poem, and his offering was quite conservative. The morning of Emerson's oration, the same committee chose Caleb Stetson to be the following year's speaker. Although also a member of the Transcendental Club, he, too, was politic and well liked. True to form, Stetson presented a balanced and convivial talk that was acceptable to conservative Unitarians but disappointing to fellow Transcendentalists. Emerson, it seems, was caught between a society in which some of its members might welcome new ideas, but only gradually, and Transcendentalist colleagues who desired a forceful statement.[14]

Emerson had other considerations to weigh (ones that we will examine in detail in subsequent chapters). Thirteen years earlier, with Lafayette in attendance, Edward Everett had delivered a rousing, star-spangled Phi Beta Kappa oration that catapulted him to Congress. Everett had there assumed and exalted the homogeneity of his Cambridge audience, his "brethren of one literary household." Emerson, who would call Everett his "old idol," had proclaimed that talk "the high water mark which no after tide has reached." Public success, the self-reliant Emerson conceded, was his ambition, too: "I do not fully disclaim the vulgar hunger to be known, to have one's name hawked in the great capitals in the street." Just ten months before giving his own oration, he reminded himself of a desire that "the high prize of eloquence may be mine[,] the joy of uttering what no other can utter & what all must receive." Pursuing a career as public speaker in conscious emulation of Everett, Emerson had to think of the expectations of his audience.[15]

Someone nearer to Emerson was also on his mind. His late father, William, played an ambiguous role in his life. At the same graduation at which Everett delivered his celebrated oration, Emerson's younger brother Edward gave a highly acclaimed commencement address, publicly acknowledging their deceased father. Edward understood that it would have sentimental appeal, for their father was beloved at Harvard. William had even been the society's orator half a century earlier, and his talk, according to a witness, earned him "great applause." Yet Waldo, who closely resembled his father in appearance and temperament, was to leave an embarrassing legacy by denigrating William's contributions to Unitarianism and Boston civic life. When he appeared before Phi Beta Kappa in 1837, Emerson was facing the memory of his father—a ghost he had not as yet put to rest.[16]

But most immediately, Emerson felt the pull of his own friends. With Transcendentalists locked in battle with Harvard Unitarians, Bronson Alcott, in his own journal which Emerson had read, anointed their savior: "Emerson is destined to be the high literary name of this age. . . . [His] whip of small cords . . . shall do somewhat to drive the buyers and sellers of slang and profanity from this sacred place. . . . sham-image killer, is he!" Many friends were to attend the talk, including more than a dozen Transcendentalists or sympathizers who were fellow members of Phi Beta Kappa. Several of them planned to meet the following night at Emerson's home, and his oration would inevitably be on their mind. After months of agonizing about speaking out on public controversies, Emerson believed Transcendentalists awaited his leadership. Yet his friends were divided, and it is not at all clear how much they looked to him. When Emerson delivered his remarkable oration, there was, then, opportunity and challenge before him.[17]

And it didn't all come from family and friends. While crafting the talk, Emerson could hear rumblings from part of the anticipated audience. Immediately after the publication of *Nature* the previous year, the influential dean of the Divinity School, John Gorham Palfrey, wrote retired Harvard professor George Ticknor that Emerson's "Carlyle-like book" had some beautiful passages, but much of it was unintelligible and parts were simply noxious. The same criticisms were then publicly expressed in a punishing review by a young Harvard instructor under the thumb of the Unitarian establishment. A few months later, Harvard divinity student George Ellis recounted to Theodore Parker that Emerson was ridiculed there. Worse, a mere five weeks before Emerson was to speak, Samuel Osgood described to James Freeman Clarke the Divinity School graduation exercises that had just occurred: "The Dean seems to have imposed the *authority* principle very deeply upon the minds of these graduates." The speeches, Osgood judged, "were very strongly anti-transcendental." Parker, Osgood, and Freeman were part of Emerson's circle: he must have known what awaited him.[18]

Rather than give him pause, the news may only have confirmed his resolve. Ten days before delivering the oration, in a heart-stopping journal entry he wrote: "A dream of a duel. . . . Dreams are the sequel of waking knowledge. . . . In dream I turn that knowledge into fact; and it proves a prophecy. In like manner the Soul contains in itself the event that shall presently befal it." Although rarely taking note of his dreams, five years before, at the beginning of the spiritual crisis that led to his resignation from the ministry, Emerson had "hideous dreams" and worried "whether they were any more than exaggerations of the sins of the day." Nearing another defining moment of his life, he was haunted this time not with fears of his own moral imperfections, but by a vision of aggression. Emerson had made up his mind: he was going to Harvard to have a duel.[19]

It takes two to duel, and Emerson usually managed to avoid confrontation. Transcendentalist colleagues—especially George Ripley, Orestes Brownson, and Henry Hedge—were busy publishing scholarly articles attacking Harvard and Unitarianism. Holding little back, they gave as well as they got. But polemics weren't Emerson's style. As a preacher and lyceum speaker, he was accustomed to an approving audience. And so a few days after his dream and despite his determination, Emerson had a disturbing revelation: "Draw circles. The man finishes his story how good! how final! He fills the sky. Lo! On the other side rises also a man and draws a circle around the circle which we had just pronounced the outline of the sphere; then already is our first speaker not Man, but only a first speaker. His only redress is forthwith to draw a circle outside of his antagonist." Emerson capitalized "man" whenever he meant Man the Scholar, Man the Teacher, Man the Prophet. He worried that he would be drawn into a debate that would trivialize his pronouncements and reduce him merely to man.[20]

To be the Man whom Alcott thought a sham-image killer, there had to be no ambiguity, no other circles. Because measured phrases might admit of rebuttal, Emerson needed a rhetoric different from anything he had used as minister and lecturer—and, in fact, a rhetoric different from anything heard before at Harvard. And so five days later, looking down on his former teachers and ministerial colleagues, the graduating seniors, the many visitors, and a convivial and distinguished alumni, Emerson confronted his audience, welcoming condemnation in return: "For the ease and pleasure of treading the old road . . . [the scholar instead] takes . . .

the state of virtual hostility in which he seems to stand to society, and especially to educated society."[21]

To prove himself such a scholar, in bold strokes Emerson attacked the institution he was expected to honor. Rather than offering the traditional declaration of being inadequate to so august a task, Emerson began by expressing impatience with the gathering: "I greet you on the re-commencement of our literary year. Our anniversary is one of hope, and, perhaps, not enough of labor." Emerson announced that the education being celebrated that day suffocated him: "The book, the college, the school of art, the institution of any kind . . . pin me down. They look backward and not forward." And not just Emerson, for "Meek young men grow up in libraries. . . . instead of Man Thinking, we have the bookworm . . . the restorers of readings, the emendators, the bibliomaniacs of all degrees." Therefore, "The scholar is decent, indolent, complaisant." He then added viciously, perhaps peering from his text to the audience below: "See already the tragic consequence."[22]

Knowing that Governor Everett, Justice Story, and Harvard president Josiah Quincy, a former congressman and mayor, were present, and aware that a Harvard education was often a stepping-stone to public office, Emerson scolded: "Men such as they are, very naturally seek money or power; and power because it is as good as money,—the 'spoils,' so called, 'of office'. . . . Wake them, and they shall quit the false good and leap to the true, and leave governments to clerks and desks." And at a ceremony at which previous speakers urged their audience to solicit contributions from the commercial class, Emerson warned that university, already far the wealthiest in the land, that "[g]owns, and pecuniary foundations, though of towns of gold, can never countervail the least sentence or syllable of wit. Forget this, and our American colleges will recede in their public importance, whilst they grow richer every year."[23]

No previous orator had ever asserted the right to advise, much less admonish, the university on its direction or principles. The prior year's speaker, Francis Wayland, according to an eyewitness, "paid a generous and earnest tribute to our University. . . . At [the talk's] termination the expression of unmingled applause was long, loud, and universal." As Holmes testified about the reaction to Emerson's oration, "The dignity, not to say the formality of the Academic assembly was startled."[24]

Now, were Emerson by nature a polemicist, the tone of the "The American Scholar" might be understandable. But until then, Emerson's lyceum and other public talks were mild and purposely nonconfrontational. Even in his several other speeches on education in surrounding years there are virtually no explicit criticisms. "Literary Ethics," given at Dartmouth a year later, elaborates the central themes of "The American Scholar." Yet save for a single mild cautionary, in which he called the scholar a pedant, Emerson articulated the theory of "The American Scholar" without attacking the institution or audience. Emerson had not suddenly turned complaisant. From Hanover, he wrote his wife about a fellow speaker who "is one of those men that churches & colleges are not apt to like,—quite incalculable—no man can tell which way his arrows may fly. . . . I like him very well." Privately still impatient with the academy, publicly at Dartmouth, and everywhere except at Harvard, Emerson was restrained.[25]

The polemics, as we'll see later, were an important part of the talk. But far more importantly, "The American Scholar" presents a plan for personal intellectual transcendence. Emerson began where he had left off in the last chapter of *Nature*, by proposing (largely in the spirit of Carlyle's 1829 work *Signs of the Times*) a myth in which humans in their primordial state had been fully integrated morally and intellectually. Evolving social and economic tasks caused them to splinter into specialized identities—the farmer, tradesman, priest, attorney, mechanic, or sailor. "The state of society is one in which the members have suffered amputation from the trunk, and strut about so many walking monsters,— a good finger, a neck, a stomach, an elbow, but never a man." Those who were once true scholars have become in the current divided state merely thinkers. It is the American scholar's responsibility to restore to the original condition "Man Thinking." This "old fable," as Emerson called it, evoked the figure of Adam in a perfect state of harmony, at one with himself and with nature. In echoing the Romantic belief that modern life fractured rather than improved humankind and in asserting that something had gone wrong at the beginning that needed repair—in a sense inverting the Calvinist notion of original sin—Emerson defied the presentist and materialist values of his audience.[26]

Emerson's "influences" on the reborn scholar are three in number. Nature is "first in time and the first in importance." Emerson had identified several interpretations of nature in his earlier essay of that name. He meant by it here natural law and its underlying connection to Reason. For, harmoniously organized and beholden to pattern, nature's truths run parallel to the moral sensibilities inherent in the human condition: "[T]he ancient precept, 'Know thyself,' and the modern precept, 'Study nature,' become at last one maxim." Second is "the mind of the Past," of which books are the best example. Although books have great worth, no knowledge external to the self should have prime authority over the development of the individual. So long as conventional colleges are built on such authority, they cannot be the site of transformational learning. The third influence is action inevitably turned into insight: "[E]xperience is converted into thought, as a mulberry leaf is converted into satin. The manufacture goes forward at all hours."[27]

Emerson's exaltation of individual experience as the foundation of understanding would be embraced by American pragmatists and Friedrich Nietzsche alike. But it was hardly satisfying to an audience which believed that a Harvard education should mold students into members of Boston's ruling elite. Instead, that day they heard that the knowledge emerging from nature and experience—essentially what comes from trusting one's own intuition—is to be valued more highly than the learning derived from books and teachers. And once Man Thinking has been created, his duties "may all be comprised in self-trust. The office of the scholar is to cheer, to raise, and to guide men by showing them facts amidst appearances." Anticipating that society, especially educated society, will scorn the scholar who follows his own path, Emerson urged courage: "He is to find consolation in exercising the highest functions of human nature. . . . He is the world's eye. He is the world's heart."[28]

Because it was the *American* scholar, democracy, too, had to be considered. Attempting to resolve the tension between individual accomplishment and the collective impulse, Emerson argued that the source and substance of the scholar's insight derived from a naturally reciprocal arrangement between genius and the populace: "Linnaeus makes botany the most alluring of studies, and wins it from the farmer and the herbwoman." The present age—the "Age of Introversion"—heralded the rise of popular literacy and culture: "The literature of the poor, the feelings of the child, the philosophy of the street, the meaning of household life, are the topics of the time. It is a great stride. It is a sign,—is it not? of new vigor, when the extremities are made active, when currents of warm life run into the hands and the feet." Until the creation of an American vernacular, the language of the ordinary had been appreciated only by certain continental authors, such as Goethe, Wordsworth, and Carlyle—anathema to most Unitarians. Emerson nodded approvingly: "This writing is blood-warm. . . . [T]he worth of the vulgar is fruitful in discoveries." For what should be despised is not the common or coarse, but the mediocrity that society had come to embrace: "The mind of this country, taught to aim at low objects, eats upon itself. There is no work for any but the decorous and the complaisant. Young men of the fairest promise . . . turn drudges, or die of disgust."[29]

The proposal was a complete break with the values of its audience. Harvard-Unitarian culture found spiritual and intellectual confirmation in empirical proof, scientific progress, and material success. Emerson acknowledged understanding derived from observation of external phenomena, but believed that the more important truths are eternal and intuitive, emerging from within. Ostensibly a struggle between the schools of Locke and Kant, after 2200 years it still pretty much came down to Aristotle versus Plato. But Emerson's scholar wasn't the elite Guardian of

Plato's *Republic*; it was instead Socrates, son of a stone mason. The committed scholar avoided social pretense, appreciating that truths of the spirit and the body emerge from the simplest common surroundings.

In offering a poetic appeal for humankind restored to nature and instinct, Emerson made a no-holds-barred effort to affirm spiritual and intellectual ideals that Romantics felt had been lost in the Enlightenment. Statements of such pure idealism are always difficult. They embarrass the audience, which naturally feels unworthy of the vision, and they embarrass the speaker, who has revealed so much and stands vulnerable to a cynical reception. At times of stress, idealism can offer hope and may carry the day. But at times of calm, few look for or wish to ponder so challenging a vision.

Little wonder, then, that the address caused something of a stir. In England, it was soon quoted by the young William Gladstone, M.P., and strongly praised in Harriet Martineau's popular work on America, *Retrospect of Western Travel*. But privately to Thomas Carlyle, Martineau was more circumspect: "Some say it is inspired, some say it is mad." During her visit to Boston two years earlier, Martineau had met Emerson, as well as Harvard faculty. Yet here she was, back in Great Britain and, only a few months after the publication of the speech, passing on gossip. Word had spread quickly.[30]

And the reception, as Martineau rightly suggested to Carlyle, was not one of universal acclaim. Two months later, in reviewing the printed version, William Henry Channing opined: "We have been not a little amused and somewhat edified by the various criticisms on this address, which we have seen and heard of all kinds, from kindling admiration to gaping wonder, shrewd caviling, sneering doubt, and even offended dignity." The nephew of Harvard professor Edward Tyrrel Channing and Unitarian leader William Ellery Channing was well positioned to judge the reaction.[31]

John Pierce, a Unitarian minister who kept a diary of extraordinarily rich detail, including descriptions of several dozen Phi Beta Kappa orations he witnessed, testifies to Channing's judgment. Uncharacteristically critical, Pierce thought the talk "incoherent" and "unintelligible." If Emerson "professed to have method . . . I could not trace it." Although Emerson "spoke severely of our dependence on British literature," he was obviously influenced by Coleridge and Carlyle, in whose "misty, dreamy, unintelligible style" he discoursed.[32]

Pierce was on the conservative side of Unitarianism, and his reserve is understandable. Other eyewitnesses were enthusiastic. Emerson's closest friend, Bronson Alcott, "[could] not forget the delight with which I heard it, nor the mixed confusion, consternation, surprise and wonder with which the audience listened to it." James Russell Lowell recollected it as

Figure 2. The 1848 "rainbow portrait" by David Scott (1806–1849). Emerson in a pose he frequently struck while speaking. Courtesy of the Concord Free Public Library.

"an event without any former parallel in our literary annals. . . . What crowded and breathless aisles, what windows clustering with eager heads, what enthusiasm of approval, what grim silence of foregone dissent!" Oliver Wendell Holmes pronounced, "This grand Oration was our intellectual Declaration of Independence. . . . [T]he young men went out from it as if a prophet had been proclaiming to them 'Thus saith the Lord.' "[33]

Some young men may well have. Only a week later, a graduating senior wrote classmate Henry David Thoreau in Concord, noting that his hometown was also home to Emerson, "one of our most distinguished Apostles of the Future." Edward Everett Hale, however, Harvard junior, nephew of Governor Everett, and future author of "The Man without a Country," recorded in his diary a different view of the speech: "It was not very good, but very transcendental." One student's prophecy was another's silliness.[34]

Massachusetts school reformer Horace Mann concluded at least that Emerson's performance "was very good for any body else—but hardly so for him." And even some of Emerson's closest colleagues, more committed than he to social activism, couldn't accept the profound and elemental idealism that placed individual conscience over collective norms. What was more easily appreciated were the explicit insults. But they were just his line in the sand, his way of announcing to the world that there would be no compromise, no obfuscating circles drawn in response. Orestes Brownson, whose own views differed significantly from Emerson's, nevertheless recognized the Old Testament–like prophetic courage, writing, "I do not know what the world is coming to, if such a voice as that may be heard in old Harvard. You bearded the lion in his den."[35]

What motivated Emerson suddenly to be so bold is constantly debated. Because Emerson's scholar refused to yield to the politics of the moment, the address might be understood as a transcendent response to the economic uncertainties caused by the Panic of 1837. Or, having heard a dull sermon a month before, Emerson might have been especially prone to stressing personal experience over what could be taught. A closely associated explanation, perhaps the most often embraced, draws on Emerson's identity crisis. Having been a school teacher and then minister of some repute who was now attempting a career as a public speaker, Emerson in turn demanded that the American scholar reject narrow specialization.[36]

There is probably some truth to each of these explanations. But even taken together, they do not adequately explain why this politic and still undistinguished child of Harvard—dependent on well-placed friends for the high honor of the moment—decided to beard his alma mater in front of so many acquaintances, teachers, and dignitaries. Nor do they begin to address the fundamental philosophical and cultural differences between the audience and the speaker. "The American Scholar" is not attributable to a single narrow event in Emerson's life. At the time of the oration Emerson was wrestling with a great many demons: with what he perceived to be the regressive direction of his college, with the constraints of his Unitarian upbringing, and with his place among friends whom he feared he had disappointed. What propelled Emerson to extraordinary heights of idealism were not calculated thoughts about events but feelings and concerns emerging from within. Committed to living a life of self-reliance, it was his very emotional dependencies that in the end motivated him. Emerson's experience supplies a salutary reminder that it is real people, with all their limitations, who lay claim to ideals. But to understand fully the several influences on Emerson, we need first to appreciate the revolutionary vision of his oration.

Chapter Two

AMERICA IN "THE AMERICAN SCHOLAR"

WHEN THE YOUNG EMERSON STOOD BEFORE AN ASSEMBLAGE
of some of the most important intellectual and civic leaders of his day, he
was driven by both a desire to achieve self-reliance and, conversely, a
deeply felt need to defend himself and friends that would compromise
that self-reliance. In responding to this inner conflict, what Emerson did
precisely was to offer an entirely new interpretation of what it meant to
be an American scholar. It was a problem as old as the United States itself.
Coming to a new land, Puritans had hoped to establish a City on the Hill
to provide light unto all the nations. With the country's independence,
the search only intensified for a literature to match the brilliant political
achievement. Phi Beta Kappa, first established at the College of William
and Mary in that year of independence, 1776, was originally a forum for
contemporary political debate. When the press of politics receded, annual
orators spoke instead of the need for the independent American scholar.
As a teenager, Emerson had hoped his brother would address the theme
in a college essay. Then he assumed the conventional understanding of
American scholar as a writer substantially free from European influence.
The question became so much the standard fare of the literate class that
even in his oration Emerson acknowledged the subject as the expected
theme: "I accept the topic which not only usage, but the nature of our
association, seem to prescribe to this day,—the AMERICAN SCHOLAR. Year
by year, we come up hither to read one more chapter of his biography."[1]

James Russell Lowell believed that Emerson fully succeeded: "The Puritan revolt had made us ecclesiastically, and the Revolution politically independent, but we were still socially and intellectually moored to English
thought, till Emerson cut the cable and gave us a chance at the dangers

and glories of blue water." But how exactly did he cut that cable? Little in the talk pertains to anything specifically American. Nearing his conclusion, Emerson acknowledged, "I have dwelt perhaps tediously upon this abstraction of the Scholar. I ought not to delay longer to add what I have to say, of nearer reference to the time and to this country." He then recommended to his audience the study of popular culture, citing as models European writers—Goldsmith, Burns, Cowper, Goethe, Wordsworth, and Carlyle—and following with an odd allusion to the beliefs of Swedish mystic Emanuel Swedenborg. What to Emerson was especially American about the scholar, if so controversial to his audience, had to be far more complex than meets the eye. To a country with a fragile hold on its new identity, it was uncompromisingly iconoclastic. To those in the audience, it was a particularly shattering vision.[2]

A decade before Emerson entered Harvard, the religious environment of the college, growing increasingly liberal and rational during the previous seventy-five years, took an even more dramatic turn. After a struggle within the Harvard Corporation, the Hollis Professorship of Divinity was offered in 1805 to Henry Ware, Sr., an anti-Trinitarian and follower of what would soon become known as American Unitarianism. A few years later, Harvard elected a president of the same faith, and by 1831 the *Christian Examiner* could proclaim of Harvard Divinity School: "Now we do not deny, that the Professors of the School are Unitarian; and we rejoice in the fact. We do not deny, that the probability is, that the students will come from the School impressed with the truth of the Unitarian faith. God forbid that it should be otherwise." Because training ministers was still perhaps the most important duty of the university, the rest of the institution followed pretty much in lockstep.[3]

Then, with the 1833 disestablishment of the Congregational Church in Massachusetts, Unitarians began to exert fully their intellectual and economic influence. Evangelist Lyman Beecher, trained at Yale under Timothy Dwight and sent to Boston to oppose Unitarianism, only mildly exaggerated when he complained: "All the literary men of Massachusetts were Unitarian. All the trustees and professors of Harvard College were Unitarians. All the elite of wealth and fashion crowded Unitarian churches. The judges on the bench were Unitarian, giving decisions by which the peculiar features of church organization, so carefully ordained by Pilgrim fathers, had been nullified." Octavius Brooks Frothingham, a Transcendentalist whose father, Nathaniel Langdon Frothingham, was one of the most prominent Unitarian ministers, testified similarly: "[Unitarianism] was the religion of the most intellectual men in the community. . . . [T]hey cherished a sentiment of deep rational piety, principles of strict personal morality, and a remarkably high standard of public virtue. They knew nothing of theological subtleties or critical refinements." Liberal in religion, conservative in political and social instinct, Unitarians took hold of Boston culture.[4]

And they did so with conscious purpose. In the half century following the Revolutionary War, the nation's wealthy and powerful feared that descent into mob rule would crush America's fragile political experiment. For their part, Unitarians believed that secular literature, growing far more abundant because of the Industrial Revolution, could serve the cause of moral regeneration and social stability. Harvard intellectuals launched in 1815 the *North American Review*, perhaps the most influential of all contemporary magazines, in order "to foster American genius, and, by independent criticism, instruct and guide the public taste." Hundreds of surviving letters discussing their contributions to the *Review* show how it united Harvard faculty in common cause.[5]

Brothers William Ellery Channing and Edward Tyrrel Channing, Henry Wadsworth Longfellow, Edward Everett, and brothers-in-law George Ticknor and Andrews Norton—to name some of the most prominent, all of whom, except the first, Harvard professors—expressed full confidence in Unitarian culture and leadership. Ticknor, whom Henry Adams called the social arbiter of Boston and Merle Curti labeled "scholar of scholars and patrician of patricians," described the Hub: "Boston is a happy place to live in, because all the people are educated, and because some of them, like Dr. Channing, Mr. Norton, and Mr. Prescott [the renowned historian and close friend of Ticknor's], who have grown out of this state of things, and Mr. Webster, and others, *who could have been produced in no other than this state of things*, are men who would be valued in any state of society in the world." In 1823, even before becoming a minister, Emerson wrote a friend criticizing the Unitarian preaching he heard: "An exemplary Christian of today, and even a Minister, is content to be just such a man as was a good Roman in the days of Cicero or of the imperial Antonines." Nothing Ticknor wrote suggests that he would have disagreed. A rational, orderly, and highly prosperous society—governed by what Henry Adams would later refer to as "the old Ciceronian idea of government by the *best*"—was Ticknor's rock-solid desire and belief.[6]

The best, of course, meant those who thought similarly, and their leading purveyor of civic and cultural virtue, their Cicero, was Ticknor's brother-in-law, Andrews Norton. He pronounced that "in this land, where the spirit of democracy is everywhere diffused, we are exposed, as it were, to a poisonous atmosphere, which blasts everything beautiful in nature and corrodes everything elegant in art." Consequently, "a correct and refined moral taste is the most important constituent of a correct and refined taste in literature." And that all began at Harvard: "Very much must depend upon the tastes here cultivated, the sciences here taught, the principles here inculcated, and the views here opened to those, who are to go abroad into society, and to be its teachers, guides, and governours."[7]

If Norton was "the Moses in the Exodus from the orthodox realm, [then] Dr. Channing [was] the Aaron," proclaimed the *Christian Examiner*. William Ellery Channing's 1830 essay "Remarks on National Literature" was a foundation text of Unitarian leadership. "[A national literature] is plainly among the most powerful methods of exalting the character of a nation, of forming a better race of men," wrote Channing. "We know nothing so fitted to the advancement of society, as to bring its higher minds to bear upon the multitude; as to establish close connexions between the more and less gifted." Channing might have been more ecumenical and populist than most Unitarians, but organized religion remained for him the bulwark of secular culture: "Christianity was given, not to contradict and degrade the rational nature, but to call it forth, to enlarge its range and its powers. . . . It ought to be so explored and so expressed, as to take the highest place in the nation's literature, as to exalt and purify all other literature."[8]

No matter how confidently they appeared in staking a claim to moral leadership, however, Unitarians suffered the inevitable fate of a group that had effected half a revolution. Observed Andrew Delbanco: "Channing and his colleagues moved with deep insecurity, less in celebration than in flight from an old house collapsing. The Unitarians, in the end, committed themselves to living in a world of ambiguity between two worlds of clarity, the orthodox and the romantic. And they knew it." Moses Stuart, the premier polemicist at rival Andover Theological Seminary, in 1819 called Unitarianism "the half-way house to infidelity." A dozen years later, Unitarian apologists were still smarting from the remark. Unitarians were attacked from all sides. It was no accident, but it was their misfortune, to have spun away fully from Calvinism during the Second Great Awakening. Revivalists who harkened back to simpler beliefs claimed that Unitarians were not Christians, while the conservative Princeton Theological Seminary blamed them for spawning Transcendentalism. Caught in this cross fire, it is little wonder that Unitarians felt compelled constantly to trumpet their own virtues and destiny.[9]

One of the showplaces for the celebration of their culture was the annual Phi Beta Kappa oration. As Harvard's literary society, its orators often talked about the need for a national literature led by Harvard Unitarians. And to counter the public charges that, because Phi Beta Kappa was secretive in election and initiation it was somehow tied to Freemasonry and French radicalism, orators eagerly proclaimed their patriotism and loyalty to conservative politics.[10]

The great Unitarian minister Joseph Stevens Buckminster, who briefly taught at Harvard and introduced to America modern biblical criticism,

Figure 3. William Ellery Channing, 1838, by Spiradone Gambardella. Oil on canvas. Courtesy of the Harvard University Portrait Collection, Gift of Frederick A. Eustis, Class of 1835, in accordance with the will of Mary Channing Eustis. Copyright President and Fellows of Harvard College.

delivered the 1809 address. He blamed the democratic spirit of the American and French Revolutions for "the foul spirit of innovation and sophistry [that] has been seen wandering in the very groves of the Lyceum." The intellectual must become a moral leader, avoiding the excessive temptations of the temporal life. And yet Buckminster, ever true to his alma mater and to the Unitarian emphasis on material evidence of success, urged an alliance with the commercial class: "You, then, who are alive to the reputation of this ancient university . . . [g]o to the rich and tell them of the substantial glory of literary patronage! . . . Show them that island of the blessed, where so many rich endowments of schools and of literary institutions have mingled forever together with the glories of commerce and of science!" Few college presidents even today would dare be so bold.[11]

Edward Tyrrel Channing, soon to be appointed Boylston Professor of Rhetoric, in his 1818 oration called for the development of—with these very words—the American scholar. He urged his audience to "cultivate domestic literature" for personal pleasure and enlightenment, "that your countrymen, in every part of the union may feel a close . . . intimacy" and "a source of national pride and unity." In the address of the following year, James Walker, Unitarian minister and future president of Harvard, repeated the demand that America establish a literary and moral elite and, like Buckminster, albeit with less flourish, suggested an alliance between the intellectual and moneyed classes.[12]

The declaration of cultural and material leadership continued and intensified. Joseph Story, the U.S. Supreme Court's most important conservative voice and perhaps the most powerful member of the Harvard Corporation, expressed satisfaction in his 1826 talk that "the literature of the age [has] superior moral purity. . . . He who would now command respect, must write with pure sentiments and elevated feelings; he, who would now please, must be chaste as well as witty, moral as well as brilliant." Attacking the contemporary Romantic poetry that was becoming the heartbeat of Transcendentalism, Story defended the classics, for "[o]nce the reverence for authority is shaken, there is apt to grow up in its stead a cold skepticism respecting established opinions. . . . There is not a remark deducible from the history of mankind more important than that advanced by Mr. Burke, that 'to innovate is not to reform.'"[13]

Just two years before Emerson delivered "The American Scholar," distinguished lawyer Theophilus Parsons gave another strongly conservative oration. Under the shadow of class riots in neighboring Charlestown and soon after Harvard faculty and corporation members strongly protested the awarding of an honorary degree to Andrew Jackson, Parsons passionately decried Jacksonian politics. Like Story, he presented a classically Whiggish argument that rich and poor alike must affirm the sanctity of property. A Swedenborgian by faith but a Unitarian by culture, Parsons grafted a moral agenda on top of a desire to control the volatile social conditions by inviting the educated to create a national voice and oppose what he saw as the dangers of majority rule.[14]

It might have been by then predictable Phi Beta Kappa fare, but Harriet Martineau, a friend and admirer of Emerson's, was appalled. She wrote her British readers that "[Parsons] diverged into a set of monstrous suppositions, expressed or assumed: that men of letters are the educated men of society in regard not only to literature and speculative truth, but to morals, politics, and the conduct of all social affairs; that power and property were made to go eternally together; that the 'masses' are ignorant

... that they are, consequently, opposed to law. .... This extraordinary collection of fallacies was not given in the form of an array of propositions, but they were all taken for granted when not announced." The values inherent in Parsons's address were equally implicit in the society: "There are a thousand mechanics' shops," Martineau claimed, "a thousand loghouses where certain members of the Phi Beta Kappa Society, the orator of the day for one, might learn new and useful lessons on morals and politics, on the first principles of human relations."[15]

Martineau had left the United States before Brown University president Francis Wayland gave the following year's oration. Although Wayland's unpublished talk is now lost, an eyewitness recounted that "he alluded with deep feeling to the dangers of our Republic from the despotism of the *many*, in the language of the passionate and unprincipled appeals to the prejudice of the vulgar, and in the form of mobs and other ways in which justice is anticipated or perverted by those not immediately authorized to dispense it." Wayland knew well his audience, which, according to the same eyewitness, greeted the talk with thunderous applause. It could not have been a surprise: the chapter was so cautious that when in his 1813 oration Alexander Everett, brother of the future governor, criticized Edmund Burke's famously conservative *Reflections on the Revolution in France*, the president of the chapter made sure the talk wasn't published.[16]

It was within this consistent tradition of materialism and moral guidance that the young Emerson was invited to speak. Attending or reading most of the previous orations, he had earlier accepted the standard Federalist view of elite moral leadership. Even in his Phi Beta Kappa poem of 1834, in contrast to Henry Hedge's prescient 1828 offering that ridiculed those unable to understand German idealism ("And thou, great Goethe, whose illustrious name,/ So oft mis-spelt and mis-pronounc'd by fame"), Emerson produced a celebration of Whiggish chauvinism and only obliquely suggested any of his new thinking ("For, the true man, as long as earth shall stand,/ Is to himself a state, a law, a land"). Because he was simultaneously putting the finishing touches on *Nature*, it wasn't for lack of Transcendentalist passion that he spoke so cautiously. Likely intimidated by the prospect of performing at Harvard, Emerson immediately afterwards chastised himself and belittled the effort throughout his life. Now, three years later, his belief in transcendent idealism ever more refined, he came into direct conflict with community values publicly sworn to on this very occasion. How could his American scholar possibly do the theme justice?[17]

Although in breaking free from European control the new country had adopted a more enlightened form of government, expectations that America would also surpass Europe in arts and letters had so far been disappointed. Emerson, whose grandfather had died in the Revolutionary War and whose own journals reflect a passionate pride in the American polity, struggled with America's seeming lack of cultural imagination. At times he tried to rationalize the failure, in Hegelian terms, as a natural reflection of broader historical trends: "The history of America since the Revolution is meagre because it has been all that time under better government, better circumstances of religious, moral, political, commercial prosperity than any nation ever was before. History will continually grow less interesting as the world grows better." Yet he persisted in worrying that "there is yet a dearth of American genius."[18]

But by the time he gave his talk, he had developed a way out. At the earliest meetings of the Transcendental Club in 1836, discussion turned to the question of American culture. "Emerson," Alcott noted in his journal, "gave us many good things as usual," exploring why on "this Titanic Continent where Nature is so grand, Genius should be so tame." The problem partly stemmed of course from American writers falling under European influence. But guided by his current reading—Coleridge, Carlyle, Goethe, and de Staël—and perhaps in discussion with his more politically minded friends in the Transcendental Club, Emerson also began to understand how genius could attend to and even be produced by popular culture. American artists and writers, he discovered, "are not called out by the necessity of the people." Pondering the link between individual genius and popular culture, Emerson turned to what Stanley Cavell has called "the investment in the ordinary." Just months before giving the oration, he reflected that "the roots of what is great & high must still be in the common life."[19]

This went directly into "The American Scholar," where Emerson argued that popular culture could be the actual seedbed of genius:

> One of these signs [that the current age is one of revolution] is the fact, that the same movement which effected the elevation of what was called the lowest class in the state, assumed in literature a very marked and as benign an aspect. Instead of the sublime and beautiful; the near, the low, the common, was explored and poetized. . . . The literature of the poor, the feelings of the child, the philosophy of the street, the meaning of household life, are the topics of the time. It is a great stride. It is a sign,—is it not? of new vigor. . . . I ask not for the great, the remote, the romantic. . . . I embrace the common, I explore and sit at the feet of the familiar, the low.

In obvious anticipation of his eventual protégé Walt Whitman, Emerson identified himself with the rich potential of popular culture and with all individual creation, whatever the social or intellectual station of its creator. Unitarians wanted secular literature to have a high moral purpose, to approach, yet never reach, the inspiration of sacred literature, and always to be produced by the "best." Emerson joined other Transcendentalists in believing that all literature contained the potential for truth and revelation. But he expressed a far greater reliance on the power of creativity than did even most of his colleagues when, in the midst of writing "The American Scholar," he exalted in a perfectly formed Gnostic vision: "To create, to create is the proof of a Divine presence. Whoever creates is God, and whatever talents are, if the man create not, the pure efflux of Deity is not his." Part of that sentiment went directly from his journals into the oration.[20]

And yet, was that the destiny of everyone in America—to be a god? Throughout his life Emerson struggled with the obvious conflict between the uniqueness of genius and the weight of collective culture. Using what he called compensation, reciprocity, and rotation, Emerson tried to reconcile the charmed individual with the masses from which that individual arose. Genius, Emerson stressed in "The American Scholar," merely represents humanity, which would some day lay claim to the individual accomplishments and discoveries: "Each philosopher, each bard, each actor, has only done for me, as by a delegate, what one day I can do for myself." No single type of genius remains dominant, for opportunity and talent are rotated: "The books which once we valued more than the apple of the eye, we have quite exhausted. . . . First, one; then, another; we drain all cisterns, and, waxing greater by all these supplies, we crave a better and more abundant food. The man has never lived that can feed us ever."[21]

Attempts to resolve individual excellence and society's collective identity recur throughout later essays, but Emerson never did attain the balance he was after. The belief that inevitably there will come a sort of compensation—something Stephen Whicher has called "without question the most unacceptable of Emerson's truths"—is hardly convincing. No matter how much one wants to believe that genius represents humanity and that in the end humanity gets its due, it certainly seems that the accomplished individual has greater advantages. If an honest balance couldn't result, one side had to dominate. In the end, Emerson made society supportive of genius, rather than fully triumphant. Nearly immediately after celebrating popular culture as the proper subject of the American scholar, Emerson emphasized that the true scholar must still live a solitary and defiant existence.[22]

Emerson's scholar, in fact, had to free himself from all institutions. In his 1830 "Remarks on National Literature," Channing had moved a good distance from the strictly nationalist claims made in response to European, and especially British, criticism of American culture. But his perspective was limited by association. Most of his Harvard friends had European training or were at least admirers of continental thought. If they demanded an American voice that reflected American values, it was still a voice recognizable to a European. Channing conformed to the general nationalistic trend of promoting American institutions in competition with European ones: "We must enlarge our literary institutions, secure more extensive and profound teaching, and furnish helps and resources to men of superior talent for continued, laborious research. . . . We boast of our primary schools. We want universities worthy of the name." And just a year before Emerson gave his oration, a speaker at Union College, delivering an address entitled *The Advantages and the Dangers of the American Scholar*, once again defined the scholar in the traditional terms of America's national character and institutions.[23]

Because Europe had shaped those very categories of thinking, Emerson understood that the scholar could not break free through competition. His response was instead to leap over the question of who had or ought to have the better institutions and therefore literary expressions. The New World might provide inspiration, for "It is a mischievous notion that we are come late into nature; that the world was finished a long time ago." But seeing clearly the limitations of that argument, Emerson stressed the reintegration of all essential human characteristics and vocations. If the American scholar was also the Transcendental scholar, each one unique and self-cultivated, a European could then be such a scholar. Witness Thomas Carlyle's ecstatic reception: "I *have* a kinsman and brother: God be thanked for it! I cou[ld have] *wept* to read that speech." Wherever there is fresh insight and reinvention of the individual, there will be found the American scholar.[24]

Emerson's decision to define the American scholar without dwelling on what is uniquely American not only disturbed an audience expecting to hear extolled the Harvard intellectual. It also created tension between Emerson and some of his friends who understood the scholar as the American everyman, fully committed to democratic principles and social justice. Orestes Brownson, political radical and occasional Transcendentalist, urged Emerson to strengthen his identification of the scholar with qualities that were specifically American: "American scholars we shall have; but only in proportion as the scholar weds himself to American principles, and becomes the interpreter of American life, " he wrote in his periodical, the *Boston Quarterly Review*. William Henry Channing, in his review of "The American Scholar," reflected the thoughts of more socially progressive Transcendentalists in arguing that Emerson should have emphasized common genius rather than the rare, representative individual: "And yet would we see [Emerson] more fully warmed with the great social idea of our era,—the great idea, which he has hinted at in this very address—of human brotherhood, of sonship to God. . . . Every man is or should be a 'student,' 'man thinking.'"[25]

Three years later, in the autumn of 1840, some of his friends called upon Emerson to join them at Brook Farm, their experiment in communal living. Emerson's refusal is generally considered the beginning of the end to harmony among Transcendentalists. But the division had already been announced in "The American Scholar." Emerson did not call for the establishment of a scholar with any political characteristics. That vision would become as stultifying as the established literatures he attacked in this very speech. In referring to the American scholar, Emerson fully subverted an established phrase. Used previously with nationalistic and moral overtones, for Emerson it signified freedom from all prescribed culture and convention. The American scholar became Man Thinking—who was no more merely a producer of literature than Socrates had been. And just as Socrates defended and ultimately died for Athenian freedom without ever feeling comfortable with Athenian democracy, Emerson embraced American liberty without feeling beholden to the institutions that supported it. When he proclaimed in his oration that "if a single man plant himself indomitably on his instincts, and there abide, the huge world will come around to him," he not only defied the Unitarian call for elite leadership of American culture. He also refused to ally himself fully with those Transcendentalists who believed in popular sovereignty. Other Phi Beta Kappa orators of the period—at Harvard and elsewhere—might recommend social, legal, or political reform. Emerson alone, however, argued for reform of the soul. And yet, as we'll see next, the impatience and even anger that he expressed in pursuit of spiritual reform put him on course, almost despite himself, to greater social awareness and commitment.[26]

Chapter Three

THE SCHOLAR TRANSFORMED

IN REDEFINING THE DUTIES OF THE INTELLECTUAL, EMERSON went far beyond his Transcendentalist colleagues—and about as far as anyone has gone since. Friends such as George Ripley and Henry Hedge argued that Harvard faculty lacked the requisite intellectual disposition to understand Transcendentalist beliefs. Emerson converted their attack into an elevated, poetic vision, so much more messianic than his lyceum talks or even his church sermons. Punctuating the oration with staccato-like bursts of intentional insult that reflected his highest ideals and deepest personal disappointment, Emerson questioned the very essence of the academic enterprise. There were important practical reasons why Emerson delivered so harsh an oration and why he freed his American scholar not only from the influence of European institutions, but from American ones as well.

Polemics didn't come naturally to Emerson, and a year later he reflected that "there is no scholar less willing or less able to be a polemic." In fact, with the exception of "The American Scholar" and the Divinity School address, Emerson never attempted to alienate his audience. Both talks, given eleven months apart, were delivered at Harvard. Had he been, as he claimed in composing his Phi Beta Kappa oration, merely intent on "advising the young men at Cambridge," he would have done so circumspectly, as he later did at Dartmouth. But enthralled by Harvard as a student, Emerson was now contemptuous of its increasingly corporate approach to education. A close look at the institution that was his patrimony will help us understand the sudden polemics and how they helped produce a unique American rhetoric.[1]

Emerson was, to be sure, eternally grateful for his own college experience. He remarked poignantly after Harvard's bicentennial in 1836: "I found my old friends the same; the same jokes pleased, the same straws tickled; the manhood & offices they brought hither today seemed masks; underneath, we were still boys." But even by 1830, teachers he had venerated looked more human. Edward Everett, whom Emerson had earlier considered in the company of Milton and Shakespeare, was now "all art & I find him nowadays maugre [in spite of] all his gifts & great merits more to blame than to praise." George Ticknor, the other instructor he had admired most, became an emperor without clothes.[2]

Demythologizing professors might be part of the inevitable process of maturation, but Emerson was deeply disturbed by Harvard's new direction in education. His own education had come during the quiet period of John Kirkland's presidency. To both contemporaries and posterity the most beloved of all Harvard presidents, Kirkland had been a college classmate of Emerson's father and his close confidant during their years together in the ministry. After William's death, Kirkland remained a family friend, making it financially possible for Emerson, then almost desperately poor, to attend Harvard. And when in 1827 he invited Waldo's brother Edward to give the master's oration, Kirkland offered "heartfelt remembrance to your grandfather and to your mother."[3]

The warm family feelings were fully reciprocated. Waldo wrote his older brother, also named William, in 1818, noting that "our good President" was to meet President James Monroe, confident that he "will do himself as much honor as a man of the world as he will as a literary character." Kirkland was indeed a visionary. To increase the intellectual rigor of his faculty, he sent to Germany his finest young talent: George Ticknor, Edward Everett, and George Bancroft (who took along Professor Levi Hedge's thirteen-year-old son, Henry, one of the future founders of the Transcendental Club). They returned to Harvard with an appreciation of critical thinking, refined pedagogy, and German Romanticism, somewhat inadvertently providing much of the spark for the Transcendentalist movement. Kirkland's presidency also witnessed Harvard's shift from a predominantly Calvinist to Unitarian institution. For more than a century, Harvard's single greatest source of financial support had been the Commonwealth of Massachusetts. But because the lower legislative house, which controlled finances, was dominated by rural, religiously conservative members, Harvard's embrace of liberal Christianity jeopardized its state support. Kirkland in response turned to the Unitarian commercial elite of Boston. During his presidency, the number of endowed chairs more than doubled.[4]

Kirkland was less successful in the latter days of his presidency. A student rebellion in 1823 led to the expulsion of a large part of the senior class and made Harvard further unpopular with the Commonwealth. Enrollment fell nearly in half by 1826, and Harvard seemed to be drifting financially. There followed a terrific and complex fight between faculty and administration over governance, which faculty utterly lost, and a struggle over pedagogy, which they effectively lost. The contests were led by two of Harvard's most distinguished professors, George Ticknor and Andrews Norton. Although married to daughters of the late Samuel Eliot, a Harvard benefactor said to be "the richest man who has ever died in Boston," these brothers-in-law and former teachers of Emerson's clashed strongly over strategies and goals.[5]

In 1827, Kirkland suffered a partially incapacitating stroke and the following year faced a corporation critical of his financial management. Against the bitter opposition of the college seniors, led by Emerson's brother Charles, the corporation readily accepted his resignation. Whatever underlay the situation, Kirkland certainly appeared to have been treated badly, and there was public protest. "His retiring from the College was universally regarded as a great public calamity, an irreparable loss to the State, as well as to the republic of letters," wrote one contemporary. "This whole community felt that the sun of Harvard had suffered disastrous eclipse, and that the glory had departed from Cambridge." There was a general sense, as Andrews Norton suggested years later, that the corporation "quarreled with him, and he was compelled to resign."[6]

Emerson, who always seemed to have reliable inside information, took the loss personally, as did his whole family. In the initial draft of his 1828 class oration, brother Charles proposed that, although his class ought to give thanks that not one of their number had died, "a single grievous calamity has befallen us. . . . The good shepherd, whom we followed, for we knew his voice, by whom we had hope to be this day led out of the fold, was removed from over us." Kirkland, a benefactor of the Emerson brothers and their late father's close friend, had been ripped from office.[7]

Many years later, Emerson reflected: "When the great man comes, he will have that social strength that Dr Kirkland or Franklin or Burns had, and will so engage us . . . [that] we shall say behold I am enlarged[;] how dull I was! how grand of late has my horizon grown! This man[,] this man must be divine." George Ripley, another prominent Transcendentalist, believed that Kirkland helped spark their passions through "the magnetic charm of his conversation, the sweet amenity of his manner,—the quaint and original suggestions of his fertile imagination . . . his sympathy with whatever was rare and beautiful in literature."[8] It is entirely possible that, had Kirkland remained president, Emerson might not have been able to say what he did in his Phi Beta Kappa oration. Conversely, that a very much different type of administrator became the next president contributed significantly to the defiant tone of the talk.

Figure 4. John Thornton Kirkland, president of Harvard, 1810–1828, no date. Courtesy of the Manuscripts and Archives Department, Andover-Harvard Theological Library, Harvard Divinity School.

The corporation selected as the new leader Josiah Quincy. College presidents were then customarily chosen to teach the required course on moral philosophy that demonstrated the unity, through natural law, of the entire curriculum. Kirkland was venerated as such an intellectual; Quincy certainly was not. Neither minister nor scholar by profession, Quincy had been a politician—a remarkably independent congressman and more recently a successful mayor of Boston. Wealthy, outspoken, and enormously energetic, Quincy, noted Samuel Eliot Morison, had "a distaste for the new West, for nationalism, and for democracy; a love of good conversa-

Figure 5. Josiah Quincy, president of Harvard, 1829–1845. Gilbert Stuart painting of 1824. Courtesy of the Museum of Fine Arts, Boston. Gift of Miss Eliza Susan Quincy.

tion, good books, classical letters, and English culture." He had been graduated first in the class of 1790 (the year after Emerson's father), was Phi Beta Kappa orator in 1794, and president of the society, from 1809 to 1812. He maintained throughout his life an interest in letters, having already penned decent satire and later producing a number of small-scale histories, including one of Harvard that was more than mere triumphal propaganda. But Quincy was above all politic. Although voicing opposition to slavery before and after his presidency, he used the influence of his office to keep that tumultuous issue off campus. Besides his concern that it would provoke student reaction, he was beholden to the Cotton Whigs among Harvard fellows and overseers whose commercial interests depended so heavily on trade with the South.[9]

Quincy's lack of academic standing created doubts from the beginning. Edward Everett, by then a member of Congress, wrote John Gorham Palfrey in January, 1829: "I am exceedingly surprised at Mr Quincy's nomination, and not a little disturbed. I do not consider him qualified. He has no literary eminence, tho' a fair scholar, for a man who has led so active a life. His nomination is a hasty, unconsidered thing." Quincy never shook off the perception that he was the corporation's president alone. Years later, Andrews Norton told Palfrey that the corporation "belonged, as they still do, to the world of business, not the republic of letters;—and consequently as a means of raising the literary character of the College, and encouraging literary ambition, their first act was to appoint as President one . . . whose recommendation was that he was an efficient man of affairs."[10]

Upon Kirkland's resignation, Emerson wrote a despairing letter to his brother William: "President Kirkland you will have learned has resigned—compelled to that step by some slights if not insults put upon him by the Salem junta in the Corporation. . . . The College has got into a hand gallop on a wrong road. Tis queer that little men should show Everett & Bigelow & Judge Parker the door, & now spill the President out of the window." Everett had been asked to give up his faculty position after his election to the House of Representatives, and Jacob Bigelow gave up a chair that required public lectures, apparently in order to spend more time with medical activities. Isaac Parker, chief justice of the Massachusetts Supreme Court until his death in 1830, had been the founding faculty in law at Harvard. There may have been honest questions about his devotion to his academic duties, and in late 1827 the corporation, likely guided by that great expert on navigation Nathaniel Bowditch, abruptly asked him to step down.[11]

The "Salem junta" that spilled Kirkland out the window consisted of that same Bowditch—"fearless, tactless, and inflexible"—and his close ally Joseph Story. U.S. Supreme Court justice, director of two banks, and Harvard fellow, Story had in 1824 written the report that assured the control of his alma mater by its wealthy board rather than by the faculty. Then, in 1827, after initially boosting George Ticknor for the presidency, he read the political winds correctly and switched support to Quincy. At Quincy's inauguration, it was announced that Story would receive an appointment in jurisprudence, in effect replacing Parker as the head of a law program that was now to become a professional school. (The Supreme Court did not then require full-time service.) Emerson attended Story's own inaugural ceremony and ridiculed his remarks. Story soon became, according to the recollection of an undergraduate, "a special friend of Quincy."[12]

Quincy proved a meticulous and efficient organizer. During his long presidency, a significant number of programs were introduced and the budget was at last stabilized. Increasingly the fellows and overseers consisted of wealthy Boston merchants, and Harvard's endowment dwarfed that of peer institutions. But if to the likes of powerful insiders like Joseph Story and John Gorham Palfrey he provided the necessary managerial skills and a steady hand, to others, including Emerson, Quincy suffered by comparison to the scholarly and extraordinarily beloved Kirkland.[13]

Almost all of the faculty who had earlier attempted to expand faculty governance soon resigned. George Ticknor, perhaps the most progressive teacher at Harvard, held on until 1834. He had pushed hard for electives in the modern languages. But Quincy, along with many other Unitarians, had been impressed by the influential Yale Report of 1828 that affirmed the primacy of the Classics. When Ticknor left Harvard, finally admitting that reform would not occur, he wrote a friend that, although admiring Quincy, "We differ, however, largely, both as to what the College can be, and what it ought to be." His brother-in-law Andrews Norton had resigned three years earlier, claiming Quincy had falsely promised greater faculty governance. Accordingly, Theophilus Parsons caused "no little stir," attested a contemporary, in arguing in the pages of the *Boston Daily Advertiser* just months after Emerson's "The American Scholar" that the quality of Harvard faculty had diminished.[14]

Yet even Parsons would have conceded that, at least economically, the value of a Harvard degree had increased. To Quincy, an essential part of education was proper dress and social associations. Scheduling regular receptions for faculty and students at his home and urging the same of faculty, he intended his students to be, recollected his son, "high-minded, high-principled, well-taught, well-conducted, well-bred gentlemen"; in other words, like himself, perfect members of the Boston commercial class. And that's whom the college attracted. While the financially needy began to flood other schools, Harvard, whose tuition rose much faster than that at comparable institutions (to double Yale's), became known for drawing most of its students from the economic elite. Wealthy Boston children attended the college, observed Henry Adams, "for the sake of its social advantages."[15]

Harriet Martineau, visiting Cambridge in 1835, published a blistering attack on Quincy's Harvard that reverberated two years later in "The American Scholar." Accusing the "managers of Harvard University" of opposing "the great body of the American people," Martineau conceded that "she will probably receive sufficient patronage from the aristocracy, for a considerable time to come, to encourage her in all her faults. She has a great name . . . and the sons of the wealthy will therefore flock to her." And yet, "[t]he attainments usually made within her walls are inferior to those achieved elsewhere, her professors . . . being accustomed to lecture and examine the students, and do nothing more.[16]

The students may have been passive learners, but they could fight, and it was Quincy's businesslike efficiency that nearly brought on disaster. Student behavior had long been troublesome, and it is important to remember that the student body, with fourteen- and fifteen-year-old freshmen, was quite different from today's. Wrote a close observer: "Harvard College was then and long afterwards, as far as the instruction went, very much a boys' school, such as boys' schools then were. The students were boys, and the business of the place was to give and receive a certain dose of learning, without much thought on either side of there being anything of intrinsic interest in it." Insistent on teaching proper manners to his wealthy students, Quincy ran the college very much as a boys' school.[17]

Competition for class rank had long dominated Harvard education. An exacting manager in the age of the Industrial Revolution, Quincy brought the competition to an absurd level, instituting the infamous "Scale of Comparative Merit." Every aspect of college performance and life—recitation, declamation, written exercise, attendance, and behavior—was graded on a scale of eight, with a total of 29,920 possible points. The newly produced *Harvard Annual Report* grew thick with statistics of hours studied and of student transgressions, averaged by class and rationalized to indicate efficiency. Quincy himself closely oversaw the merit process. But when he attended class, the result was not always of assuring quality. In 1838, Longfellow wrote Ticknor, whom he had succeeded in the chair of modern languages: "The President frequently honors my lectures with his presence; and as soon as I begin, he gives his spectacles three whirls (you remember the gesture) and then falls into a deep sleep, highly flattering to the lecturer, and highly conductive to decorum among students."[18]

At the end of his freshman year in 1831, Richard Henry Dana, Jr., future author of *Two Years before the Mast*, joined other classmates in rebelling against Quincy's system. Dana later wrote about the resulting semester's suspension and study with a private tutor: "I can hardly describe the relief I felt at getting rid of the exciting emulation for college rank, & at being able to study & recite for the good of my own mind, not for the sixes, and sevens & eights, which, at Cambridge, were put against every word that came out of a student's mouth."[19]

After a few years of smoldering troubles, in 1834 there arose a great student rebellion, for which Quincy expelled the entire sophomore class and had lawbreakers prosecuted. Quincy was hung in effigy, and the undergraduate secretary of Phi Beta Kappa wrote dramatically in the chapter's minutes: "[M]ay our *Alma Mater* never again be so unnatural as to

send her own sons, nourished by her own milk, lulled to sleep by the
soothing sounds of her own instructions, to be *tried before a criminal
court.* . . . The sons of Madam Harvard tried as culprits! Verily she is a
step-mother unto us." The seniors published a circular, proclaiming that
"[President Quincy's] defective memory, and the natural impetuosity of
his character, often give the appearance of acting in an arbitrary and capri-
cious manner." Local newspapers reprinted the circular, some adding a
call for his resignation. That was averted, but only narrowly, as cousin
John Quincy Adams carried the day with the overseers. Nerves were still
raw the following year, as Martineau witnessed: "The unpopularity of the
president among the young men was extreme, and the disfavour was not
confined to them." Even three years later and months after Emerson's
"The American Scholar," a plot to destroy the college library was attributed to the same conflict.[20]

It was also in 1834 that the contract of the popular professor of German, Charles (Karl) Follen, was not renewed. Because German literature
had not been previously offered at Harvard, friends and relatives had
initially funded his chair for five years, hoping that the university would
sustain it permanently. Despite Follen's reputation as a remarkable
teacher, Quincy decided not to continue his services, and there were suspi-
cions that he acted punitively. Follen had become a leading abolitionist
and claimed to have been warned by Quincy to cease that activity. And
like Ticknor, Follen wanted to break free from Quincy's strict scale of
merit and allow students greater liberties. "He wished," recounted his
widow in a biography of her late husband, "to see less outward government in College, and to induce the young men to govern themselves."
Nor did it help that Follen's outspoken wife was a Cabot, for there was
bad blood between the Cabots (into whom Kirkland had also married)
and the Quincys.[21]

If public perception was that a promising professor had been let go for
all the wrong reasons, that was bad enough for the college. But to Transcendentalists, there was the added insult that German literature—which
fueled American Transcendentalism—was once again absent from the
Harvard curriculum. George Ripley had celebrated the inauguration of
Follen's chair in the pages of the *Christian Examiner,* seizing the occasion
to attack his former teachers by accusing them of holding "a confused
idea, taken up with very little or no examination, that [German scholars]
are all given to mysticism, rhapsody, wild and tasteless inventions in poetry, and dark and impenetrable reasonings in metaphysics." Transcendentalists believed that Follen was sympathetic to their views. The subsequent
decision to eliminate his position was inevitably interpreted as a way of
keeping dangerous knowledge out of the hands of Harvard students.[22]

Emerson, during the time of all these troubles in 1834, wrote despairingly in his journal of Harvard and of Quincy's exacting system of merit: "A young man is to be educated & schools are built & masters brought together & gymnasium erected & scientific toys & Monitorial Systems & a College endowed with many professorships and the apparatus is so enormous and unmanageable that the e-ducation or *calling out of his faculties* is never accomplished, he graduates a dunce. See how the French Mathematics at Cambridge have quite destroyed the slender chance a boy had before of learning Trigonometry."[22] But far worse was to come. As we'll later see, two years afterward and a year before Emerson spoke at Harvard, there arose a furious and widespread public debate between certain Transcendentalists and Harvard-based Unitarians over the significance of Jesus's miracles to Christianity. Andrews Norton and George Ripley in particular attacked each other viciously over whether proof of his divinity derived from a certainty that Jesus had indeed performed deeds and wonders or instead from the belief that his moral teachings had entered the soul of humanity. Several months later, Emerson's closest friend, Bronson Alcott, suffered public humiliation when the book he wrote about teaching children was ridiculed by the press. Although the attack did not originate at Harvard, there were indirect ties to that institution.

This was the Harvard Emerson knew when he delivered "The American Scholar," and just weeks later George Bancroft gave a (now lost) address at the Democratic State Convention at Worcester in which he apparently criticized Harvard for elitism. The following year Martineau attacked the college for being the private refuge of the wealthy, and the next year still Orestes Brownson noted in the *Boston Quarterly Review* that Harvard "has not of late years been renowned for her reverence for the people, her faith in democratic institutions, or her efforts to establish universal suffrage and equal rights." Harvard, in fact, did not take "any peculiar pains to educate her sons in harmony with those free principles which are the just pride of all true Americans." Bancroft, Martineau, and Brownson criticized Harvard's emphasis on class and status. Emerson, far less liberal politically, drew a somewhat different conclusion. Emerson wasn't so concerned that Harvard's emphasis on wealth might be undemocratic. To him, it was intellectually constraining. Any economic or political path, narrowly framed and fiercely practiced for the sake of self-preservation, prevented the transformational teaching that Emerson demanded. Franklin Benjamin Sanborn recounted that Emerson hoped for a "good crop of mystics at Harvard," to which observation Sanborn responded that Harvard was "the last place in which many of that class were to be found."[24]

Just as he fought the Unitarian consensus on national literature, Emerson also opposed an institution that, from its president on down, was preoccupied with the mere mechanics of education. Precisely because he had a deep appreciation for the education he had received, he reacted strongly to Harvard's increasing compromise of intellectual inspiration. Emerson's other talks of the period, with the exception of the Divinity School address, are mild and reserved. At Harvard, it was the passion arising out of personal experience that forced his rhetoric to soar.

And soar it did. To punctuate the separation of his scholar from that characterized by previous orators and to chasten the host institution for its failings, Emerson used speech so raw that it, rather than the substance of his talk, drew the greater notice. Observed Oliver Wendell Holmes:

> The dignity, not to say the formality of an Academic assembly was startled by the realism that looked for the infinite in "the meal in the firkin; the milk in the pan." They could understand the deep thoughts suggested by "the meanest flower that blows," but these domestic illustrations had a kind of nursery homeliness about them which the grave professors and sedate clergymen were unused to expect on so stately an occasion. But the young men went out from it as if a prophet had been proclaiming to them "Thus saith the Lord."[25]

Emerson had already begun employing realism in recent lyceum lectures, but "The American Scholar" was its first significant manifestation. The result, as Holmes suggested, shocked the audience. No previous Phi Beta Kappa orator had ever used—had ever thought it desirable to use— the language of the street. Emerson tied his attack on conventional language to the very heart of his message, that humanity, in its modern condition, was eviscerated: "The state of society is one in which the members have suffered amputation from the trunk, and strut about so many walking monsters,—a good finger, a neck, a stomach, an elbow, but never a man." Alternating between the high style and the low, Emerson employed ordinary language to keep listeners off balance and exalt the enterprising scholar above his staid audience. Describing how childhood memories turn into adult insight, he teased: "Observe, too, the impossibility of antedating this act. In its grub state, it cannot fly, it cannot shine, it is a dull grub. But suddenly, without observation, the selfsame thing unfurls beautiful wings, and is an angel of wisdom." He taunted his listeners indecorously: "I have heard it said that the clergy, who are always, more universally than any other class, the scholars of their day,— are addressed as women; that the rough, spontaneous conversation of men they do not hear, but only a mincing and diluted speech." Emerson's words had an impact that was immediate, disturbing even his friend William Henry Channing.[26]

Emerson's use of realism, the grotesque, and earthy humor was to exert enormous influence on American letters. Yet he in turn had his own obvious influences. Eyewitness John Pierce described "The American Scholar" as written in "the dreamy, unintelligible style of Swedenborg, Coleridge, and Carlyle." Emerson was first introduced to Swedenborg by Sampson Reed, who himself possessed "an oracular, cryptic style." But it was especially through Coleridge, de Staël, and Carlyle—who also provided through his translations a portal to Goethe—that Emerson came to understand the power of the vernacular. Three months before the oration, Emerson admonished himself in his journals that he must speak out on *Wilhelm Meister's Apprenticeship*, Goethe's most controversial work, recently translated by Carlyle. He then sent off to the *Christian Examiner* a review of Carlyle's own *The French Revolution*, which revealed the extent of the Scotsman's influence: "One thing has for some time been becoming plainer, and is now quite undeniable, that Mr. Carlyle's genius, whether benignant or baleful, is no transient meteor, and no expiring taper, but a robust flame self-kindled and self-fed, and more likely to light others into a conflagration, than to be speedily blown out." Emerson became closely identified with Carlyle, whose interest in everyday language and popular culture was naturally threatening to hierarchical religion and society. When faculty of the Princeton Theological Seminary attacked Emerson's Divinity School address, they described it as "a rhapsody, obviously in imitation of Thomas Carlyle, and possessing as much of the vice of his mannerisms as the author could borrow, but without his genius."[27]

For the fire and blood of his prose, Emerson, still a practicing minister if one without a permanent congregation, also drew on fellow preachers. Edward Thompson Taylor, the evangelical minister of the Seamen's Bethel Church and model for Father Mapple in *Moby-Dick*, gave sermons full of ejaculatory admonitions and colorful language. It is often rightly recognized that Emerson admired and to some extent emulated Father Taylor, believing that he spoke from experience which he then imprinted on the world. But rather than focus on an individual, it is more accurate to put Emerson's explosive rhetoric into broader, more deeply rooted traditions that Taylor, too, had tapped.[28]

Brought to America by Puritans, the jeremiad, as reinvented in the new country, was used both to remind congregations of their present failings and to inspire them to higher goals. Jeremiads began by noting the scriptural text that confirmed the communal norm under discussion, then detailed how the community had strayed from those values, and finally declared a prophetic vision that reconciled an ideal vision with what was practically attainable. Emerson had occasionally resorted to the jeremiad in his ministerial sermons, and, after his own fashion, this is what he did in "The American Scholar." He began by citing the primordial myth of the integrated human: "The old fable covers a doctrine ever new and sublime; that there is One Man,—present to all particular men only partially, or through one faculty; and that you must take the whole society to find the whole man." With harsh polemics, he then chastised the academy for failing to produce such an integrated scholar—"instead of Man Thinking, we have the bookworm . . . the restorers of readings, the emendators, the bibliomaniacs of all degrees"—and for being more interested in narrow materialism: "Gowns, and pecuniary foundations, though of towns of gold, can never countervail the least sentence or syllable of wit." Emerson evoked the higher vision of the American scholar as prophet, defiled especially by the educated, but eventually redeemed. He concluded by grounding this elevated vision of the scholar in concrete examples of individuals whom he could commend: those who drew on popular culture, continental Romantic writers, and Emanuel Swedenborg. Full of harsh language and accusations, Emerson's jeremiad made the sedate Unitarian audience feel judged and found wanting. When, while writing the address, he referred to the intended audience as "our saints," Emerson was sarcastically recalling the Puritan term for their own elect. It was those elect whom with his jeremiad he would humble.[29]

The fiery visionary proclaimed: "Young men are shut up in their schools, confined to books and shut out of the intercourse with the common people, or contact with the common mind." A reader of Emerson might well identify that passage as coming from "The American Scholar." That reader would be wrong. What Emerson said was: "Meek young men grow up in libraries, believing it their duty to accept the views, which Cicero, which Locke, which Bacon, have given, forgetful that Cicero, Locke, and Bacon were only young men in libraries, when they wrote these books." Although making much the same point with similar imagery, the first passage comes from a book of sermons published two years earlier by Charles Grandison Finney, that century's most powerful revivalist preacher. There is no obvious connection between the Boston Brahmin and the travelling minister and no direct evidence that Emerson read Finney's book. But Finney did visit Boston in 1831–1832, and Unitarian clergy paid special interest in attending—perhaps policing—his sermons. Then minister of the Second Church, Emerson may well have been one of them, for he acknowledged the power of Finney's preaching.[30]

Unitarian clergy would have had reason to pay attention. Protestant church attendance in the first third of the nineteenth century grew rapidly, with the number of churches in Boston increasing fourfold. Yet most of that increase was due to the revivalism of the Second Great Awakening, drawing even in the eastern United States far more followers than did Unitarianism. Refined revivalist meetings, akin to the Edwardsian experiences of the First Great Awakening, had recently given way to the intensive and less controlled gatherings that had also come to pose a social threat in the later stages of the First Great Awakening. Revivalist fires so illuminated the sky that parts of Ohio and New York became known as "burned-over districts." Finney was the acknowledged leader of the aggressive stage, which included public confrontation of sinners, wildly evocative praying, claims of prophetic visions, and attacks on less enthusiastic ministers. As did Emerson, Finney used a powerful oratory drawn from the vernacular: "[A]mong farmers and mechanics and other classes of men I borrowed my illustrations from their various occupations. . . . I addressed them in the language of the common people." For the minister to neglect the principle of using the language of common life would be, he claimed, "wicked." Revivalists visited slums and shouted about the need for action. Unitarians certainly had their own commitment to social reform, but announced they would be responding to the vices of society in a rational, restrained voice.[31]

Of course, Unitarians "were outraged," Perry Miller caustically observed, "both as theologians and as gentlemen." Unitarian minister Ephraim Perkins characterized Finney's preaching style as you "raise your voice, lift high your hand, bend forward your trunk, fasten your staring eyes upon the auditors, declare that they know it to be God's truth that they stand upon the brink of hell's gaping pit of fire and brimstone, and bending your body and bringing your clenched fist half way from the pulpit to the broad aisle, denounce *instant and eternal damnation* upon them unless they repent forthwith." In contrast, the ideal of Unitarian sermonizing, testified Octavius Brooks Frothingham, was "a quiet, even strain of public speech, manly and elevating. . . . The 'water of life,' if cold, was pure; if not sparkling, it was fresh. There was no fanaticism, little enthusiasm." To John Locke, patron saint of Unitarian philosophy, enthusiasm was antithetical to reason-based religious faith.[32]

Harvard, the center of Unitarian training and theology, also felt the pressures of revivalism. Although enjoying its bicentennial in 1836, the nation's oldest college was rapidly changing. Partly in response to Jonathan Edwards's earlier religious revival, Harvard had become a center of scientific rationalism. Then, in the first decade of the new century and somewhat in reaction to the Second Great Awakening, the institution filled its presidency and the Hollis Professorship of Divinity with men of a liberal Christianity. Calvinist Jedidiah Morse, who also happened to be a Harvard overseer, furiously assailed the decisions in print and in 1808 helped found Andover Theological Seminar. Supported by Yale president Timothy Dwight, who was infusing his own students with religious fervor, Andover became the first professional graduate school in the country and a center of revivalism. Harvard's president Kirkland responded in 1811 by establishing the Divinity School and then, in 1819, the year the Divinity School was fully operational, by appointing Andrews Norton the Dexter Professor of Sacred Literature. Norton attacked both Yale and Andover that year in *A Statement of Reasons for Not Believing the Doctrines of the Trinitarians*, a work that went through several editions.[33]

Harvard needed the help. The year that Finney published his call-to-arms for the modern revivalist minister, the *Christian Examiner*, edited by ministers trained at and often on the faculty of Harvard, reviewed a volume on the history of its favorite college. Even the *Examiner*, however, could not help noting with some annoyance that the glory of Harvard had been reduced by revivalism: "The temporary phrenzy of religious party may for a time diminish the number of her students, but cannot permanently lessen her usefulness or obscure her fame." The Divinity School especially suffered, and, once in decline, matriculation remained low for most of the century.[34]

The challenges to Harvard, however, were coming not just from the religiously conservative. As we'll see later, Norton's own students—the Transcendentalists—were accusing him and his Harvard colleagues in the pages of the same *Christian Examiner* of not being liberal enough. It was only in 1825 that the American Unitarian Association was established, and even in the 1830s many members preferred to be called simply "liberals." Unitarians, with a fragile hold on their own fate, were stung by the attacks of their epigoni.

Then suddenly, on a day of great pomp and circumstance, Emerson, one of their very own, rose to assault them. When he portrayed the ideal scholar wondering through villages and appealing directly to the common people in their own language, Unitarians must have feared that revivalists and Transcendentalists, despite great differences, had somehow ganged up on them. Previous Phi Beta Kappa orators, with their emphasis on gradual self-culture, annually reinforced their community's beliefs against rapid social and spiritual change. Emerson departed from the traditional prescription, promoting radically new ideals in education and culture and using a radical way to express them. Unconcerned with charges of barbarism or antinomianism, Emerson fearlessly proposed ideals and language that lacked the formal constraints Unitarians demanded.

Revivalism was only one of many urgent movements sweeping the land. Most important was abolitionism, in large part spawned by the Second Great Awakening. Redemption from sin, possible and necessary for the revivalist, came by word and deed. But how could those who were enslaved and without recourse to voluntary action redeem themselves? Salvation, revivalists argued, depended on manumission. Unitarians, on the other hand, who did not believe in original sin and strove more for perfection than redemption, were not, until very near the Civil War, enthusiastic about abolition. They were also uncomfortable with the intensity of the rhetoric, for abolitionist meetings often produced passionate, accusatory speech and harsh audience reaction. With mob violence against abolitionist rallies seeming to be ever on the rise, most Unitarian churches and Harvard banned public discussion of emancipation. When Emerson gave his oration, the Grimké sisters were touring the Northeast, causing special concern among cautious Unitarians. In "The American Scholar," Emerson embraced the rhetorical power of the abolitionists before he felt able to embrace the cause of abolitionism. Giving a talk which stirred his heart as well as his mind was an important beginning, as we'll see in the next chapter, in his own slow journey toward public activism.[35]

Brilliantly, Emerson mixed form and content. "The American Scholar" conforms to classical oratorical structure—his only extant speech to do so precisely—opening with an *exordium*, followed by an exhibition, and closing with the peroration. Quickly, harsh polemics, so much more appropriate to a political or forensic oration, take over. Emerson's sense of urgency converted a state occasion into a political trial. But he saved the speech from being merely an attack on its audience by imposing the substructure of the jeremiad. That focused the polemics not on the listeners but on human nature generally and provided an optimistic vision for the future. His feelings for Harvard's current direction fueled his passions, but he took control of the anger by putting it in the service of his idealism. Emerson did not want to defeat his audience; he wanted, much more, to shake it. "Colleges . . . can only highly serve us, when they aim not to drill, but to create; when they gather from far every ray of various genius to their hospitable halls, and, by the concentrated fires, set the hearts of their youth on flame."[36]

"The American Scholar" most certainly did set on flame the hearts of at least some of the attending youth. Even so, Emerson's rhetoric, drawn from authentic American experiences of the jeremiad and the revival, was only the stylized part of an argument for new substance as well as new form. The American scholar need attend not only to its expression but to its essence. Ignoring the constraints not only of European institutions but American ones as well, the scholar must live from within. If that was lost on most of Emerson's audience, it was not lost on his literary offspring— as diverse and gigantic as the country that produced them—from Thoreau, Whitman, and Dickinson to Stein, Ellison, and Bellow.

Chapter Four

SELF-RELIANCE

AS ICONOCLASTIC AS THE VISION OF "THE AMERICAN
Scholar" might have been, delivering the address proved the easy part.
The hard thing for Emerson was to come before friend and foe, confident that he would remain his own master. Self-reliance, despite pious
proclamations, never came readily, if at all, to Emerson. Feeling tor-
mented that speaking in support of ideals might draw him into conflict
and therefore compromise his self-reliance, and equally concerned that
such candor might cost him revenue on the lyceum circuit, he hesitated
to speak out and then rebuked himself for hesitating. How Emerson
struggled to achieve for himself what he demanded of the American
scholar is as important as the speech itself, for it connects Emerson's
idealism to his humanity.

Self-reliance was to become a lifelong goal, first fully articulated in
"The American Scholar." In sermons and lyceum lectures, Emerson had
expressed a vague desire for intellectual and moral independence. But at
Harvard, on fire with a vision of the intrepid scholar, he directly linked
the courage to speak the truth with the self-reliance he made famous in
the essay of that name written two years later: "[I]t becomes [the Scholar]
to feel all confidence in himself, and to defer never to the popular cry.
He and he only knows the world. . . . In silence, in steadiness, in severe
abstraction, let him hold by himself; add observation to observation, patient of neglect, patient of reproach; and bide his own time. . . . In self-
trust, all the virtues are comprehended." So much did Emerson think of
himself as the self-reliant scholar that he claimed to be impervious to
audience reaction: "For this self-trust, the reason is deeper than can be
fathomed. . . . I might not carry with me the feeling of my audience in

stating my own belief. But I have already shown the ground of my hope, in adverting to the doctrine that man is one."[1]

Despite his bold declaration "to feel all confidence in himself, and to defer never to the popular cry," however, personal insecurities became manifest immediately following the oration. His wife, Lidian, preserved the only record of the Transcendental Club's discussion, held the night after his talk: "I think it not unlikely," she wrote her sister the next day, "you will hear that his discourse was not generally interesting—(interesting to the generality—I mean to say) but Mrs Ripley of Waltham tells me he fully answered the hopes of his most devoted literary friends. Hedge—Stetson—G P B[radford] &c. . . . I do not think the audience looked particularly edified—(though I am told that they did—uncommonly so)." The double negatives and qualifying parentheticals indicate just how cautiously the Emerson family viewed the reaction, and how much friends hastened to reassure them.[2]

For at least the next month, Emerson tried to gauge the reception. His first journal entry after the oration was hopeful: "It seemed the other day a fact of some moment that the project of our companion be he who he may, & that what it may, is always entitled in courteous society to deference and superiority." But a week later he required more precise confirmation: "It occurred the other day in hearing some clapping of hands after a speech, that the orator's value might be measured by every additional round after the first three claps. . . . [For] the first & second roll come very easily off, but it gets beyond the third very hardly." He soon fussed: "I suppose there was seldom a person of my age & advantages whom so little people could pull down & overcrow. The least people do most entirely demolish me . . . a snippersnapper eats me whole."[3]

Emerson looked back on the talk with regret and even repression. Governor Edward Everett, one of Emerson's early idols, presided over the dinner that evening, and in a toast fulsome and tempered declared the talk "a train of original remark and ingenious speculation, clothed in language the most exquisite and uttered with a natural grace beyond the reach of art." Everett then recalled with far greater sincerity the memory of Emerson's two recently deceased brothers, Charles and Edward. A month later, brother William asked Emerson why he had not sent him a copy of the remarks. Everett's empty praise was nothing to share with family.[4]

At the same dinner, longtime friend Charles Warren offered his own toast, which Emerson recorded: "Mr. President, I suppose all know where the orator comes from; and I suppose all know what he has said; I give you *The Spirit of Concord; it makes us all of One Mind.*" Many assume that Emerson's reaction, that "it was the happiest turn to my old thrum," expresses his confidence that the audience was unanimous in its approval. Its placement suggests otherwise. Emerson slipped the anecdote into his journal nearly three weeks after the oration. His notation reflected the need to confirm his success as he continued to look back on the event.[5]

His spirit must have risen when Henry Hedge urged him to publish the talk (only about half the Harvard Phi Beta Kappa orations of that period were published, and none from the immediately surrounding years, 1836 and 1838–1840). The first printing sold out within a month. But Emerson's continued anxiety is evident, not only because he recorded the fact in the *Journals*, but because of how he did so. "I find in town the Φ.B.K. Oration, of which 500 copies were printed, all sold, in about one month." He then crossed out the "about" and substituted "just." Emerson felt the need to boast, if only to himself.[6]

Yet by December, he seemed reconciled to seeing "The American Scholar" sink into oblivion. Wrote Lidian to Elizabeth Palmer Peabody, "He says he has never thought of having a new edition of the P.B.K. address—none is as yet called for; and most likely never will be." But within weeks of Lidian's letter, Emerson sent off the text for another edition. His initial miscalculation probably resulted from the aftermath of his November abolition speech, which clearly was not a success, even to his friends, and the lack of consistent acclaim for "The American Scholar." Emerson was not yet able to assess his achievement independently of public criticism. Although he would in the future continue to feel pessimistic and even fearful of critical response, by the following year he did at least begin to sense that controversy brought commercial success. After the harsh reaction to his Divinity School address, Emerson hastened to make the piece ready for purchase at Harvard's commencement six weeks later. Certainly he wanted to assure an accurate record of his speech. But, along with his great influence on American letters, Emerson may have been the first to develop the idea of convention book sales.[7]

The bold vision of "The American Scholar" belied, then, the doubts Emerson felt. Emotionally dependent on relationships and the opinion of others, he was at his best when he drew on people and their reactions. In fact, because Emerson's most celebrated lectures, "The American Scholar" and the Divinity School address, were in front of people he knew well, we shouldn't confuse his proclaimed moral and intellectual self-reliance with a physical reclusion so often and mistakenly attributed to him. Emerson was hardly a recluse. He frequently preached on Sundays until 1838, and usually attended church even after giving up the pulpit. He was on numerous municipal committees, belonged to social clubs, and was quite savvy about village politics. He lived with his mother and then with her and his growing family—he was not shy about courting or marrying. He invited friends frequently to his Concord home, often for long stays. Emerson's desire for self-reliance did not include physical isolation. As he wrote Carlyle, "A new person is always to me a great event, & will not let me sleep," and as he admitted to himself, "Solitude is fearsome & heavy hearted . . . leave me alone a few days, & I creep about as if in expectation of a calamity." "He lectured everywhere, and knew everyone," concluded John Updike.[8]

Self-reliance for Emerson meant depending upon one's innate moral sensibilities—one's Reason—and limiting the influence of the external world, perceived through one's Understanding. In practical terms, it meant being with people and yet forming one's thoughts independently. That is how he understood it in his most famous essay, "Self-Reliance," composed in the summer of 1839: "It is easy in the world to live after the world's opinion; it is easy in solitude to live after our own; but the great man is he who in the midst of the crowd keeps with perfect sweetness the independence of solitude." Or so he hoped. If to some he appeared detached and had difficulty committing fully to friends and movements, the very fact that he struggled and even agonized over that detachment indicates his dependency. He grew up with brothers on whom he closely relied. In utter collapse over the death of Charles in 1836, he wrote to Aunt Mary: "In him I have lost all my society. I sought no other and formed my habits to live with him"; to Thomas Carlyle: "I have put so much dependence on his gifts that we made but one man together"; to Harriet Martineau: "In Charles, I found society that indemnified me for almost total seclusion from all other. He was my philosopher, my poet, my hero, my Christian"; and to Lidian: "[Y]ou must be content henceforth with only a piece of your husband; for the best of his strength lay in the soul with which he must no more on earth take counsel. How much I saw through his eyes." Emerson certainly had other society, but there is truth in the statement of how much he could develop a dependence on others.[9]

People and opinion could bring him low. He worried constantly, as we have seen, about the reception of "The American Scholar," fussing that "the least people do most entirely demolish me." He wrestled most of his life with the memory of his long-deceased father, and what he wrote publicly about him would not redound to his credit. Guilt, especially in the early years, is manifest in his journals. And a devoted husband, he opened himself to complex emotional involvement with other women. Margaret Fuller, very much Emerson's intellectual equal, was, like him, also blessed with considerable charm. She "was not beautiful," recalled a near-contemporary, "but she was more than beautiful. A sort of warm glow surrounded her, and warmed those who listened." Despite his reminding her of Aristotle's aphorism that "*O my friends*, there are no friends," their rich correspondence attests to an only slightly repressed erotic relationship, about which he clearly fretted. He wrote in despair

Figure 6. Margaret Fuller. Engraving from a painting by Alonzo
Chappel in Evert A. Duyckinck, *Portrait Gallery of Eminent Men
and Women with Biographies* (New York: Johnson, Wilson, 1873).
Courtesy of the John Hay Library, Brown University.

after she, along with her husband and young child, was drowned in 1850:
"I have lost in her my audience." And audience, to Emerson, was just
about everything.[10]

   He was also not above social pretense. After learning of Henry Hedge's
reservations about him, Emerson confided to Fuller spitefully, "I owe him
gratitude for all his manifest kindness to me, though he is wrong to say
he loves me, for I am sure he does not quite." He triumphantly reported
to his Aunt Mary that he dined with the governor "by invitation, at his

Figure 7. Emerson's Concord home, into which he moved in 1835. He owned two acres of land. From *Ralph Waldo Emerson: His Maternal Ancestors*, by David Greene Haskins (Boston: Cupples, Upham, 1887).

house—The other company were people of no interest to you or to me." And despite his attacks on materialism, he could become absorbed with business affairs—fighting hard for his share of his first wife's estate, lamenting when he missed opportunities to profit more from his lectures, and worrying about his (at times) significant land holdings and house full of servants.[11]

Even in "Self-Reliance" he admitted to falling short of his ideal. Attacking institutionalized charity, Emerson asked, "Are they *my* poor?" and denied that he should contribute: "[T]hough I confess with shame I sometimes succumb and give the dollar, it is a wicked dollar which by and by I shall have the manhood to withhold." In 1839, he had not yet attained sufficient self-reliance to resist even the simple request for charity. But promising future perfection was uncharacteristic of Emerson and more akin to the Unitarian notion of progressive self-cultivation than to the Transcendentalist creed of constant reinvention. There is, to be sure, some self-parody in echoing what Jesus had said about the poor (John 12:8). Yet written at a time when friends still hoped he would join them in social activism, Emerson was also signaling his separation from organized reform movements. Positioning himself among his friends intruded into his statement of ideals.

Although denying that he should give to charity for its own sake, he then admitted in the same essay to a general social commitment, for "there is a class of persons to whom by all spiritual affinity I am bought and sold; for them I will go to prison, if need be." But he followed this with the complaint that "[a]t times the whole world seems to be in conspiracy to importune you with emphatic trifles. Friend, client, child, sickness, fear, want, charity, all knock at once at thy closet door and say,— 'Come out unto us.' But keep thy state; come not into their confusion. The power men possess to annoy me, I give them by a weak curiosity." He would go to jail for his friends, but would not answer their knock on the door. Yet without first attending to them, how does one determine what is trivial and what a matter for which one should go to jail? And how does one build friendships without the trifles?[12]

Perhaps the tensions and contradictions are intentional. Perhaps Emerson used irony, ambiguity, and self-contradiction to bring out the full range of possible truths within the human condition. But perhaps this was also the best Emerson could do to write himself out of his own social dependency. If writing is an act of self-discovery, for those who produce primarily for a public, the therapy tends to be done in public. Emerson, on the other hand, wrote first for himself in his journals. Composed almost exclusively of material selected from these journals, the seemingly candid essays were in fact carefully filtered and rigorously redacted. Polished gems, they reflect his strongest claims to independence. But the *Journals*— what Harold Bloom calls simply "his authentic works"—contain a thick residue of often agonizing dependency.[13]

Just after composing, but before publishing, "Self-Reliance," Emerson compared himself unfavorably to his closest friend, Bronson Alcott. By Emerson's definition of self-reliance as expressed in the essay of that name, Alcott fit the bill perfectly. But not Emerson himself: "In all companies I sympathize too much. If they are ordinary & mean, I am. If the company were great I should soar: in all mere mortal parties, I take the contagion of their views & lose my own. I cannot outsee them, or correct, or raise them. As soon as they are gone, the muse returns; I see the facts as all cultivated men always have seen them, and am a great man alone." Here is a signed confession that the Emerson of the lofty essays was not the Emerson who privately worried so about social acceptance. In "Fate," Emerson openly acknowledged his dual persona with the term "double consciousness" (later modified and made famous by DuBois in *The Souls of Black Folk*). Emerson described it this way: "A man must ride alternately on the horses of his private and his public nature, as the equestrians in the circus throw themselves nimbly from horse to horse, or plant one foot on the back of one, and the other foot on the back of the other." Because he struggled mightily with identity, it is willful to believe, as many do, that Emerson achieved the sort of self-reliance he preached in his essays.[14]

As a practical matter, in fact, the lived experience is essential to understanding the formal statements of moral philosophers. How compelling would the words of Socrates or Jesus seem if we didn't know the price either paid for them? Emerson himself tied ideas to life by arguing that history is always biography, that the past does not exist outside of one's own confrontation with it. The tone and substance of "The American Scholar" is especially close to Emerson's lived experience. As we'll see later, he composed the oration in just a few weeks and in a white heat, full of anger and fear. Desperate to jump start his creativity, he drew much of the material from journal entries of those very weeks and depended for inspiration on a visit from a friend. He used polemics to anticipate the reaction of his audience and yet worried for months afterward about the reaction. To view the talk apart from the dependencies is to elevate Emerson's intentions but misunderstand his genius.[15]

Precisely one month before being invited to address Harvard Phi Beta Kappa, Emerson entered into his journals a startling admission that he was losing the respect of his friends because he had not acted:

> You think that because you have spoken nothing when others spoke and have given no opinion upon the times, upon Wilhelm Meister, upon Abolition, upon Harvard College, that your verdict is still expected with curiosity as a reserved wisdom. Far otherwise; it is known that you have no opinion: You are measured by your silence & found wanting. You have no oracle to utter, & your fellowmen have learned that you cannot help them; for oracles speak.[16]

During the following year and in direct response to this painful confession, he delivered "The American Scholar," his first speech on abolition, and the Divinity School address. "The American Scholar" attacked Harvard's narrow pedagogy and took indirect note of Goethe's *Wilhelm Meister's Apprenticeship* and *Travels*, both recently translated by Carlyle. Goethe and Carlyle, along with Wordsworth, Coleridge and de Staël, had presented Transcendentalists with powerful new ways of interpreting both the spiritual and everyday worlds. In "The American Scholar," Emerson rose to their support. Two months after that oration, Emerson delivered his first, tentative public thoughts on abolition. "The times" that Emerson referred to in the journal entry almost certainly had to include the miracles controversy, which had been raging for the past year and which he turned to in the Divinity School address with sudden fury.

What is absolutely essential to appreciate is that Emerson's actions were prompted by what he thought were the expectations of his friends. If he wanted to serve as an oracle to Transcendentalists and, in particular, if he wanted to live up to the high ideals of his emotional anchor, Bronson Alcott, who was then under exceptional stress, he needed to speak out on questions in which they were already engaged. The noble proclamation of self-reliance espoused in "The American Scholar" was largely guided by perceived obligations to friends.

Emerson's remorse that he had not spoken as an oracle arose because of his failure in the public forum he already had at his disposal. Having resigned his ministry in 1832 and upon returning from his European trip a year later, Emerson was offered his first lyceum date. The lyceum movement had just been started in 1828 by the Boston Society for the Diffusion of Useful Knowledge, on which board sat Emerson's cousin, George Bliss Emerson. The movement spread quickly, giving Emerson ready access to a public he missed after giving up his pulpit. Speaking from the late fall through the early spring, Emerson might offer several lectures in a concentrated period of two to four weeks in (say) Salem or New Bedford, but his main presentation took place in Boston. In 1836, his weekly lectures at the newly built Masonic Temple were on such topics as "Humanity of Science," "Literature," "Politics," "Religion," "Society," "Trades and Professions," "Ethics," "and "The Individual." Lyceum revenue that year almost matched what he made as a part-time preacher (netting about $360 for the Boston series), and, rather than work through a middle man, he himself rented space, placed advertisements, and sold tickets. In the spring of 1838, Emerson wrote his mother, Ruth, that, because "lecturing . . . promises to be good bread," he would give up his occasional ministerial responsibilities in East Lexington and "shall not preach more except from the Lyceum." He had found the vocation he had been searching for.[17]

If the profits began to accrue, staking his intellectual reputation on lyceum lecturing was risky business. Oliver Wendell Holmes painted a dismal picture of his own experience: "Front seats: a few old folks—shiny-headed—slant up best ear towards the speaker—drop off asleep after a while. . . . Bright women's faces, young and middle-aged, a little behind these. . . . Here and there countenance, sharp and scholarlike, and a dozen pretty female ones sprinkled about. An indefinite number of pairs of young people—happy, but not always attentive." What Emerson's friend described was a social event without expectation of deep illumination. Certainly there was no expectation of being exposed to profound, disturbing, or controversial thoughts. When the lyceum movement began in 1828, it was announced that the speaker should talk in "a plain, familiar way, fitted to the comprehension of all members." The Salem lyceum invited Emerson to address their organization in 1837, provided that "no allusions are made to religious controversy or other exciting topics upon which the public mind is honestly divided." Emerson declined.[18]

Despite Holmes's colorful description, lyceum audiences were largely populated by middle-class merchants, who, desiring upward mobility, were looking for information they could use. After all, the movement was

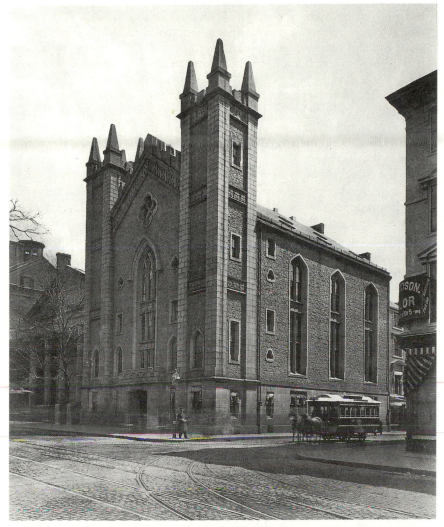

Figure 8. The Masonic Temple, where Emerson gave lyceum lectures and Bronson Alcott had his Temple School. Courtesy of the Boston Public Library, Print Department.

overseen by the Boston Society for the Diffusion of Useful Information. Henry Hedge as early as 1834 sharply criticized the evident utilitarian expectations, lamenting in the *Christian Examiner*, "The sentiment which this institution expresses is respect for knowledge, but it is a kind of respect . . . for the results of knowledge rather than for knowledge itself. It is the applicability to the practical purposes of life, rather than the inherent,

essential worth, which our people prize." Emerson well understood
Hedge's concern, writing in his journals: "Do, dear, when you come to
write Lyceum lectures, remember that you are not . . . [to say] what they
will expect to hear but what is fit for me to say." Rightly worried, as it
turned out, that he might compromise his intentions, when he began lecturing in 1834 Emerson swore an oath of faithfulness to his inner light:
"Hail to the quiet fields of my fathers! . . . Bless my purposes as they are
simple & virtuous. . . . I will say at Public Lectures & the like, those things
which I have meditated for their own sake & not for the first time with a
view to that occasion."[19]

Emerson's decision to earn a living as an independent speaker is generally applauded as a demonstration of his self-reliance. That's certainly the
way he presented it publicly, in his optimistic 1843 lecture "New England:
Genius, Manners, and Customs." But in private he saw it otherwise, expressing deep anxiety that he was falling short of his own expectations
and a bitter belief that he was working only for money. From the very
beginning, he considered public speaking "this new drudgery," and approaching the start of the 1837–1838 lyceum season he told Margaret
Fuller: "I have promised in the newspaper some more lectures[.] I thought
once I had made up my mind to the dignity & beatitude of silence, but
who can defend us from wallowing if that is our weird." Perplexity
quickly turned to despair: "I wake up in the morning & think, Well, I
need not go to Boston or New York. . . . If I were master of Millions I
should not feel such vexation but should control the circumstances[,] &
inasmuch as I am master of hundreds or thousands, I do." And a bit later:
"I will, I think, no longer do things unfit for me. . . . Why should I read
lectures with care & pain & afflict myself with all the meanness of ticket
mongering, when I might sit, as God in his goodness has enabled me, a
free poor man with wholesome bread & warm clothes though without
cakes or gewgaws, & write & speak the beautiful & formidable words
of a free man?" Twice Emerson juxtaposed the lyceum lecturer with the
free (and poor!) man. If he believed that, where was the idealism he had
expressed in the oath of 1834?[20]

Voicing a reluctance to continue, Emerson claimed financial need drove
him on: "I see plainly I shall have no choice about lecturing again next
year; I must do it," he wrote William in the summer of 1839. As he pre-
pared for the lyceum season, he conceded that until he achieved financial
independence, "I submit to sell tickets again." He admitted to Fuller that
his lectures sounded so dull that they "would walk with due decorum in
the columns of the Christian Register" and agonized in his journals:
"These lectures give me little pleasure. I have not done what I hoped when
I said, I will try it once more. I have not once transcended the coldest
selfpossession. I said I will agitate others, being agitated myself. . . . Alas!

alas! I have not the recollection of one strong moment." The depths of frenetic despair to which professional speaking drove him and his incessant struggle over work, candor, and, ultimately, money are revealed in that same entry:

> I ought to seek to lay myself out utterly,—large, enormous, prodigal, upon the subject of the week. But a hateful experience has taught me that I can only expend, say, twenty one hours on each lecture, if I would also be ready & able for the next. Of course, I spend myself prudently; I economize; I cheapen; whereof nothing grand ever grew. Could I spend sixty hours on each, or what is better, had I such energy that I could rally the lights & mights of sixty hours into twenty, I should hate myself less.

Little wonder that, after finishing the Boston series, he wrote William: "unhappily the lectures are ended—ten decorous speeches & not one extacy, not one rapture, not one thunderbolt." Friends were relieved. Wrote Sophia Ripley to John Sullivan Dwight: "I am not sorry the lectures are drawing to a close, for he is tired of them & their life is departing." Emerson confided to Carlyle that he talked for money and glory and despaired that attendance in Boston was on the way back down. But when a few months later he repeated the talks in New York to large crowds and a great purse, he could write his brother, "[I] crowed unto myself on the way home."[21]

Emerson never did hurl thunderbolts on the lyceum circuit. Commented a Cincinnati newspaper after a 1850 lecture stop there: Emerson was "as unpretending as . . . a good old grandfather over his Bible. . . . [H]is most remarkable trait is that of plain *common sense*." In his eulogy to Thoreau, Emerson admitted that he was always concerned about reception: "Talking one day of a public discourse, Henry remarked, that whatever succeeded with the audience, was bad, I said 'Who would not like to write something which all can read, like "Robinson Crusoe"; and who does not see with regret that his page is not solid with a right materialistic treatment, which delights everybody.' Henry objected, of course, and vaunted the better lectures which reached only a few persons." With the exception of his two academic talks at Harvard and until his embrace of abolitionism, Emerson could bring himself neither to alienate nor abandon his audience. Committed to public lecturing to pay his bills, Emerson remained in an emotional purgatory of fame and (at times significant) fortune.[22]

This was not the first time Emerson felt that, in speaking publicly, he was compromising principles. He had had a similar experience during his years in the ministry. Moving quickly past the liberal Christian embrace of both a single godhead and a divine Christ, Emerson viewed Jesus as the exemplar of the human who allowed God to reside fully within him, so that man and God spoke as one. That same unity, Emerson believed, should be the sacred hope of every individual. But the heterodoxy was not an easy position for the young minister to express, and modern research indicates that Emerson put his most controversial statements in the parts of his sermons where congregants would least take notice. For the year before his resignation from the Second Church, Emerson's journals are filled with harsh self-recrimination: "Who opposes me, who shuts up my mouth, who hinders the flow of my exhortation? Myself, only myself. Cannot I conform myself to my principles? Set the principles as low, as loose you please, set the tune not one note higher than the true pitch[,] but after settling what they shall be, stick to them[.]" And when he finally came to realize that, to be true to those principles, he would have to surrender his pulpit, he made the quick financial calculation: "I believe a hundred dollars a year would support me in the enjoyment of what I love best. Why toil I then for 20 times as much?"[23]

In the end, Emerson did resign. But changing profession, he soon came to realize, did not increase his candor. As he later did with the essays, in composing the lyceum lectures Emerson carefully culled and stitched together material drawn from journal entries. In anticipation of his audience, however, he reined in the passion and honesty expressed in the *Journals*. Struggling to discuss the miracles controversy and abolition, he was bold in front of audiences he knew well but constrained in the lyceum hall. Occurring just after and as a result of the "The American Scholar," these talks illuminate how Emerson wrestled with his sworn obligation to speak his mind. They are essential to understanding the urgency of his Phi Beta Kappa oration and his need then to speak out on behalf of friends and principle.

In November, 1838, angry at those who thought Jesus's physical works alone miraculous, he wrote in his journals:

> "Miracles have ceased." Have they indeed? When? They had not ceased this afternoon when I walked into the wood & got into a bright miraculous sunshine in shelter from the roaring wind. Who sees a pine cone or the turpentine exuding from the tree, or a leaf the unit of vegetation fall from its bough as if it said "The Year is finished," or hears in the quiet piny glen the Chickadee chirping his cheerful note, or walks along the lofty promontory-like ridges which like natural causeways traverse the morass, or gazes upward at the rushing clouds or downward at a moss or a stone & says to himself "Miracles have ceased?"

The next month, Emerson used this passage in his lyceum talk "The Eye and the Ear," but slight changes in the first two sentences produced a modulated rhetoric: "'Miracles have ceased,' says the citizen. The poet knows they had not ceased when ever he last walked the wood into bright miraculous sunshine. Who sees a pine cone . . . ?" Rather than preserving the original conflict between Emerson himself—who took that walk that very day—and those who believed otherwise, Emerson disengaged by substituting the poet and the citizen. The contrast of the poet's embrace of nature's creations with the citizen's faith in historical miracles invited the audience to consider two plausible beliefs. Would his middle-class listeners feel compelled to follow the view of a poet who, by custom, interprets the world differently than they? Years earlier, he had criticized brother Charles's commencement address because "you may hear it or not as you choose. The orator leaves you to your opinion." This is precisely what Emerson himself did here: remove the strong focus that would have forced his audience to concur. Gone, too, is the pointed challenge to the claim that miracles, because they were Jesus's work, had ended—"Have they indeed? When?"—that gives the journal passage its moral indignation and urgency.[24]

Two months later, in the lyceum talk "Holiness," Emerson returned to the subject of religion. Acknowledging his concern about controversy— "In approaching this subject I feel very sensibly its difficulty"—Emerson didn't even broach the miracles question. Alcott thought Emerson necessarily cautious: "He treated the topic in a wise manner, but did not venture into the depths of it before a popular audience," Alcott wrote in his journal. Although some contemporaries considered "Holiness" a controversial talk, modern scholars judge it a "particularly evasive performance." Emerson felt similarly. He excluded it from *Essays: First Series* and chastised himself: "I regret one thing omitted in my late Course of Lectures; that I did not state with distinctness & conspicuously the great error of Modern Society in respect to religion."[25]

Yet five months later, in talking to a handful of ministers and graduates of the Divinity School, Emerson held back nothing: "[Jesus] spoke of Miracles; for he felt that man's life was a miracle, and all that man doth, and he knew that this his daily miracle shines, as the character ascends. But the very word Miracle, as pronounced by Christian churches, gives a false impression; it is Monster. It is not one with the blowing clover and the falling rain." Largely on the basis of this single bold statement before perhaps a dozen clergy, Emerson reignited the miracles controversy. At Harvard, he faced a different audience with a clearer vision and purpose.[26]

After the outcry over the Divinity School address, Emerson seemed eager to engage the public: "I have a great deal more to say that will shock you out of all patience . . . and as fast as these become clear to me you may depend on my proclaiming them." Lidian, however, urged him to hold his counsel, so Emerson kept still. Perhaps believing that discretion was the better part of valor, he also worried that the publicity could affect lyceum attendance: "The farmer, the laborer, has the extreme satisfaction of seeing that the same livelihood he earns, is within the reach of every man. The lawyer, the author, the singer, has not." Emerson wrote William, "I mean to lecture again in Boston the coming winter & perhaps the people scared by the newspapers will not come & pay for my paper & pens." He was wrong about that, later telling William that "the lecturing thrives[.] The good city is more placable than it was represented & 'forgives.'" Attendance was a constant concern in Emerson's attempt at candor and self-reliance.[27]

The miracles controversy, as we'll see in the next chapter, captivated Boston ministers and Harvard faculty; it even brought in some of the lay population. But it was, in the end, a fight over an abstraction. The question of slavery was very much a concrete issue, and it divided Boston—and the nation—like no other. When, in May, 1837, Emerson began challenging his own silence, he asked himself specifically why had he not spoken out on abolition. In the lyceum, he had a perfect venue. Because slavery was the most contested question of the day, one that troubled Emerson for several years, the distinction between his public and private thoughts reveals a great deal about his struggle for self-reliance.[28]

Despite being surrounded by friends and relatives who were anti-slavery activists—Lidian, Charles, Aunt Mary, step-grandfather Ezra Ripley, Abigail ("Abba") Alcott, her father Samuel May, the Hoars (father and daughter), Ellis Gray Loring, novelist Lydia Maria Child—Emerson was not quick to take a strong stand for abolition. As a Boston minister, he occasionally expressed guarded outrage. "Let every man say then to himself—the cause of the Indians, it is mine; the cause of the slave, it is mine . . . and speak and act thereupon as a freeman and a Christian," he preached in 1832. But when William Lloyd Garrison founded the New England Anti-Slavery Society in the same year, pressure to identify with the cause increased. Mary hoped Waldo would abandon the subject of great men in his lyceum talks and "take the gauge of slavery," but it was instead brother Charles who began speaking publicly. Lidian and Aunt Mary then contrived to have Waldo breakfast with Samuel May and British abolitionist George Thompson, who was on a fiercely contested speaking tour. They came for Emerson's support, but he would not commit: "I said also, what seems true, that if any man's opinion in the country was valuable to them that opinion would be distinctly known."[29]

There was, as he noted in his diary entry of May, 1837, the strong expectation of his friends that he declare his allegiance to abolition. Defining himself as a public figure, Emerson could hardly fail to consider this most topical of issues for his lyceum talks. Perhaps he had already tested the waters in the previous year's lecture on "Milton," when he quoted approvingly another writer who had stated that the Puritan "had constantly employed his strength and faculties in . . . direct opposition to slavery." Soon after, Emerson seemed to be getting ready to speak for himself. In the fall of 1836, he devoted a notebook—one hundred pages long in its present published form—to ideas for his impending lecture series, and they included by far his most extensive thinking on slavery.[30]

Like even some fully fledged abolitionists, he confessed there that he did not care much for black slaves: "I think it cannot be maintained by any candid person that the African race have ever occupied or do promise ever to occupy any very high place in the human family." And yet, "no man can hold property in Man. . . . Reason is not a chattel; cannot be bought & sold; and . . . every pretended traffic in such stock is invalid & criminal." Emerson's strategy for abolition, as he understood that term—for the modern distinction between anti-slavery and abolitionism, that is, between limiting the expansion of and entirely abolishing slavery, was not then consistently kept—was "to awaken the conscience of the Northern States in the hope thereby to awaken the conscience of the Southern states." The Northerner had to develop a firm conviction, "so that whenever we are called to vote in the matter, we may not dodge the question; we may not trifle with it." If both painfully bigoted and politically naïve from today's vantage point, at least Emerson put some thinking into this most controversial of questions. Yet, how much of this actually found its way into the lyceum talks?[31]

Publicly, Emerson would only name abolition as one of many contemporary issues that "I stand here to describe, not to praise," and he fleetingly suggested that "the growing moral power of individuals" by itself would abolish slavery. And then there is this sorry observation, that in the era of global commerce "We have the beautiful costume of the Hindoo, the Chinese, and the Turk in our street. Our domestic labor is done by the African. Our trench dug by the Irish. The South Sea Islander is on the wharf. The Indian squaw sells mats at our doors." Although slavery had been outlawed in New England for a generation, from Emerson's description one might think the country's entire African-American population was engaged in free enterprise. Essentially nothing, then, of Emerson's nuanced journal entry became part of the year's lyceum talks. With abolition being so controversial and Emerson so concerned about attendance at his lectures—he detailed expenses and profits in the same notebook—perhaps he thought better of discussing the issue. That is why the following May, just before being invited to address Phi Beta Kappa, he agonized over his failure to talk about abolition.[32]

Then, a year later, on November 7, 1838, after repeatedly smashing his printing press only to have him order a new one, an Illinois mob finally managed to kill the Reverend Elijah P. Lovejoy, a publisher of abolitionist material. The murder stirred a divided Massachusetts. William Ellery Channing tried to organize a rally in protest but was initially denied a permit, to the delight of Andrews Norton, whose wife's family money was invested in Lowell cotton mills. When Channing eventually created enough political pressure to stage a rally on December 8, the state's attorney general came to argue that the Illinois mob had acted in the best tradition of Revolutionary War heroes and claimed that Channing's own published statement was "the doctrine of Insurrection." For his part, Channing condemned the violence without demanding the end of slavery.[33]

During the past few years, Concord had become a hotbed of anti-slavery sentiment. "[E]very third man [here] lectures on Slavery," observed Emerson. But even in so liberal a town, abolition was a controversial issue. When Emerson was asked to talk on the Lovejoy tragedy, organizers had difficulty finding a hall. He was at last offered the vestry at the Second Church for, almost certainly, the evening of November 14. It was Emerson's first political speech, yet all that survives is a brief excerpt by friend and biographer James Elliot Cabot. Historians today generally follow Cabot's assessment that Emerson spoke mainly on the question of freedom of speech.[34]

Cabot, however, who wrote of the incident precisely half a century after it occurred, tended to portray Emerson as an anxious and unwilling reformer. And here, it's especially easy to assume that Emerson was more concerned with free speech than with abolitionism, for the two issues were tightly linked. Abolitionist meetings often resulted in such violent rioting that Massachusetts governor Edward Everett—who later would precede Lincoln in speaking at Gettysburg—tried unsuccessfully to ban discussion of slavery in his state. Stifling free speech became the surest way to stifle abolitionism, as the murder of Elijah P. Lovejoy, a printer as well as abolitionist, proved.[35]

It is obvious even from the little Cabot preserved that Emerson's talk did not please abolitionists, for he placed the blame for slavery equally on the slaves themselves: "The degradation of that black race . . . is inevitable to the men they are, and nobody can redeem them but themselves. . . . The negro is imitative, secondary." Emerson had actually spoken better of African-Americans in a sermon of a few years earlier, asserting that "[the good and wise] feel . . . no distinction of skin and color."[36] But not now. Emerson also referred brutally to abolitionists as "an altogether odious set of people, whom one would shun as the worst of bores and canters." And yet, "my conscience, my unhappy conscience, respects that hapless class who see the faults and stains of our social order, and who pray and strive incessantly to right the wrong."

Although Emerson must surely have disappointed abolitionists, his address, it is obvious, did have plenty to do with slavery. Everything Cabot recorded pertains to that question, and for the rest of the speech Emerson drew extensively on his earlier, unused journal notes on slavery. One passage (that the plantation owner should be pitied as much as despised) is found in both the journal entry and Cabot's excerpts of the talk, and Emerson put diagonal lines—his characteristic method of keeping track of passages he used in talks and essays—through virtually the entire journal entry. Although he could not bring himself to discuss slavery with his lyceum audience, at Concord and in front of people he knew well, he surely did. A few days earlier, Emerson had reflected in his journals: "Right minded men have recently been called to decide for Abolition." Emerson, when he spoke at a Concord church, thought he was one of them.[37]

But Emerson's struggle between self-reliance and joining a common cause soon returned to bedevil him. Just a few weeks later, he wrote in despair: "When a zealot comes to me & represents the importance of this Temperance Reform my hands drop—I have not excuse—I honor him with shame at my own inaction. Then a friend of the slave shows me the horrors of Southern slavery—I cry guilty guilty!" These are hardly the thoughts of the self-reliant scholar who made up his own mind quite apart from the influence of others.[38]

Finally, on January 24, 1838, he at long last took on slavery at the lyceum, where, once again, he proceeded to lose his nerve. There Emerson proclaimed: "Human virtue demands her champions and martyrs, and the trial of persecution always proceeds. It is but the other day, that the brave Lovejoy gave his breast to the bullets of a mob, for the rights of free speech and opinion, and died when it was better not to live." This time, we are sure that the question he raised is one of free speech alone. He did not even hint that the right to speak freely involved the most divisive issue in American history. Two months earlier, Emerson had written that it was the duty of all who were opposed to slavery "to open our halls to the discussion of this question steadily day after day, year after year until no man dare wag his finger at us." No one had a better opportunity to do this than he. In avoiding the question of abolition in his lyceum lectures, Emerson kept silent before a public he did not wish to alienate.[39]

That April, Emerson joined a protest against the Federal removal of the Cherokee Nation from the eastern to the western shore of the Mississippi. The action was transparently illegal and opposed (in vain) by notable politicians and jurists, including Chief Justice John Marshall. Along with other Concordians, Emerson was asked to talk after church on the twenty-second. The following day, at the urging of neighbors, he fired off an angry letter to the newly inaugurated Martin Van Buren that he allowed to be published and that brought him national attention. "Sir, does the Government think that the People of the United States are become savage [a neat reversal of stereotype] and mad? From their minds are the sentiments of love and of a good nature wiped clean out? The soul of man, the justice, the mercy, that is the heart's heart in all men, from Maine to Georgia, does abhor this business," is how he addressed the president. Emerson, however, simultaneously had deep regrets, describing his effort as "a letter hated of me." Thinking he had compromised his self-reliance, Emerson then withdrew from political activism: "I will let the republic alone until the republic comes to me. I fully sympathise, be sure, with the sentiment I write, but I accept it rather from my friends than dictate it. It is not my impulse to say it & therefore my genius deserts me, no muse befriends, no music of thought or of word accompanies. Bah!"[40]

His friends judged the letter brilliant—which it surely is—but to Emerson it represented a compromise of principle. In his one address on slavery, he offered a complex argument to a controversial issue and managed to offend everyone: slaves, slaveholders, and abolitionists alike. The question of the Cherokee removal was just too easy. Because everyone he knew seemed to concur, Emerson feared that he was merely embracing the positions others had already staked out. That's pretty much what he wrote a few months later about reaction to his Divinity School address: "As long as all that is said is said *against* me, I feel a certain sublime assurance of success[;] but as soon as honied words of praise are spoken for me, I feel as one that lies unprotected before his enemies."[41]

It wasn't until 1844, when, having grown more confident in every way, Emerson became a committed abolitionist. Moved by Lidian's feelings about the harsh realities of the slave trade and deeply affected by the vivid accounts of brutality he himself read while researching the talk, Emerson rose to denounce the impending annexation of Texas, which would extend slavery. After that, despite his continued private reservations, abolitionists could count on him to speak at rallies or lend his name to the cause.[42]

Emerson's initial foray into public activism began in May, 1837, when he reluctantly acknowledged that, to keep pace with his friends, he must speak "upon the times, upon Wilhelm Meister, upon Abolition, upon Harvard College." Although fearful of offending his lyceum audience, at Harvard he presented an image of the scholar reflecting his newly found courage and candor:

> Free should the scholar be,—free and brave . . . for fear is a thing which a scholar by his very function puts behind him. . . . It is a shame to him if his tranquility, amid dangerous times, arise from the presumption that like children and women, his is a protected class; or if he seek a temporary peace by the diversion of his thoughts from politics or vexed questions, hiding his head like an ostrich in the flowering bushes. . . . Let him look into the eye [of danger] and search its nature. . . . The world is his who can see through its pretension.

Here Emerson extended the limits of self-reliance and linked freedom with commitment. But a year later, he cautioned himself about going further. Reflecting on the public debate around "The American Scholar" and the Divinity School address, he asked: "Why need you rail, or need a biting criticism on the Church & the College to demonstrate your holiness & your intellectual aims? Let others draw that inference which damns the institutions if they will. Be thyself too great for enmity & fault-finding." Having attacked with unbridled passion the church and the college, Emerson then withdrew from the resulting controversy. Emerson believed that continuing his assault on what were, after all, *his* church and *his* college would make him even more dependent on both institutions. Protecting what he perceived to be his self-reliance, he failed to consider that his words had further emboldened his friends, whom by his subsequent silence he abandoned.[43]

Emerson compromised his intellectual freedom by being selectively candid. Avoiding conflict in the lyceum, the place where he made his living, was an uncomfortable concession to practicality. Bringing that conflict to Harvard and Concord, the institutions and people to which he was tethered, was an equally uncomfortable compromise of his self-reliance. There was a side of Emerson that always strove to be ethereal, bodiless: "I believe that I shall some time cease to be an Individual, that the eternal tendency of the soul is to become Universal." Around the time of his Phi Beta Kappa oration, however, he chose not incorporeal contemplation, but action. To extol and demonstrate the self-reliance of the scholar, he himself had to be less self-reliant. A year later, Emerson felt unable to pay the price. He needed to be involved with, but ultimately detached from, others. As we saw in the last chapter, a large reason for his engagement at Harvard had to do with his immediate anger at his alma mater. But other forces were at work as well. In the next chapter, we'll consider Emerson's complex relationship to his Transcendental colleagues in the shaping of "The American Scholar."[44]

Chapter Five

FRIENDS

LOOKING BACK A CENTURY AND A HALF, EMERSON'S ENOR-
mous influence on American letters and thought may seem obvious. As a
result, Transcendentalism is almost inevitably interpreted through his eyes
alone, with virtually every entry in reference works on Transcendentalism
acknowledging his prominence. Because he commanded so great a presence, there were in his lifetime and certainly are in posterity several Emersons. The public Emerson of the essays is a powerful, searching figure striving for exceptional candor and self-reliance. As dominating as that persona
may seem, in private Emerson could be insecure and heavily dependent on
others. His friends played an important role in his decision to speak out.
They served to shame him into action; by their own example, they helped
define what he didn't want to say; and they made him desire a kind of
recognition they would never give him. Emerson's relations with other
Transcendentalists formed an essential aspect of his imperfect struggle for
self-reliance and his decision to risk so much in "The American Scholar."

Emerson's troubled dealings with friend and mentor Frederic Henry
Hedge illustrate his complex relations with colleagues. Son of a Harvard
professor, Henry had as a youth gone with George Bancroft to study in
Germany as part of the first wave of Americans receiving European training. A few years after graduating from the Divinity School, Hedge took a
pulpit in Bangor, Maine, a decision with which he was never fully satisfied.

Emerson's relationship with Hedge is most easily understood if first
viewed from the end of the period, when Emerson expressed his feelings
more fully. In 1841, four years after Emerson's oration, Hedge delivered
his own Phi Beta Kappa address at Harvard. Emerson, as he recorded in
his journals, believed "Conservatism and Reform" was simply another ex-

ample of Hedge's indiscriminate pugnacity: "He is a warrior, & so only there be war, he is not scrupulous on which side his aid is wanted. . . . The sentence which began with an attack on the conservatives ended with a blow at the reformers: the first clause was applauded by one party & the other party had their revenge & gave their applause before the period was closed." Others saw it as having a greater purpose, namely to understand the claims of conservatives as well as those of fellow Transcendentalists. Margaret Fuller called it "high ground for middle ground," and Hedge's closest friends, Caleb Stetson and Convers Francis, thought the oration "a survey, rather than . . . an opinion of the two conflicting elements."[1]

But contemporaries—as well as modern readers—missed the principled stand that Hedge did take. Following Coleridge more faithfully than did any other American Transcendentalist, Hedge argued in the first half of the talk that institutions and traditional beliefs were essential for the continuity of society: "Authority is not only a guide to the blind, but a law to the seeing." Although not once criticizing Transcendentalists for denigrating institutions and authority, in the second half, when turning to praise Transcendentalism, he did simultaneously chastise its opponents: "[T]he actual Conservatism of the present day . . . is with most men a mere prejudice. . . . [A]ll philosophy is to them *suspect*, and has a guilty, revolutionary look. They see a traitor beneath the stole." Transcendentalism, despite the "war [that] is waged against new views by conservative minds," had succeeded "in furnishing a new impulse to thought, and enlarging, somewhat, the horizon of life."[2]

The oration concluded with a strong defense of Transcendentalism and an attack on conservatism as it was then practiced. It was that ending which was undoubtedly intended to leave the lasting impression. Orators trained in the classical tradition know full well that a supposedly balanced speech tilts to the position last presented. When, for example, Emerson himself, in his great essay "Fate," first set out Nature's restrictions followed by an assertion of the human capacity for freedom, he left no doubt where his own inclination lay. And in fact, Edward Everett's brother Alexander, living in Louisiana and sympathetic to the Transcendentalists, heard that Hedge had given "a full blast of transcendentalism" at Harvard. The society was so polarized by 1841 that there were high expectations that Hedge would come down strongly on the side of Transcendentalism. That he produced something subtler may have naturally been viewed by his closest friends as equivocal.[3]

Yet Emerson—whose own oration had been criticized by friends for equivocating between individual genius and society—was so bitter that the following year he refused Hedge's offer to have the oration printed in the Transcendentalist periodical, the *Dial*. No matter how delicately Emerson put it, the rejection must have stung, for previously Emerson

Figure 9. Frederic Henry Hedge in the 1860s. Photograph by John A. Whipple. Courtesy of the Manuscripts and Archives Department, Andover-Harvard Theological Library, Harvard Divinity School.

and Fuller had urgently requested any contribution from Hedge. Emerson felt that Hedge, for many years his friend, fellow intellectual traveler, and even mentor, was not fully committed to *his* kind of Transcendentalism.[4]

Hedge's recent participation in the club that he helped found had already raised questions with his colleagues. But his disillusionment was not the only fracturing in what historians see as an earlier Transcendentalist unity. Hedge's detachment coincided with the establishment of Brook Farm, led by George and Sophia Ripley. Even if they visited often and lent moral support, Emerson, Alcott, Fuller, and Parker were conspicuously not members of the experiment in communal living, and George Ripley's resentment, especially, grew. By this point as well, Orestes Brownson's politics had pushed him so far from most of his Transcendentalists colleagues that in the final issue of his own periodical, the *Boston Quarterly Review*, he attacked the beliefs of his old friends. Meanwhile, Parker's radical theology was becoming unpalatable to some, and Emerson, Alcott, and Thoreau pursued their self-reliance in Concord.[5]

"The 1840s witnessed the slow fragmentation of the Transcendentalist movement and the departure of its members upon paths of their own," suggested Barbara Packer in perhaps the finest survey of the subject. In the 1840s there were, to be sure, pronounced differences among Transcendentalists. But is the consensus of modern scholarship correct, that those differences mark a clear departure from an earlier harmony? Perry Miller wrote eloquently that "the unity of sentiment within the group, which a few short years before had seemed sufficient guarantee of their unanimity, was lost in the abyss between society and solitude." In basing "their unanimity" on the "unity of sentiment," Miller resorted to a tautology to define just what it was that tumbled into the depths below. Perhaps in the end it was too elusive to name.[6]

Perhaps too elusive also were its beginnings. Packer proclaimed that "Transcendentalism had generated several scriptures in 1836. . . . It was ready to mount an offensive." Miller identified instead 1833, with Hedge's article on Coleridge, as "the point at which Transcendentalism went over to the offensive." Asynchrony aside, Packer's and Miller's identical military metaphor of going on the offensive reflects the general belief that the Transcendentalists were initially engaged in conscious, concerted action. Yet the Transcendental Club was formed by happenstance: Henry Hedge had thought about it at least as early as 1833, but undoubtedly feelings of isolation over his move to Bangor finally spurred him to action. Certainly not everyone who occasionally attended belonged to the tight circle that eventually "grew apart." The likes of James Walker, William Ellery Channing, and Nathaniel Langdon Frothingham were also invited to the meetings. Although they rarely, if ever, attended, they played their own roles on the periphery. Many contemporaries, as we'll see at the end of this chapter, considered Channing the leader of the Transcendentalists, while scholars today debate whether he was even sympathetic. Orestes Brownson, who attended the early meetings, was so stridently political that he "became unbearable," recalled a near-contemporary, "and was not afterward invited." What is to be made of William Henry Furness? His own essay on miracles came out simultaneously with Ripley's and was at least as strongly stated. Yet he somehow managed to win Norton's prior approval, and, although he was initially suggested for membership in the Transcendental Club, scholars today continue to debate whether he was a Transcendentalist or an opponent. Transcendentalists are more accurately known for their similarities in background and temperament than for specific thoughts or actions held in common. James Freeman Clarke suggested the group ought to be called the Club of the Like-Minded, "because no two of us thought alike." Looking back, the club's main architect agreed. "There was no club, properly speaking; no organization, no presiding officer, no vote ever taken," recalled Hedge. "How the name 'Transcendental' given to those gatherings and the set of persons who took part in them originated, I cannot say. It certainly was never assumed by the persons so called."[7]

When trying to identify dramatic, axial events in history, historians are naturally drawn to formal expression and public documents. Because Transcendentalists produced important texts in 1833 and 1836, those years would seem to be essential moments of concerted action. But surviving personal journals and correspondence suggest a very different picture. They indicate that there was likely never a time when the Transcendentalists decided "to go on the offensive" nor when their sympathies were fully attuned. It is within this dynamic and rapidly shifting social group that Emerson struggled for his own public voice.

Emerson's opinion of Henry Hedge amplifies the tense relations that seem always to have existed among Transcendentalists. When he harshly, and unfairly, judged Hedge's Phi Beta Kappa address in 1841, Emerson had, in fact, already secretly learned that Hedge disapproved of his beliefs. Margaret Fuller, as editor of the *Dial*, had the year before solicited material from Hedge, her longtime friend. Declining to contribute, Hedge revealed his fears that Transcendentalism was turning away from rigorous philosophical inquiry. He followed up three months later, telling Fuller that his associations with the group could result in his being labeled an atheist and separated himself from the ideas of Emerson and Alcott.[8]

Fuller, despite being Hedge's friend far longer, had by then become closer to Emerson and showed him that letter. Emerson's response to Hedge's concerns reveals a great deal about how he viewed his relationship with his colleagues and the struggle against Unitarianism. With empty bravado, he evoked the marshal spirit of loyalty to a cause: "If the outer wall gives way, we must retire into the citadel. . . . So in the matter of strength I cannot regret any loss of numbers." This he wrote to Fuller while at the very same time claiming in "Self-Reliance" that "there is a class of persons to whom by all spiritual affinity I am bought and sold; for them I will go to prison, if need be." In real life, he could not help but take offense at Hedge's letter: "But I am very sorry for Henry Hedge. It is a sad letter for his biography: he will grieve his heart out by & by & perhaps very soon, that he ever wrote it. As I have told you, we (H. & I) never quite meet; there is always a fence betwixt us. . . . I owe him gratitude for all his manifest kindness to me, though he is wrong to say he loves me, for I am sure he does not quite." Expressing false pity, Emerson repeated for good measure: "All this makes me heartily sorry for him,— but I know he will nigh kill himself with vexation at his own letter, after a few months be past."[9]

Although Emerson sought to distance himself emotionally from Hedge—a strategy he often used when he feared failure in a relationship— Hedge did feel close to him. He avidly sought Emerson's company during his stays in Boston and hoped in vain that Emerson would visit him in Bangor. After Emerson delivered "The American Scholar" and continued to be anxious about its reception, it was Hedge whom Lidian specifically mentioned as supportive, and it was Hedge who urged him to publish the oration. Emerson, for his part, wrote Hedge in 1838, "I believe that we belong to each other." It is "the uncharacteristic harshness" of Emerson's response to Hedge's own Phi Beta Kappa oration that has set historians looking for what happened between Hedge and Emerson in the early 1840s.[10]

Yet—and this is essential to understanding relations among Transcendentalists—Emerson had had his doubts all along. Although exhilarated by Hedge's article on Coleridge in 1833, he quickly qualified that enthusiasm. He may have noticed that, in a 1834 review of Everett's Phi Beta Kappa oration at Yale, Hedge anticipated his own Phi Beta Kappa address in arguing that institutions ought to change with the times but must still be honored as preservers of tradition. The next year, and well before the formation of the Transcendental Club, Emerson recorded in his journals: "Hedge united strangely the old & the new; he had imagination but his intellect seemed ever to contend with an arid temperament." Uniting strangely the old and the new: that is precisely what six years later Emerson criticized in Hedge's oration. All the while that Emerson was welcoming Hedge as a fellow traveler—indeed, acknowledging Hedge's leadership—he was keenly aware of their differences. For his part, Hedge, so admired for his careful writings on German philosophy and literature, had early on substantial doubts about Emerson's critical faculties. Hedge's confidant Convers Francis reported to Hedge in 1837 that Emerson's lyceum lectures were inspiring, although "his train of thought (or, to use your expression, *dots* of thought) was such as you would expect from your knowledge of his intellectual character."[11]

The relationship then followed a predictable course. By 1839, Emerson recorded in his journals that Hedge was unhappy with Emersonian idealism: "Hedge thinks I overlook great facts in stating the absolute laws of the soul." And so Emerson would a short time later criticize both Hedge and their mutual friend Margaret Fuller, who "must have talent in their associates & so they find that, they forgive many defects. . . . I require genius &, if I find that, I do not need talent: and talent without genius gives me no pleasure." Relations between Hedge and Emerson, then, always had a sharp side. After Fuller turned over Hedge's critical and confidential letter the following year, there could be no doubt how Emerson would subsequently view Hedge's Phi Beta Kappa talk.[12]

With the exception of his friends of the heart—Bronson Alcott, Margaret Fuller, and (a bit later) Henry David Thoreau—Emerson left in his journals and correspondence a far more extensive trail about his feelings toward Henry Hedge than about any other Transcendentalist colleague. As we'll see near the conclusion of this chapter, it is possible to speculate that Emerson's relations with George Ripley, which were certainly tense at the end of the decade, may have had the same edge earlier. This should come as no surprise. Three years after "The American Scholar," Orestes Brownson outlined the nature of the debate between Transcendentalism and Unitarianism: "The movement is properly threefold; philosophical, theological, and political or social . . . and on these three subjects, the new school and the old are at issue." These related but complex aspects of the movement—the philosophical, theological, and sociopolitical—could not develop in tandem for all its members. There would be different opinions and different alliances within the circle.[13]

Retrospectively, Emerson confirmed as much. Transcendentalists, he believed, were in fact surprised to learn that they were considered a movement, for "there was no concert, and only here and there two or three men or women who read and wrote, each alone, with unusual vivacity." Rather than seeing cohesion, Emerson noted the shifting affections and alliances within the larger group: "As these persons became in the common chances of society acquainted with each other, there resulted certainly strong friendships, which of course were exclusive in proportion to their heat: and perhaps those persons who were mutually the best friends were the most private." An inventory of extant correspondence among Transcendentalists would almost certainly reveal, like tracks in a cloud chamber, the existence of the very social patterns Emerson described.[14]

Emerson's journals show that in the spring of 1837 he felt under pressure from friends to speak more boldly. His response to those perceived expectations was the two Harvard addresses which largely determined his subsequent reputation. In examining key acquaintances by their affinity to Brownson's categories of philosophical, theological, and sociopolitical belief, it becomes clear that in "The American Scholar" Emerson was struggling for his own voice within the fluid relationships of fellow Transcendentalists.

Back in 1830, well-known Unitarian minister Samuel Gilman published a screed in the standard Unitarian journal, the *Christian Examiner*, under the title "Unitarian Christianity Free from Objectional Extremes." It was customary for Neo-Calvinists and Revivalists to condemn Unitarians as atheists whose wanton religious experiment was nearing an end. Unitarians had no difficulty retaliating in kind. What makes Gilman's argument interesting is that he began with an attack, not on Calvinism or Revivalist preaching, but, strangely enough, on religious liberals: "When will it be fully understood that freedom is not riot . . . that fearless inquiry after truth is not synonymous with sneering skepticism or reckless infidelity?" Choosing as his initial target those whom he considered too liberal was partly, of course, a rhetorical strategy designed to demonstrate that mainstream Unitarians were not atheists. But it was a plausible strategy.[15]

An article appearing just two issues later in the same journal proved that, indeed, there was a liberal wing of Unitarianism worth worrying about. The article was written by the brilliant young Unitarian minister George Ripley. It has aptly been said of Ripley that "[his] gold-rimmed spectacles betokened the scholar, but the intense black eyes behind them betrayed the reformer." Ripley, who had been raised so conservatively that he had thought about attending evangelical Yale, quickly rebelled against his father as he fell under the liberal Unitarian influence of Harvard. Soon thereafter he rebelled against the very teachers who had helped him become so liberal.[16]

The *Christian Examiner* was the essential public forum for Unitarian theological and philosophical inquiry. Proclaimed "the grand bulwark of *our* faith," it was made more important because Unitarians believed in spreading their gospel through publication rather than by denominational organizing. Over much of the next decade, while the *Examiner* was edited by the exceptionally tolerant James Walker, Ripley was to publish some of the most important and polemical Transcendentalist pieces, most of them aimed against his former Harvard teachers and other Unitarian intellectuals.[17]

In this initial contribution, Ripley railed against Scottish Enlightenment and English moral philosophers as bloodless and lacking in social compassion. Coleridge was the only living writer of England whose combination of speculative and practical philosophy appropriately addressed the moral improvement of society. Ripley here fired the first shot at his Harvard

Figure 10. George Ripley, no date. Courtesy of the Manuscripts and Archives Department, Andover-Harvard Theological Library, Harvard
Divinity School.

mentors: "We are aware that it has been usual among certain classes with us, as well as in England, to speak with contempt of [Coleridge's] speculations . . . but, for ourselves, we consider him as in possession of a treasure of valuable truth." Coleridge provided the essential epistemological blueprint for the distinction between Reason and Understanding, while the beliefs of Locke and his successors belonged to "the age of a superficial, sensual philosophy, [which] is passing away. Its foundations were first effectually laid bare by the strong thinkers in Germany." Most importantly for Ripley, since Reason, as Coleridge understood it, was a common gift to humankind, moral philosophy had to be democratic: "Moral progress is a career open to all. It does not consist in producing extraordinary men. It may be found in the destiny and condition of every one, and may be adapted to the most ordinary occasions."[18]

When Ripley published this piece in 1830, his cousin Ralph Waldo Emerson was still a practicing minister and happily married to Ellen. He had begun reading Coleridge with difficulty the previous year, but there is no indication until 1834 that he had seized the implications. Unitarians, meanwhile, had just five years earlier formally organized and were struggling to shape their identity. They hardly needed opposition from within. Just as the *Christian Examiner* was going to press with Ripley's article attacking what he considered the conservative nature of Unitarianism, the Unitarian minister Orville Dewey—another, older cousin of Emerson's—gave the Phi Beta Kappa address. Dewey preached to the choir in attacking popular literature for its low standards and for being too abundant, but saved his subtler polemics for contemporary thinkers of greater pretension: "I should be glad, at least, to *understand* Kant and Coleridge, before I can agree with it. I should be glad to understand that some of their language has any meaning, or any that answers to the mystical depths of their phraseology." Traditional Unitarians were gradually becoming aware of the revolution before them.[19]

Two years later, Ripley reviewed in the *Examiner* Charles Follen's inaugural lecture on assuming a chair at Harvard. Because Follen helped make German Romanticism accessible to students, Ripley saw an opening and rushed through, praising Follen and explicitly attacking his own former teachers for dismissing Kant and Coleridge: "Nothing shows more forcibly the blinding influence of a popular prejudice, than to hear this stale conceit from the mouths of men at whose feet we would gladly sit and learn wisdom, and who would be the first to discard it, should they study each of those great writers as they deserve." Having been graduated first in the strong Harvard class of 1823, Ripley was to produce academic writing that was probably better—certainly more spirited—than that done by his own former instructors.[20]

But it was Henry Hedge who delivered perhaps the most influential statement of Transcendentalist principles. In the 1833 *Examiner*, Hedge illuminated Coleridge's interpretation of Kant. Subtly attacking the Lockean philosophy taught at Harvard (or as Harriet Martineau described the process, "indoctrinat[ing] the students with a certain number of chapters of Locke"), Hedge made a plea for understanding German idealism that anticipated his Phi Beta Kappa oration: "Not all are born to be philosophers, or are capable of becoming philosophers, any more than all are capable of becoming poets or musicians. The works of the transcendental philosophers may be translated word for word, but still it will be impossible to get a clear idea of their philosophy, unless we raise ourselves at once to a transcendental point of view."[21]

Hedge's concern that Transcendentalism might be misunderstood by those insufficiently diligent or sympathetic wasn't idle anxiety: an actual duel had been fought in Germany over whether one could master Kant's philosophy without decades of study! And in fact, Hedge, likely the first American to devote himself to German metaphysics, worried throughout his life that even Transcendentalists failed to appreciate Kant's complex epistemological linkage between what is intuitively perceived (Transcendentalist "Reason") and what is experienced (Transcendentalist "Understanding").[22]

Emerson, who had since buried Ellen and traveled to Europe where he met Carlyle and Coleridge, on his return read Hedge's article. In a letter to his brother Edward, he described it as a "living leaping Logos" and proclaimed Hedge, whom he had known since student days, "an unfolding man." Emerson later claimed to have derived his own philosophical tenets from Kant. But whether he appreciated the complexity of Kant's work or Hedge's concerns is an open question. Having resigned his ministry and now radically redirecting his life, Emerson was hoping to rely on Hedge for intellectual inspiration and for assistance in starting a periodical. Never one to look at the finer points of philosophy, he read Hedge the way he wanted.[23]

The confrontational rhetoric of Ripley and the urgent appeal of Hedge were fully matched by the political radicalism of Orestes A. Brownson. A tobacco-chewing preacher with farming and working-class roots who had gone from agnosticism to denouncing atheist Abner Kneeland for blasphemy, Brownson had no patience with halfway measures. In an 1834 review in the *Examiner*, he proclaimed: "Every religious denomination must run through two phases, the one destructive, the other organic. Unitarianism could commence only by being destructive. . . . But that work is done; that negative character which it was obliged to assume then, may now be abandoned. The time has now come to rear the new temple,—for a positive work, and, if we are not mistaken, we already see the workmen coming forth with joy to their task." The new temple for Brownson was Transcendentalism. As he wrote two years later in the *Examiner*: "[T]he philosophy [of John Locke], which has hitherto prevailed and whose results now control our reasonings, cannot sustain religion. Everybody knows, that our religion and our philosophy are at war. . . . The result cannot be doubtful. [Transcendentalist] philosophy will gain the victory."[24]

Transcendentalists could not have imagined the bitterness of that war. Much of the opposition came from Andrews Norton. Having lost a good many fights with the administration over faculty governance and in poor health, Norton had resigned from Harvard in 1830. But he was still a commanding presence, enjoying by marriage great social prominence and enormous wealth (public records show him by far the largest taxpayer in Cambridge). Called by contemporaries "the Unitarian pope," Norton was a complex soul, perhaps best described by James Walker, at the time president of Harvard: "Few men have ever lived who had less of ill-will or unkindness; nevertheless his nature was the opposite of genial, understanding that word to mean a readiness to take up and sympathize with, and, in this way, to enter into and comprehend, a great variety of characters and convictions." Walker added, "He came before his classes, not as one in the act of seeking after the truth, but as one who had found it."[25]

Norton met his match in his pugnacious former student George Ripley, and the flashpoint was the validity and significance of New Testament miracles to authentic religious belief. Theodore Parker, recognizing that German critical source theory, as applied to the Bible, had raised difficult questions about the historicity of miracles, warned Ripley that "the first one who lifted a hand in this work would have to suffer" and suggested that his friend "push some old veteran German to the forefront of the battle, who would not care for a few blows." Ripley probably took this more as a challenge than a warning.[26]

In the November, 1836, issue of the *Christian Examiner*, Ripley expressed doubt as to why miracles were necessary to Christianity. Ripley personally believed in the historicity of Jesus's works. But here he argued that it was Jesus's teachings, reflecting universal Reason, that established Christianity, rather than mere deeds, which were susceptible to individual Understanding and historical challenge. After all, electricity, when first discovered, had appeared miraculous. It would be foolhardy to ascribe a divine nature to one who simply produced initially inexplicable physical events. The validity of a religion must instead rest on whether "the image of God [is] in the Soul of Man." That might seem reasonable enough. But because investigation of the soul defies any known critical method, Ripley's suggestion threatened formalists far more than did the application of German source-criticism to the synoptic tradition. Unitarians,

Perry Miller observed, "had publicly renounced the doctrine of original sin, but they had secretly hung onto it by requiring the dignity of man to be sustained through supernatural intervention. They did not, after all, trust humanity." Denying the value of miracles as an independent measure of religious authenticity meant denying any external and objective proof of Christianity. To Transcendentalists, that hardly mattered; to Unitarian materialists, objective proof was everything.[27]

When he accepted his chair in biblical literature in 1819, Norton had assumed the responsibility for defending Unitarianism against attacks by more conservative sects. But he was never so enthusiastic in his criticisms as when he defended Unitarianism against his own, more liberal students. He published an immediate rejoinder in the *Boston Daily Advertiser*, declaring Ripley's arguments to have been "disastrous to the progress of religious truth." Standard Norton fare, it could not intimidate Ripley, who responded with equal alacrity in the same publication. Before launching into a full technical defense, he noted sarcastically, "I must not forget the benefits I have received from the severity of your taste and the minuteness of your learning in a former pupilage." Ripley concluded with a statement so bold that it left no possibility of common ground: "You are a disciple of the school which was founded by Locke. . . . For that philosophy I have no respect. I believe it to be superficial, irreligious and false in its primary elements." Ripley had traveled a fair distance from when, as a student at Harvard fifteen years earlier, he had written his mother that "we are now studying Locke, an excellent author who has done more to form the mind to habits of accurate reasoning and sound thoughts than almost any other philosopher."[28]

Ripley's rebuttal, according to student George Ellis, was all that was talked about at Harvard Divinity School. Writing classmate Theodore Parker a few days after it appeared, he acknowledged that the general sentiment was against Ripley but that the contest was far from over. And Ellis, no obvious friend of Transcendentalism, thought Ripley was gaining support: "Mr. Ripley is a good man for it. If I am not much mistaken his name will be widely known & honored." Excessively optimistic, however, is Elizabeth Palmer Peabody's assessment that Ripley had the sympathy of most practicing ministers and that "the theological students almost to a man have come to see Mr. Ripley—& are extremely interested in his views." Instead, throughout the next year, under their strong-willed dean John Gorham Palfrey, who was Norton's friend and neighbor, Divinity School students remained, in their public expressions at least, decidedly anti-Transcendentalist.[29]

The year 1836 witnessed a number of Transcendentalist writings, including Emerson's own *Nature* (published anonymously). Yet it was Ripley's essay on miracles and his debate with Andrews Norton that defined for the public the division between the Harvard-Unitarian establishment and the young Transcendentalists, almost all of whom were Harvard graduates. Ripley had been attempting to articulate this division since his first publication in the *Christian Examiner* in 1830, and in many subsequent articles he consistently framed his support for continental thinking by his opposition to Harvard's allegiance to Lockean sensualism. At the time of "The American Scholar," Transcendentalists looked to the combative Ripley. Theodore Parker, far the most erudite of the Transcendentalists, was especially taken with him: "[Ripley and Parker] were drawn together by a deeply rooted sympathy in philosophical ideas, by a common philanthropical aim, and by an irrepressible buoyancy of spirit. They walked and talked by the day," reported O. B. Frothingham.[30]

Attempting in vain to prevent Transcendentalists from publishing in the *Christian Examiner*, Norton received encouragement from other Unitarian ministers. John Brazer, former Harvard professor and current overseer, proved a passionate opponent of the Transcendentalists, writing Norton that the young rebels were "virtually undermining the basis of Christianity." In the same letter, which seems to have been made public, he proposed a meeting of like-minded persons so that their religious community "receive no harm." An accomplished classicist, Brazer chose the language of the ultimate decree of the Roman Senate, issued only when the safety of the republic was in jeopardy and most notoriously invoked by Cicero against Catiline. Within a few years, Norton would similarly fear "the ruin of the party," and even Transcendentalist Samuel Osgood referred to one of Norton's attacks as a "philippic." There were those who talked of the Transcendentalists as a threat to the *res publica*, to their republic of letters and morality. In the pages of the *Boston Quarterly Review*, Orestes Brownson observed, "Many others, who think with [Norton], have in private circles denounced in no measured terms the men and the doctrines of what is termed the new school, but he is almost the only one who has had the manliness to bring his charges before the public, and in a tangible shape." Those who over the dinner tables expressed contempt for Transcendentalism included Cambridge elite Edward Everett, Francis Parkman, John Gorham Palfrey, and George Ticknor.[31]

An ally of the conservatives—more accurately, a foot soldier in the struggle—was the young Harvard instructor and Norton protégé Francis Bowen (later a political philosopher of some distinction). In January, 1837, he wrote for the *Christian Examiner* what was ostensibly a review of Emerson's *Nature*, but what in fact proved to be a broader examination of Transcendentalism. Dismissing Emerson's work as beautifully written but ultimately idiosyncratic and empty, Bowen gave Transcendentalists—and clearly Ripley in particular—measure for measure: "Arrogance and self-sufficiency are no less absurd in philosophy, than criminal in morals;

Figure 11. Andrew Norton. Bust by Shobal Vail Clevenger, c. 1839.
Courtesy of the Manuscripts and Archives Department, Andover-Harvard Theological Library, Harvard Divinity School.

and we cannot but think, that these qualities are displayed by men who
censure indiscriminately the objects which the wise and good have endeavored to attain, and the means which they have employed in the pursuit." To Bowen, Ripley appeared the greater threat.[32]

At the same time, having worked on the project since 1819, Norton in
early 1837 brought out the first of three volumes of *Evidences of the
Genuineness of the Gospels*. Selectively using German critical methods to
support the general historicity of the synoptic Gospels and written for the
general reader as well as the scholar, *Evidences* was greeted warmly by
the Unitarian intelligentsia and the Boston public alike. Norton and his
brother-in-law, the Spanish scholar George Ticknor, had differed sharply

on issues of instruction and faculty governance. But as traditional scholars and stalwarts of the wealthy Unitarian leadership in forging national values, they agreed on matters of religion. To Ticknor, Norton's work was absolutely definitive. Colleagues such as Furness and Story inevitably followed suit. Even traditional rival and conservative critic Moses Stuart of the Andover Theological Seminary wrote Norton that his own review, to appear in the *American Biblical Repository*, was going to be, as he put it, a "eulogy." (Stuart and Norton had become allies in the more pressing fight against abolitionism.)[33]

Transcendentalists reacted differently. Orestes Brownson, in reviewing the work, recommended to the reader who wished to gain faith in Christianity, not Norton's proof of miracles, but the sermons of Jonathan Edwards. Nathaniel Langdon Frothingham, if no Transcendentalist, was sympathetic to Emerson. That spring he sent Andrews Norton two letters questioning the conclusions of *Evidences*, earning, not surprisingly, sharp replies in return. And Bronson Alcott reflected in his journal: "On the whole, I think I have less confidence in the historical evidences of the Christian Faith, than before I read this work. . . . I doubt if this book of Mr. Norton's, will add a single disciple to the cause of truth and religion."[34]

While Norton was attacking Ripley and enjoying public acclaim for his own scholarship, Carlyle wrote Emerson, referring to Norton as "a Philistine of yours." Two years earlier, Emerson had described Norton to Carlyle oppositionally, yet respectfully, as "one of our best heads . . . and a destroying critic." But only a few days after receiving Carlyle's letter, Emerson confessed to Margaret Fuller, "[I] am sour & savage when I anticipate the triumphs of the Philistines." In a small concession to conformity, Emerson now agreed that Unitarian opponents were idol-worshippers, and the epithet "Philistines" henceforth stuck.[35]

Yet in the ensuring confrontation, it was Ripley who led the charge. Near the end of 1839, Caleb Stetson informed Hedge that "the great topic this fall has been Mr Norton's discourse & Ripley's triumphant answer in which he has done himself great honor." A month later, Convers Francis wrote Parker with a mild criticism of Emerson's current lyceum lecture, but with a ringing endorsement of Ripley's performance in the miracles controversy. Following his Divinity School address and with so many of his colleagues supporting the principles he espoused but refused to defend, Emerson was fittingly described by Oliver Wendell Holmes as a latter-day Patroclus, whose body was fought over by Greeks and Trojans.[36]

Why during this period Emerson consistently kept to the side of the contest goes to the heart of understanding "The American Scholar." Emerson certainly worried about offending his lyceum audience; and he had not yet fully settled on what he meant by self-reliance. But he had another concern. Back in 1834, Emerson was corresponding with James Freeman

Clarke, a former classmate and an emerging Transcendentalist, who had obeyed the call to do Unitarian missionary work in Louisville and Cincinnati. Clarke had written an essay on Goethe and Carlyle—Emerson's intellectual signposts and the bêtes noires of more traditional Unitarians. Emerson urged him to publish it. Clarke declined, saying, "Here I am, a young man, just entering my profession . . . & my first act is to launch an arrow at a respectable senior, who has taught me much, & treated me well. . . . It would be easier to write a new article at once, & abuse Nortonism instead of Mr. Norton." Reading the letters today, one might suspect that Emerson, who early on had labeled Norton a bully, was pushing Clarke forward. Clarke, however, turned the tables, perhaps unconsciously: "But why do not you write something of this kind—the review you speak of, of Carlyle's Diderot & Sartor Resartus?. . . Now if you have read [Schleiermacher], pray write something about him in the Examiner— if not read him, & then you will write."[37]

Unlike Ripley, Hedge, and Brownson, however, Emerson would not engage in philosophical discourse. When considering the ministry in 1824, Emerson had admitted that "My reasoning faculty is proportionately weak, nor can I ever hope to write a Butler's Analogy or an Essay of Hume." The same specter arose the year after his correspondence with Clarke, when Hedge wrote Emerson from Bangor, saying that a Mr. Bowie was soliciting manuscripts for a new periodical, and "for you who are so rich in unpublished manuscripts & so productive, a splendid repository & show gallery is herewith promised." Emerson never did respond. Until "The American Scholar," what he did produce were a few minor pieces and his poetic narrative *Nature*—most of which, including *Nature*, were published anonymously. Soon after the exchange with Emerson, Clarke, as editor of the *Western Messenger*, wrote spirited defenses of Carlyle, Ripley, Alcott, and Emerson.[38]

Emerson himself served as an editor—of the *Dial* in the early 1840s. Yet a periodical of some sort had been the dream of his and of fellow travelers throughout the previous decade. From the moment he resigned his pulpit, Emerson thought of starting a journal but worried that it was too much to do alone. By early 1835, however, Hedge was contemplating something more academic—"a journal of spiritual philosophy in which we are to enlist all the Germano-philosophico-literary talent in the country"—and his co-editor would be not Emerson, but George Ripley. Emerson was to be solicited for contributions, but Hedge and Ripley, having established their credentials publicly, were together drawn to the analytical side of Transcendentalism. When, a few months later, Hedge decided to take a pulpit in Maine and realized that he would be too preoccupied to edit the journal, he suggested that Carlyle, not Emerson, take his place as editor. Retrospectively, Hedge intimated that Emerson did not have the taste for rigorous inquiry, recounting that while both were students at the Divinity School in 1828, "I tried to interest him in German literature, but he laughingly said as he was entirely ignorant of the subject, he should assume that it was not worth knowing."[39]

Hedge did at least succeed in interesting him in Carlyle, who would become the single most important influence on Emerson's thinking. In fact, devoting himself fully to Carlyle, Emerson developed a personal relationship that perhaps substituted for intellectual legitimacy. Emerson visited him in 1833 and soon thereafter spread the gospel. Armed with just four copies of the recently published *Sartor Resartus* and lending them strategically, Emerson was able to create an extraordinarily avid demand for the work among Boston intellectuals. He then became Carlyle's unofficial literary agent in the U.S., helping to have *Sartor Resartus* reprinted in Boston in 1836 and the following year getting *The French Revolution* circulated and royalties paid its author. That effort, at considerable financial risk to Emerson, actually created an initially stronger market for the Scot's work in America than it enjoyed in Great Britain. Deeply beholden and somewhat at a loss to explain such loyalty, Carlyle offered that Emerson had "become an Accountant for my sake."[40]

As *Sartor Resartus* became "the Bible of the new Transcendental movement," the friendship with Carlyle strengthened Emerson's intellectual stature. When James Freeman Clarke vainly urged Emerson to write something strong on Transcendentalism, Emerson responded not by publishing an essay, but by showing Clarke his correspondence with Carlyle. Clarke in turn wrote William Henry Channing excitedly: "I have read lately, some letters, written by T. Carlyle to Mr Emerson. They are beautiful, & overflow with affection & love—sparkle with true wit—& glow with those truths which are a central fire in his faithful mind." That same year, George Ripley tried to communicate with Carlyle, but wrote too effusively and confided in Emerson that he felt embarrassed. Emerson had the right tone and the primary relationship. Ripley's subsequent relationship with Carlyle was mediated through Emerson. At nearly the same moment, Emerson arranged an introduction to Carlyle for both Longfellow and Lydia Maria Child. He was also later to bring George Bancroft together with Carlyle in correspondence and, despite Carlyle's acknowledged dislike of the Unitarian leader, tried to put William Ellery Channing in the Scot's good graces. But Emerson's exclusive hold was slipping. As others began to discover Carlyle on their own, Emerson wrote him revealingly: "I only tremble to see my importance [to you] quite at an end." It has rightly been noted that Emerson's transatlantic reputation grew when Carlyle wrote the preface to his 1841 *Essays: First Series*. But even earlier, Emerson's reputation within his own circle was assisted by the personal,

nearly exclusive relationship. It helped compensate for his lack of demonstrated analytical weight.[41]

Emerson's preferred medium, of course, was the essay. Yet it is a common complaint of his critics in every age that the paragraphs often do not
fit together. Sometimes that is true of the sentences within the paragraphs.
Full of sparkling aphorisms and sharp but often disjointed insights, the
essays illuminate in multiple directions but rarely settle an issue. Until
the publication of *Essays: First Series* in 1841, Emerson's ideas, with the
exception of *Nature* and his two Harvard talks, were known to the public
through his lyceum presentations. Yet, as we saw in the last chapter, Emerson had justifiable concerns about whether his talks were sufficiently candid and inspirational. These were doubts substantially shared by his
friends. Emerson's motives for composing "The American Scholar" depended heavily on his perceived place among Transcendentalists, for he
wrote the address just after expressing fear that they did not listen to him,
that they did not consider him an oracle.[42]

In describing himself to his future second wife, Lidian, Emerson saw
himself as "a poet in the sense of perceiver & dear lover of the harmonies
that are in the soul & in matter." By evoking the dualism of Reason and
Understanding, Emerson anchored his self-portrait of the artist in Coleridge's interpretation of Kantian epistemology. But to contemporary intellectuals that hardly redeemed him as a philosopher. Emerson tailored his
talks to an audience with expectations quite different from those of the
company he kept. And because he avoided analytical arguments, striving
instead for spiritual transcendence, fellow intellectuals judged him by language rather than by logic. Longfellow, who had recently replaced George
Ticknor in the chair of European languages, heard Emerson give a lyceum
lecture in 1838 and was unimpressed by his analytical rigor: "He is vastly
more of a poet than of a philosopher."[43]

Longfellow leaned toward Ticknor and Norton's side of Unitarianism.
But even most of Emerson's own friends reacted less to his ideas and
more to mood and expression. In Spring, 1837, Mary Peabody, sister of
Transcendentalist Elizabeth Palmer Peabody, wrote her future husband,
Horace Mann, that "[Emerson] fascinated with his voice. . . . Beyond all
the charm of his intellect I prize that of his loveliness. . . . [His] sweetness
of disposition is the most powerful & prevailing melody." Theodore Parker, one of his most devoted admirers, reported that "Emerson builds a
rambling Gothic church with an irregular outline, a chapel here, and a
tower there, you do not see why; but all parts are beautiful, and all the
while constraining the soul to love and trust." He later told a common
acquaintance, "I do not consider Emerson a philosopher, but a poet lacking the accomplishment of rhyme." To the same effect but more critically,
Convers Francis judged after a February, 1837, lecture: "His style is too

fragmentary & sententious. . . . I find that his beautiful things are *slippery*, and will not stay in my mind." Francis later heard a better lecture, reporting to Henry Hedge: "[It] was studded thick with rich gems of thought,—more methodical & less vague than he is sometimes." Francis then alluded to Hedge's judgment that Emerson's reasoning consisted of "dots of thought." That pointillist characterization must have made the rounds, for a year later Parker wrote Francis, referring to Emerson's "golden atoms of thought." Similarly, in reviewing "The American Scholar," William Henry Channing concluded: "There are no developments of thought, there is no continuous flow in his writings. We gaze as through crevices on a stream of subterranean course, which sparkles here and there in the light, and then is lost." Orestes Brownson, commenting on Emerson's Dartmouth oration, declared in exasperation: "We cannot analyze one of Mr. Emerson's discourses. . . . He is a poet rather than a philosopher. . . . He must be read not for a work of art, which shall be perfect as a whole, but for the exquisite beauty of its details; not for any new or striking philosophical views, but for incidental remarks." A few years later, Henry Hedge gained a measure of revenge in a harsh review of *Essays: Second Series*, arguing: "We should say that moral philosophy was Mr. Emerson's peculiar province, were it not that the over-weight of poetical over the practical, in his composition, disposes him to look at things too much in the order of the imagination, not in the order of the understanding." Hedge then went on to show why Emerson wasn't a particularly good poet, either. And George Ripley later reflected that "[Emerson] is certainly no friend of profound study, any more than of philosophical speculation. . . . Emerson is essentially a poet."[44]

The line between philosophy and religion was a fine one in Unitarian Boston, and if Emerson wasn't considered a philosopher, neither did he earn much respect as a theologian. Even after his Divinity School address seemed to unite momentarily many Transcendentalists against Norton's counterattacks, friends expressed private reservations. Samuel Osgood confided to James Freeman Clarke: "I say, let Emerson preach & lecture, as much as he has a mind to—but let him never be allowed to confound himself with the Christian ministry. He has no idea of theology." Cyrus Bartol wrote George Ellis: "A sensation has been produced by the whole matter in the religious world exceeding anything from so slight a cause that I remember. The result will not be I think to gain Emerson admirers or disciples though it may be to tighten the bonds among his old friends." A year later, after Emerson gave a risky lyceum talk, Convers Francis reported to Theodore Parker: "My wife was there and liked it much, but thought it would be misunderstood and caviled at. Lucky, if it is not cried out upon, as they used to say in witch times."[45]

Francis and Parker were, in fact, friends who quite sincerely loved and admired Emerson. Yet at the end of 1839, they joked that his lyceum lectures were not only repetitions of themselves, but substantially derivative of the work of other Transcendentalists. Although Emerson's presentation was "splendid, better meditated & more coherent than anything I have ever heard from him," was not Brownson more creative and Alcott more inventive? asked Parker. Could he not identify in the talk one-sixth of Brownson, one-tenth of Alcott, one-millionth of Dwight, and one-half of Fuller? A year later, Francis congratulated Parker on his article, which he believed to be the best piece yet published in the *Dial*: "[The critics] may call Emerson superficial if they will, but let them show us a better piece of aesthetical writing than that [of yours] if they can." The perception that he did not think rigorously was so widespread that, when denying the charge of heresy after his 1838 Divinity School address, Emerson slyly took refuge in the fact that, unlike himself, a heretic could "make good his thesis against all comers."[46]

There were some, to be sure, who found Emerson intellectually coherent and profound. Besides his closest sympathizers, Margaret Fuller, Bronson Alcott, and Elizabeth Palmer Peabody ("Mr. Emerson is very luminous, and wiser than ever. Oh, he is beautiful, and good, and great!"), even Harvard professor C. C. Felton, a conservative who had strong doubts about Transcendentalism, testified in 1841 that Emerson's talks "were listened to with delight by some, with distrust by others, and by a few with something like horror. . . . One thing is certain, that they have exacted no little attention among the philosophical quidnuncs of the good city of Boston, and drew around Mr. Emerson a circle of ardent admirers, not to say disciples."[47]

Praise and criticism of Emerson's style and intellectual rigor followed him throughout his career. What is important here is the general view around the time of "The American Scholar." The abundant Transcendentalist correspondence that extols the analytical skills and philosophical daring of Hedge, Ripley, and Brownson says nothing remotely similar for Emerson. No matter how reductive the categories, contemporaries, including most of his friends, considered Emerson an accomplished poet and a philosophical dilettante.[48]

Looking back, however, many today believe that Emerson's rejection by his peers just proves that he is the authentic American philosopher. His inventive, often coarse speech is understood as actually an ordinary-language style of expression designed to subvert traditional academic—European—modes of philosophical discourse. And his apparent carelessness in building argumentative structure is seen as intended to smash ossified—again, European—philosophical categories and to expose the irony of conflicting truths. Because constant reinvention based on experience and self-discovery, rather than slavish adherence to inherited forms and problems, was for him a life's goal, might he not have used these strategies as well in a project for philosophy? Emerson's gift to the discipline could have been a chaotic brilliance and raw integrity that intentionally undermined that very discipline. To the likes of Harold Bloom, Stanley Cavell, John Dewey, and Richard Poirier, Emerson, by turning his back on traditional philosophy, became "America's Philosopher of Democracy."[49]

Yet for purposes of understanding his intentions at the time of "The American Scholar," we must ignore posterity's claim that Emerson eventually triumphed as a philosopher. When he gave his Phi Beta Kappa oration just three years after he began lecturing to lyceum audiences, Emerson was still very much at the beginning of identity formation and accepted the distinction between philosophy and what he practiced, as drawn by his critics. "I will not be chidden out of my most trivial native habit by your distaste, O philosopher, by your preference for somewhat else," he wrote to himself. "If Rhetoric has no charm for you[,] it has for me[;] and my words are as costly & admirable to me as your deeds to you. It is all pedantry to prefer one thing that is alive to another thing which is also alive." Emerson's defiant tone suggests he had not yet broken free from either public criticism or personal uncertainties about his craft.[50]

Expressing, in fact, reservations about his own ability to engage in rigorous philosophical analysis, Emerson acknowledged, even to his children, that, besides his poetic muse, his greatest interest was public speaking, pure and simple. He once asked plaintively, "Why has never the poorest country college offered me a professorship of rhetoric?" and there is no reason to doubt that he understood that position and its responsibilities in conventional terms. Journal entries sketching out what became a new form of expression—"[E]verything is admissible, philosophy, ethics, divinity, criticism, poetry, humor, fun, mimicry, anecdotes, jokes, ventriloquism"—reflect in their context not the undermining of philosophical formalism, but attempts to understand his own lyceum performance. Talks on such topics as "Politics," "Manners," and "Ethics" forced contemporaries to consider Emerson as a philosopher. But for purposes of assessing why he suddenly became so bold at Harvard, what's important to appreciate is that, however scholars today label his work, Emerson understood that peers and even friends frequently judged his lyceum efforts docile and unfocused—an opinion he often shared.[51]

It is not difficult to see why. Along with the sudden growth of newspapers, inexpensive periodicals, and personal journals, all of which Emerson considered essential to democracy, the lyceum seemed a revolutionary educational force. But allowing the orator autonomy to speak meant allowing the public the autonomy to attend. "Lectures," observed Harriet Martineau, "abound in Boston," and during the 1837–1838 winter season there were more than two dozen lyceum series and, of course, a great many individual lectures. Competition for the paying customer must have been intense. Beholden to an audience to buy tickets, all lyceum speakers, including Emerson, had to be wary about what they said. Charging admission—especially in Emerson's case where he was his own business manager—implied a contract with one's audience. Emerson, who always fretted about attendance, confessed privately that he wanted to be an oracle. That is a hard mark to hit when the audience believes it has a right to have its utilitarian expectations satisfied (and always within fifty minutes).[52]

It was, in fact, only at Harvard where Emerson fulfilled his prophetic identity and his oath to speak candidly. In part motivated by a familiar audience and a familiar setting and in part to keep pace with friends who were so gifted in writing academic-style polemics, Emerson broke free from the constraints of lyceum oratory by evoking the tough language and forms of the revival and the jeremiad. Because, whether by design or fear, he wouldn't engage Harvard faculty in subtle philosophical disputes as had Ripley and Hedge, he introduced Transcendentalist thinking descriptively rather than analytically. Hedge had written about the necessity to synthesize the old and new ways, and Ripley and Brownson, as we'll see next, demanded that Transcendentalism stand in the service of social reform. To Emerson, the scholar ought to go where the heart leads: "Character is higher than intellect. Thinking is the function. Living is the functionary. . . . A great soul will be strong to live, as well as strong to think." It was Emerson's refusal to be more specific that so annoyed his foes and disappointed his friends. But Emerson's scholar struck an honest balance between experiential learning and the constant revelation of Reason. That scholar could neither be produced by traditional university pedagogy nor serve some utilitarian purpose. The American scholar could be conjured but not defined.[53]

If Emerson would not or could not engage in the analytical aspects of the philosophical and theological debate between Transcendentalists and Unitarians, at least his sympathies were generally with his friends. But the question of social action, Brownson's third category that divided the Old and New Schools, also separated Emerson from many fellow Transcendentalists. The 1830s saw the rise of several movements designed to better humankind. Abolition, of course, led the way. Socialism, temperance, education of the physically handicapped, and anti-prostitution, dietary, and public school reform were among the many other movements that, commented one observer of the Boston scene, "worked their way from street to street like an epidemic." Because social causes required a willingness to subordinate personal belief to the greater good, Emerson struggled awkwardly. We have seen how Emerson, worried about scaring off his lyceum audience, suppressed his desire to speak out. It was only after and because of "The American Scholar" that by fits and starts he learned to offer his support without feeling a loss of self—or of revenue. Others, who were from the beginning bolder, helped force Emerson to define his position.[54]

Of those closely aligned to Transcendentalism, Orestes Brownson was the most politically committed. His activism caused some Transcendentalists to shun him so that by the summer of 1837 he was no longer invited to club meetings. Brownson had little patience with the extreme religious idealism of Emerson, believing that part of Jesus's mission was to unite Catholic spiritualism and Protestant materialism. Transcendentalism, Brownson wrote in 1836, helped serve this purpose by unifying the mind and body. He hailed Emerson's *Nature* in the *Boston Reformer* "as a proof that the mind is about to receive a new and more glorious manifestation," but worried that Emerson was retreating into the world of pure, self-referential thought: "To deny [the testimony of one's senses] is to set oneself afloat upon the ocean of universal skepticism."[55]

Brownson had quickly been befriended by George Ripley, who saw Brownson's liberal politics as a way to extend the New School to the poor. By March, 1837, while Emerson agonized over his own indecisiveness, Ripley appreciated Brownson as a man of action: "Brownson is a true prophet, Heaven-anointed, and the age to come will build a regal tomb for him, though he is now stoned," he wrote Clarke. He later asked John Sullivan Dwight about a recent Brownson essay: "Can you show a finer piece of philosophical composition than his article on Transcendentalism?" Brownson, in a letter to George Bancroft, expressed similar respect for Ripley and did so publicly in the pages of his *Boston Quarterly Review*: "Mr. Ripley's doctrine . . . rescues the mass from the power of the learned few, and places the truth of Christianity within the reach of every man." Brownson praised Emerson and Alcott as well, but was careful to qualify his support and define areas of difference. He had greater affection and sympathy for Ripley and his more democratic views. Ripley that very year resigned his ministry, telling his congregation that he must follow the two dynamic movements in his life: Transcendentalism and social reform.[56]

It was a few years later, after his deep disappointment that Emerson did not join him at Brook Farm, that Ripley criticized his "indifference to the great humanitarian movements" and expressed satisfaction that others found similar fault with Emerson. But the groundwork was laid earlier. Even the year before he established Brook Farm, George Ripley, in letters to John Sullivan Dwight, despaired over the *Dial*'s idiosyncrasies: "You have seen the Dial, of course; I hope, you like it better than I do; it is quite unworthy, I think, of its pretensions." Although he might modify his opinion, he never was comfortable with the journal. Ripley all along held out the hope that Transcendentalism would result in a greater democratic achievement, of the body and spirit. Emerson hoped for the same in principle, but felt that to work for it meant to compromise one's individuality.[57]

The desire for social justice brought Ripley and Brownson to George Bancroft. Bancroft became the head of the Democratic Party of Massachusetts at a time when its Jacksonian flavor made it unpalatable to Harvard Unitarians and Transcendentalists alike. Bancroft, however, is best known today for is his ten-volume history—in many ways the first modern treatment—of the United States. The first two volumes, published in 1836 and 1837, were well received and reflected both his sympathy for Jacksonian populism and his Transcendentalist interest in personal development. Bancroft did attend a meeting of the Transcendental Club in 1839, but likely found the discourse too ethereal. He made his point, instead, by writing sympathetically about George Fox, William Penn, and other Quakers and critically about Lockean philosophy.[58]

United in political sympathies, Bancroft and Brownson became good friends, and by the summer of 1837 the two were communicating about the evil men who supported regressive material distribution. The "monster spirit" of the mercantile interest, according to Bancroft, was Daniel Webster—still one of Emerson's greatest heroes. Brownson, in turn, praised with superlatives Bancroft's *History* and strongly recommended George Ripley to Bancroft. Ripley had long believed that philosophy should serve the cause of society, but it was Brownson who brought that desire to a flame: "The conversion of my friend George Ripley to Democracy is to me a pleasing event. He is now about right, only in danger like all new converts of becoming a little too enthusiastic." Brownson considered Ripley "one [of] the first men in our country," with a mind of exceptional clarity and vigor and a pure heart. "Several young men from the Divinity School at Cambridge are coming on well." But Brownson named Ripley alone. The following year, when Bancroft received a patronage position as collector of the Port of Boston, he appointed Brownson steward of a local marine hospital.[59]

Ripley found the practical strategies of party politics distasteful, but also admired Bancroft. Reacting to the first volume of Bancroft's history, Ripley emoted about the future, writing its author: "I do not count it clearly impossible for new life to be breathed into the languid veins of our liberal Christianity; & with such men as Brownson, & the brash, young writer in the Western Messenger." Writing three weeks after "The American Scholar," Ripley identified Brownson and James Freeman Clarke, but not Emerson, as part of that new movement. And in a letter two months later—made all the more provocative because it is torn at excruciatingly important points—Ripley praised Bancroft for having given a talk at Worcester which apparently criticized Harvard. Bancroft's address seems to have touched themes similar to Emerson's, but again Ripley did not mention his own cousin.[60]

Emerson's lack of sympathy for political activism meant that his relationship to Bancroft was not as intimate or passionate. Although they remained friends, as a committed populist Bancroft separated himself from Emerson's brand of Transcendentalism, writing in Brownson's journal, the *Boston Quarterly Review*: "For who are the best judges in matters of taste? Do you think the cultivated individual? Undoubtedly not. . . . It is alone by infusing great principles into the common mind, that revolutions in human society are effected. They never have been, they never can be, effected by superior *individual* excellence." In the next issue, Brownson himself, reviewing Emerson's 1838 Dartmouth address, continued the same line of attack: "Let Mr. Emerson, let all who have the honor of their country or of their race at heart, turn their attention to the work of convincing the educated and the fashionable, that democracy is worthy of their sincerest homage, and of making them feel the longing to labor in its ennobling cause; and then he and they may cease to be anxious as to the literary results." Bancroft, Brownson, and William Henry Channing (in his review of "The American Scholar") all felt strongly sympathetic toward Emerson, especially when he was attacked by Norton. But political differences ran as deeply as did the philosophical and religious affinities.[61]

Emerson's own political views have been endlessly debated by subsequent generations. John Dewey and F. O. Matthiessen, for example, believed that Emerson was a populist fully committed to democracy and at times even infatuated with the Democratic Party. On the other side, John Jay Chapman supposed that "if a soul be taken and crushed by democracy till it utter a cry, that cry will be Emerson." What is readily established is that Emerson believed that he must strongly resist the pressure to embrace a belief that he did not come to independently. By the time Emerson wrote "Self-Reliance," his views against sentimental humanitarian gestures were formed, if not always practiced. Ripley, Brownson, and Bancroft could not help but understand his rhetorical question "Are they *my* poor?" as a rejection of all political and social ideology.[62]

Except for his comments about Hedge, Emerson was generally cautious in criticizing friends. But his alter ego Bronson Alcott was less so. At the very beginning of 1838, he wrote in his journal of Ripley: "He is an intimate friend of Brownson. With him, and some others, he espouses the interests of the people, and pleads the authority of democratic principles. This party . . . look[s] with some distrust on the growing disposition toward Idealism and Spiritualism [of Emerson and Alcott]. . . . It is not easy, as yet, to determine which shall obtain the supremacy." And a few days later, Alcott added: "I distrust the theories of Mr. B[rownson] because in them, I recognize no provision for the formation of men. There is no allowances for human culture. Society, institutions, the forms, the organs of men exist; yet still no men." Emerson could easily have said the same. In political and social sympathies, even more so than in the philosophical and theological debates, Transcendentalists did not agree. And in the political and social sphere especially, Emerson had few allies. But then again, everyone seemed to suffer from uncertainty.[63]

Just after Emerson delivered his Divinity School address in 1838, as Transcendentalist Cyrus Bartol was damning the talk with faint praise to George Ellis, Transcendentalists James Freeman Clarke and Christopher Cranch defended Emerson in the *Western Messenger* but suggested: "If we were asked who is the leader of this New School, we should not name Mr. Emerson so soon as Dr. Channing. He leads on the new school, because from him has come the strongest impulse to independent thought, to earnest self-supported activity."[64]

Clarke and Cranch only confirmed what others had been thinking. Six months earlier, noting that "Emerson & Walker by their lectures have set the whole city agog to penetrate the mysteries of transcendentalism," Samuel Osgood implied that others were even more conspicuous: "Ripley is all alive & his book just out. There are weekly meetings of the 'Progress' Club . . . where Dr Channing & all the friends of humanity regularly congregate. . . . Dr Channing seems to take stronger & stronger ground in behalf of reform. Ripley presses on undaunted. Norton & the Dean are becoming sorer & sorer." The following year, in discussing reaction to Emerson's Divinity School address, Parker confirmed that "it is quite evident there are now two parties among the unitarians, one is for Progress, the other says 'our strength is to stand still.' Dr Channing is the real head of the first party. The other has no head."[65]

How did Channing, who in early meetings of the Transcendental Club was linked to Andrews Norton as an object of concern, emerge as the head of the new party? His 1835 tract *Slavery*, calling for the use of moral suasion to end that horrible institution, earned him a great deal of hatred in the South and a fair amount of coolness in the North. Even Channing's own Federal Street Church congregation refused to allow abolitionists to speak there. To Transcendentalists, however, caught between a desire for collective action and a search for individual truth, Channing's strategy seemed like just the right approach.[66]

A number of Transcendentalists, including at least Parker, Ripley, Osgood, Dwight, Hedge, and Follen, went to the weekly Friends of Progress meetings, led by Channing and held in the rooms of Jonathan Phillips (who, though also invited, did not attend the Transcendental Club). Parker, in the letter quoted above, by then even called Transcendentalists the party of Progress. Ripley was at the time closer to Channing than to Emerson, proclaiming himself "a child of Channing." Parker, also increasingly drawn to Channing, reported that at a meeting of the Progress Club in February, 1838, Ripley took "exception to the impersonal conception of God put forth by Mr. Emerson." There is no indication that Emerson ever attended, and, in his absence, he was criticized. But he would have his revenge years later in satirizing Channing's efforts to gather intellectual society. Guests, Emerson mockingly observed, fell to eating the oysters, altogether abandoning philosophical discourse.[67]

Conservative Unitarians also noted Channing's prominence. Andrews Norton named Channing as "at the head" of the new party, and even wrote Channing himself to that effect. But to intimate friend John Gorham Palfrey, Norton qualified that somewhat: "If [Ripley] be not checked . . . he will become a great man; and he and Brownson and Miss Fuller and Miss Peabody, with occasional aid from Dr Channing and others, will become the mystagogues of one knows not how large a portion of the community." Here Channing was colluding, but Ripley, as so often, was judged the central figure. Not once did Norton mention Emerson.[68]

Although Channing's involvement with Transcendentalism is today sharply debated, clearly some contemporaries even considered him the leader of the Transcendentalists. The ambiguity confirms Emerson's judgment. There was no formal group that congealed around 1836 and suddenly fragmented some four or five years later. It was always in flux with loyalties shifting.

Channing's illusive presence, however, cast its shadow over Emerson. About six months before "The American Scholar," Bronson Alcott, Emerson's closest friend and his moral compass, was under severe public attack. He reflected bitterly in his journal—which was read by Emerson—that Channing had abandoned him in his hour of greatest need. Emerson tried mightily to repair relations between his two friends, but a month later observed: "Once Dr. Channing filled our sky. Now we become so conscious of his limits & of the difficulty attending any effort to show him our point of view, that we doubt if it be worth while. Best amputate." The resigned tone suggests concern that he and Alcott were becoming isolated. Two years earlier, Emerson had to friends criticized Channing's stand on slavery, but had then come to respect him for it. And at least Channing had said *something* on the subject and had even lobbied hard for educational reform at Harvard. It was in the same journal entry that Emerson castigated himself for not speaking out on Transcendentalist philosophy, abolition, and Harvard College: "You have no oracle to utter, & your fellowmen have learned that you cannot help them; for oracles speak." With Ripley gravitating toward Brownson and

Clarke toward Channing, and virtually all the Transcendentalists acknowledging Ripley's boldness, Emerson felt on the margin precisely because he had not yet declared himself on these questions. His lyceum talks were hardly adequate.[69]

Emerson's need to be an oracle to friends resulted from the rapidly shifting landscape, in which Transcendentalists pursued different interests and fell under different influences. Others, as Emerson observed, had spoken, and they, his fellowmen, probably had come to the conclusion that he could not help them. But motivated by what he knew of Harvard, a desire to be a consequential voice among his friends, and commitment to Alcott, Emerson over the next year set about to speak on these very issues. Considering the opinions of his friends when composing the oration, Emerson was also aware of their differences and of his place within the group. As we saw in his feeling of self-disgust after writing an acclaimed letter supporting the Cherokee Nation, precisely because he thought of himself as one who rendered original prophecy, he could not appear dependent on the views of others. "Most persons of distinguished ability meet in society with a kind of tacit appeal. Each seems to say 'I am not all here,'" he wrote in his journals. And it was no accident that those whom he chose to be closest to were obvious outsiders: Margaret Fuller and the two non-ministers, Bronson Alcott and Henry David Thoreau. In fact, even as most friends publicly supported him in the aftermath of his Divinity School address, the only Transcendentalist colleague Emerson proposed for the faculty of his ideal university was Alcott. Defining himself apart from the struggle between Harvard professors and their students, Emerson distrusted the academic predilections of his friends as much as he did those of his enemies.[70]

For the past generation, Harvard had been in intellectual ferment. Its full conversion at the beginning of the nineteenth century to liberal Christianity, what became known as Unitarianism, opened up new areas of thought. The validity of the biblical tradition and even the divinity of Jesus were investigated. Faculty charged with teaching religion had been trained in European institutions, and they in turn exposed their students to continental literatures and philosophies. Many of these graduates became members of the first classes of the Harvard Divinity School. Ordained ministers, they used their critical skills, which had been honed at Harvard, to raise questions about the intellectual and moral political direction even of their alma mater. "The freest and widest inquiry will favor Unitarian doctrines," proclaimed *Christian Examiner* editor James Walker about his university.[71]

But as quickly as they came to life, the creative energies of the institution were refocused. The Industrial Revolution and the sudden expansion of the market economy resulted in, for the first time, more students studying law than ministry. That shift, though never fully investigated, must have had an enormous cultural impact on Harvard. Kirkland had been the sweet, spiritual president who created the Divinity School; Quincy was the managerial president, who, closely allied with mercantile interests, initiated the modern training of lawyers. Quincy symbolically resuscitated the long-forgotten university motto *Veritas*, preferring it to the then-current *Christo et Ecclesiae*. Quincy's truth, however, established through the Lockean world of the senses, was affirmed by material success. We saw in chapter 3 the harsh reaction of Emerson and his circle to the changing climate of their college. They rightly feared that their revolution in idealism was to be short lived.[72]

For the most part, Emerson's friends continued to attack Harvard faculty on questions of philosophy and theology—issues that in a rapidly changing secular world seemed less pressing. Although pulled along by colleagues, Emerson leaped over the academic debate—and again, it may well have been his lack of skill rather than greater insight—and took the extreme position of prophet. He opposed the fundamental materialism of the institution, not with a competing formalistic philosophy, but with an oracular vision uttered in a common argot. A prophet doesn't rebuke the king in the king's language, but only with the words of his god.

"The American Scholar" criticizes higher education, but, jeremiadic in form, ends optimistically, inviting all to share the ideal of the scholar. To Emerson, it was not so much that others believed the wrong thing. Rather, he encouraged everyone simply to drop all their acquired beliefs and listen to the truth within. To his friends engaged in the political struggle, that was as unrealistic as was his faith that it might be possible to produce even one such American scholar. Because of Emerson's later stature, it is especially easy to see "The American Scholar" as central to the ascent of Transcendentalism. It assuredly was not. Emerson's friends celebrated his courage, but few rallied around his ideas.

Chapter Six

∾

ALCOTT

WHILE POSITIONING HIMSELF AMONG AND YET SEPARATE
from fellow Transcendentalists, there was one friend to whom Emerson
drew ever closer. Best known today as the father of Louisa May Alcott,
Bronson Alcott was the colleague Emerson especially esteemed. Three decades later, Emerson listed him below only Aunt Mary as the most important of his lifelong influences. And just two months after his daring
oration, he reflected that "Montaigne, Alcott, M[ary] M[oody] E[mer-
son], and I, have written Journals; beside these, I did not last night think
of another." Since most of his friends and family kept journals, Emerson
was not being literal. He meant that he knew of only a few individuals
who engaged in honest self-reflection. Montaigne, of course, had per-
fected the introspective essay, a genre Emerson was beginning to embrace.
And Aunt Mary, as we'll see, was respected by all who could withstand
her brutal candor.[1]

But Alcott? Transcendentalists had growing reservations about his intellectual and practical sense. Although Theodore Parker kept his opinion
to himself in a diary entry entitled "Doubts about Alcott," both Emerson's brother William and close friend Elizabeth Hoar openly expressed
to Emerson amazement that he would devote so much attention to him.
Carlyle, after Alcott's visit in 1842, exchanged testy letters with Emerson
and finally in despair warned his friend that "bottomless imbeciles ought
not be seen in company with R Waldo Emerson, who already has *men*
listening to him on this side of the water."[2]

And it wasn't just how Alcott presented himself, for his writings
caused an even greater reaction. Alcott, as we'll see, suffered public humiliation after publishing *Conversations with Children on the Gospels*

in 1837, but he really outdid himself in 1840 with "Orphic Sayings." They begin:

> Thou are, my heart, a soul-flower, facing ever and following the motions of thy sun, opening thyself to her vivifying ray, and pleading thy affinity with the celestial orbs. Thou dost
>
> the living day
Dial on time thine own eternity.

It was Emerson who convinced Fuller, as editor of the *Dial*, to publish "Orphic Sayings," proposing that "if people are properly acquainted with the prophet himself,—& his name is getting fast into the stellar regions,—these will have a certain fitting Zoroastrian style." But the prophet went unrecognized, with one critic suggesting that reading the "Orphic Sayings" was like watching "a train of fifteen coaches going by, with only one passenger." Friends thought detractors had a point. "I have not named Mr. Alcott," recalled a later Transcendentalist in describing the giants, "because, although he was prominent in the public eye and did more than any one to bring ridicule upon the movement, he had no significant influence." Emerson understood but minimized the criticisms, claiming that Alcott "read Plato as an equal" yet hoping (in vain) to outlive Alcott so that he could be the one to write his friend's biography.[3]

Acquaintances suspected Emerson's reasons for such loyalty. "[Emerson's] relation with Mr. Alcott always seemed to me inexplicable," recalled a contemporary, "because with all kind feeling for him, I could never feel [Alcott] to be in any degree a master. . . . I think certainly that both Mr. Alcott and Henry Thoreau were very much influenced by Mr. Emerson, and unconsciously reflected him to himself. Thoreau, however, was a man who had his own qualities." Emerson seems to have made Alcott into a master in order to live up to standards he believed Alcott had set. Emerson overlooked Alcott's shortcomings, for his needs in a friend ran deeper than intellectual coherence.[4]

Until well into adulthood, Emerson had complex feelings about his late father. Perhaps the most liberal of those clergy rapidly moving toward what would become Unitarianism, William died when Waldo was just turning eight. Losing a parent so young probably contributed to what was an intense need for this apostle of self-reliance to attach himself to authority figures. To appreciate how Alcott especially played such a large role in the shaping of "The American Scholar," we must first consider Emerson's remarkable relationship with his father.[5]

Emerson rarely mentioned his father in his journals or letters. But one surviving letter offers extraordinary insight. In 1849 and 1850, no fewer than three people were soliciting information about William for inclusion in biographical collections of notable ministers and civic leaders. In February, 1850, Waldo wrote his brother, also named William, acknowledging that he had received from him a copy of Josiah Quincy's request. Quincy was writing a history of the Boston Athenaeum, of which Waldo's father was a founder. Emerson never liked the former Harvard president, and Quincy, after Emerson gave "The American Scholar" and the Divinity School address at his institution, probably had little reason to like him. Quincy wrote William in New York, rather than Waldo, who was local, because he heard that Waldo was travelling: "I should write to your brother but I am told he is not now in this quarter of ye Heaven. He is a wandering star giving light every where & I know not just now in what direction to point my telescope to find him." As scorn, lightly masked as cleverness, is the only way Waldo could have read this. Because the request came from Quincy and because it concerned his father, Emerson replied stiffly to William. It is that awkwardness which forced such revelation:

> For Mr Quincys proposition I hardly know what to say to it. This is the third application within a twelvemonth that has come to me to write a memoir of our father; the first from Dr Sprague, the second from William Ware. But I have no recollections of him that can serve me. I was eight years old when he died, & only remember a somewhat social gentleman, but severe to us children, who twice or thrice put me in mortal terror by forcing me into the salt water off some wharf or bathing house, and I still recall the fright with which, after some of this salt experience, I heard his voice one day, (as Adam that of the Lord God in the garden,) summoning us to a new bath, and I vainly endeavouring to hide myself. I have never heard any sentence or sentiment of his repeated by Mother or Aunt, and his printed or written papers, as far as I know, only show candour & taste, or I should almost say, docility, the principal merit possible to that early ignorant & transitional *Month-of-March*, in our New England culture. His literary merits really are that he fostered the Anthology & the Athenaeum. These things ripened into Buckminster Channing & Everett.

Rather than expressing satisfaction that his father was about to gain recognition, Emerson was annoyed, feeling the need to explain himself in painful detail. Joel Porte rightly intuits: "Fear, shame, and anger are thoroughly mixed in this account of Emerson's complex, and perdurable, reaction to his God-like father."[6]

Emerson's identification with a guilty and fearful Adam is extraordinary, for it was in large part by denying God's judgmental nature and rejecting Adam's sin that Unitarianism separated itself from Calvinism. Emerson usually thought of Adam as "the simple genuine Self" who "liveth on with the privilege of God, with a hope as broad as the unbounded Universe." In preparing lyceum talks, he charged himself to become, like the fatherless Adam before him, the teacher of humankind. But in this letter, Calvinist theology prevailed, with Waldo the guilt-ridden Adam and his father the punitive God.[7]

Emerson, "an irrepressible symbol-hunter," was far too careful a writer to propose the analogy unintentionally. Here the symbolism is obvious. Emerson evoked the powerful impression of Adam being confronted by God for tasting from the tree of knowledge, for which he was expelled from Eden. Likewise, in defying his father's faith, Emerson left the garden of Unitarian security for the risky world of Transcendentalism. He was forever banished from his father's protection and affection.[8]

If fear and alienation are conveyed allegorically, the anger is explicit. Emerson declared that, from what he read, his father's writings weren't very memorable ("only show candour & taste, or I should almost say, docility, the principal merit possible to that early ignorant . . ."). Emerson could not have described anything as docile and ignorant without feeling contempt.

There is quite a bit in this short letter. But far more important is what's missing. How could Emerson, at age forty-seven, claim to know so little of a father who had been such a prominent member of Boston society? And yet, if knowing so little, how could he then be full of fear and contempt, portraying himself as Adam to God?

For information about his family, Waldo relied mainly on his aunt Mary Moody Emerson, not by any measure a person to be counted on for consistent and firm guidance on emotional matters. And yet, after the death of her brother William, Aunt Mary became the "female step-father" and Waldo's early intellectual inspiration. Mary remained in Concord until 1824 and then lived mostly in rural Maine, with few trips to Concord until 1842, when her visits became more frequent. In person and by her copious and often electrifying correspondence, she maintained close contact with Waldo and his brothers. Her passion for reading widely and deeply and for spontaneous candor, with similar expectations of her nephews, played an essential role in their formation. Fatherless and always loyal to his family, Waldo willingly succumbed to her energies. He would later acknowledge her as his oracle and benefactor, putting her first among those who influenced him.[9]

But erratic and tempestuous, Mary exacted a steep price for her high counsels. Henry James, who in his youth knew Waldo, noted that scholars had not yet fully appreciated the "tormenting representative value" of this "grim intellectual virgin and daughter of a hundred ministers" (in actuality, we can trace a mere six ministers in her direct ancestry). Recently and with considerably more sympathy, her significant influence on the formation of Waldo's early Transcendentalist thinking has been explored. Yet we are still a long way from fully understanding the complex

Figure 12. Mary Moody Emerson, no date. From *Ralph Waldo Emerson: His Maternal Ancestors*, by David Greene Haskins (Boston: Cupples, Upham, 1887).

relationship between the young Emerson and the aunt who often dressed in her funeral shroud and slept in a bed designed as a coffin and whom he would refer to by the anagram "Tnamurya" and the oxymoron "Father Mum." Besides bestowing enormous intellectual gifts on Waldo, Mary, with her passionate and unpredictable nature, at times also terrorized her nephew. As one of her relatives put it, "she had a positive genius for cruelty." Especially cruel was the way that she communicated to her nephew about his father.[10]

Remarkably, there's no reason to believe that Waldo had ever asked her directly about his father. On her own, the spinster aunt occasionally expressed her differences with her late brother's liberal theology, yet conveyed also how much she loved and missed him. But in 1824, when Waldo's brother Edward acknowledged William in his Harvard commencement address, Mary wrote Waldo, wondering whether it had been appropriate: "It might be as well, as it is a protestant Country, to let the dead slumber." Her reactions probably signaled to her young nephew that he was not to ask about his father.[11]

Emerson did inquire, in 1826, about the early life of his mother, Ruth, and in response was told of the failing he shared with his father: "[Ruth] married one of the finest of men—but their rural Eden was not stocked with fruit enow for him. . . . In a new situation, [which] ambition of the Adam she sustained any occasional trial of temper with a dignity firmness & good sense that I shall ever respect." Much to Mary's great disdain, William left the small and impoverished pulpit of Harvard, Massachusetts, for the more prestigious and lucrative, if less intensively pious, First Church of Boston. He wasn't, however, the only Emerson to succumb to the temptations of Eden. At the end of the letter, Mary speculated that Ruth's current physical and mental decline were attributable to "the indulgence of her sons' frivolous ambition." To Mary, both father and son reached for more than their due and both fell from grace. Excessive ambition—especially the desire for public acclaim—was a constant worry for Mary. Another great concern of hers, characteristically, was that her family should, in fact, receive its public due.[12]

In opposing the ambitions of father and son, throughout the next several years "Father Mum" worried over Waldo's soul. Just the previous year, Mary, who never fully surrendered her Calvinist, or at least New Light, instincts, had expressed the hope that he would rid the world of the sins of Adam: "*As by means of Adam sin entered and death so by means of a divine man death & sin are destroyed*! Ah my dear Waldo, prepare . . . to preach this divine medicine to a thoughtless ambitious world." But quickly she came to fear that, rather than rectifying what Adam wrought, Waldo was, instead, Adam. "Have you thriven under evil?" she wrote in 1826, just before accusing him of being ambitious like his father. The next year, she exploded: "It is worse than idle to ridicule the fall. . . . That *literal* apple might have been the *seed* of a [government that] has dug for men the hell of sin and extends to the highest rewards of Heaven."[13]

In her Almanack, Mary recorded a lifetime of extraordinarily intense observations on philosophy and theology, providing a model for Waldo's own journals. There she lashed out at his ambitions and the college that had made him too worldly:

> He talks of the Holy Ghost, God of mercy, what a subject! "A Holy Ghost given to every man in Eden." It was lost in the great contest going on in the vast universe; . . . it was regiven embodied in the assumed humanity of the son of God; and since—the reward of prayer, agony, self immolation! . . . Would to God thou wert more ambitious—respected thyself more & the world less. Thou wouldst not to Cambridge. True they use the name *Christo* but that venerable institution it is thought has become but a feeble ornamented arch in the great temple which the Christian world maintains to the honor of his name.

Mary made sure Waldo knew her feelings, quoting this outburst in a letter to him of probably 1824 or a bit later. She needed to remind him that, like his father, he was the worldly, ambitious Adam.[14]

But Mary got worse from Waldo than mere ambition. In 1832, feeling unable to celebrate the sacrament of the Lord's Supper, Emerson gave up the ministry. Her strong reaction was only partly due to her nephew's theological wanderings. He also failed the long family tradition of religious service. Because he broke the chain, he was, she harshly rebuked him, "parrisidical," a father killer. The next year, writing Waldo's brother Charles, she lamented that "it is far sadder than, the translation of the soul by death of the body to lose Waldo as I have lost him." In 1836, after a terrible fight at Waldo's dinner table, she quickly departed Concord, vowing never to return to Emerson's home. In her Almanack for 1838, Mary listed him among the dead of her family, and in 1841, after reading his *Essays: First Series*, she wished that he actually had died. Or at least, had William lived, he would have prevented his son from straying. Mary wrote Hoar, by then her closest friend: "How bitterly did I regret that Waldo had not gone to the tomb amidst his early honors like one—who if he had lived such essays had never seen the light of a [Christian] world." Mary pitted her dead brother against his living son, and there is reason to believe that Hoar, who lived in Concord and saw him frequently, showed Waldo the letter.[15]

Mary could also forgive and admire. She wrote Waldo in 1836, acknowledging the distance between them and asking forgiveness for her part in the quarrel. The year after she wished he had died rather than having written *Essays: First Series*, in her Almanack she suddenly proclaimed, "What an ingenious & powerful lecture of Waldo's on transcendentalism!" And Waldo, in turn, continued to record in his journals only admiration for her. In 1841, some five years after their fight in his house, Waldo wrote, asking her to return and to "challenge many things that now sleep & perhaps die in me." But in their subsequent infrequent meetings, he remained on his guard. In 1847, Mary confided in Hoar: "And I don't like to be in Concord when Waldo is there. . . . Waldo delights me as much as he does you & others[. T]he less I see him the better tho' as he is reserved[. W]e get no truths or errors unveiled."[16]

Early on, Mary explicitly connected her erratic relationship with her nephews to her guilt-ridden feelings about their father. In her Almanack on May 16, 1827, likely read two years later when Waldo took it for extended study, she observed the anniversary of the death of her brother and reflected on how she had helped to raise his children: "Today 16 years have come & gone since I closed with this hand the eyes of one who was the first object of my enthusiastic love & admiration. . . . Oh for me I had not *then* a tear. And that he was released from . . . the cares of a profession in wh[ich] the views of his theology I *thought* defective—from the imitations & competition wh[ich] alas attend City ministers, I could not for him. For his widow & children I did not then as since. . . . May God forgive what I omitted and what I transgressed." The day of William's death was the only personal anniversary Mary acknowledged in her massive diary, noting it at least four times. In the entry for the following year, Mary wrote remorsefully: "Different roads & education & faith led us to view each other with indifference; but the remembrance of that death, of that day in which I erred,—will never cease to pain in this life. While he lay dead, I talked & prayed,—but not with fervor." Waldo, who later copied that passage into his own journals, was treated to these torments.[17]

Mary's anxieties about William took root in Waldo and are manifested in the journal volumes he created out of her letters and Almanack. Near the beginning of the first volume, he copied from a letter Mary wrote William in 1804. Waldo identified the recipient as "her brother W.E.," rather than as his own father. What he extracted and entered into his journals was her harsh rebuke of William: "Whenever I have had my doubts & opinions with you the dread of disgusting is lessened by the conviction of having received shafts already as severe as any your quiver may afford." A little later comes a letter, probably of 1821, from his aunt to an unidentified recipient concerning his father: "*What has*, if thou knowest anything of cause & effect, what has done the most injury to men & women since the allegory of Adam? *Sexual influence*, I would not whisper it to any one but thee: but what do I know robbed him of the highest honors of [College—Waldo's addition] Government but the waste of hours in female society at F. Place, where the sex was not forgotten in mind." That seems to be all Waldo needed to learn from Aunt Mary about her "brother W.E.," and he excerpted nothing more about his father.[18]

With all the guilt, memory of his earlier life was painful. "God have mercy and save me from the past," Mary wrote a few months before her brother died. Waldo certainly had his own reasons to regret his youth. His father's death left Ruth to raise five sons and a daughter. One of the sons, Bulkeley, was mentally retarded, and the daughter, Mary Caroline, died just three years after their father. Virtually destitute, the family was forced to move around Boston, looking for ever cheaper housing and the opportunity to take in boarders. Waldo acknowledged: "[M]y manners & history would have been different, if my parents had been rich." Aunt Mary, meanwhile, believed that her own stepfather, the respected Unitarian minister Ezra Ripley, was privately a martinet. Waldo, although putting on a good public face, apparently felt similarly. Even had William been a kindly father—and there is ample reason to think that was so—there was enough trauma in Waldo's early life to result in confused feelings. Later, mourning a wife and two brothers, Waldo deemed all his childhood memories inevitably painful: "Strange is it that I can go back to no part of youth, no past relation without shrinking & shrinking. Not Ellen, not Edward, not Charles. Infinite compunctions embitter each of those dear names & all who surround them." He might claim in "The American Scholar": "The actions and events of our childhood and youth, are now matters of calmest observation. They lie like fair pictures in the air." But his own pain is clear.[19]

In 1847, a certain Mary Botham Howitt requested information about his childhood for a magazine article accompanying his lecture tour of England. The preserved draft of his response, with its numerous corrections, reveals how much difficulty Emerson had in forming a reply. In the end, he rigorously denied the request for information, slamming shut the door to his memories: "I am concerned to say I have no history[,] no anecdotes[,] no connexion[,] no fortunes that would make the smallest figure in a narrative. . . . We will really say no more on a topic so sterile." In his letter of 1850, brother William told Waldo that, residing in New York, he no longer had access to the people and materials he would need to write the biographical sketch of their father. They were, however, available to Waldo in Concord. Instead, Waldo destroyed his own copy of his father's sermons, reusing some of the paper and covers in constructing his own journals. Even Emerson's most controversial statement about self-reliance—that he felt no more at the death of his first child than he would in suffering a financial loss—is really a question of confronting memory.[20]

Emerson admitted to recalling only a few stories about his father, but in his attending the same college as his father, preaching in the same city, and then returning to Concord, reminders were everywhere. No authority better articulates the burden of patrimony Emerson labored under than John Quincy Adams. The former president of the United States was perhaps the most esteemed of the many estimable figures around Boston. Emerson had, in 1831, proudly dined with him, and he proclaimed that his most satisfying moment politically was Adams's election as president. The respect was not returned. In 1841, Adams wrote in his diary: "A young man named Ralph Waldo Emerson, a son of my once-loved friend William Emerson, and a classmate of my lamented George, after failing in the every-day avocations of a Unitarian minister and a schoolmaster, starts a new doctrine of Transcendentalism, declares all the old revelations superannuated and worn out, and announces the approach of new revelations and prophecies."[21]

Waldo's reluctance to learn about a father apparently present to everyone but himself ended soon after the biographical requests of 1850, when, perhaps urged on by Lidian, he finally faced his Aunt Mary squarely. But in the meantime, conditioned by Mary's complex feelings toward his fa-

Figures 13 and 14. Note the similar profiles of father William (L) and Waldo (R). Both from *Ralph Waldo Emerson: His Maternal Ancestors*, by David Greene Haskins (Boston: Cupples, Upham, 1887).

ther and himself, he clearly experienced unease about his past. Because his Divinity School address of 1838 was a direct attack on the church William had helped establish, the speech has been called a rejection of the father. One might characterize "The American Scholar" as an attempt to better him. Forty-eight years earlier, William had himself been the Phi Beta Kappa orator, speaking quite successfully, we are told, on the topic of "Taste." There, he exhorted his audience, in contrast to contemporary orators but in haunting anticipation of his son, to eschew the notion of "universal taste" and to uphold the sanctity of individual expression by grasping "the powers of reason, and of the soul" and by acknowledging "not only the attributes of sound judgment, but all the warmth of imagination." William also advised that foreign books could not provide adequate intellectual guidance and that one must turn "to the American sun, and . . . [f]ollow . . . the life of native genius."[22]

Yet to what extent Waldo had William in mind when he took up similar themes while berating his father's friends and university we can never know. Emerson himself could not know. After all, they were also *his* friends and it was *his* university. The important point is this: it is not necessary to posit an Oedipal struggle to appreciate that his own history was deeply confusing to him and that his distress may have affected his conscious behavior. Wrestling constantly with dependency and self-reliance, Emerson lionized friends, elevating them to inflated levels to which he, too, should aspire. Disenchantment often followed. Perhaps because of the complex notion of a father figure formed through Mary's erratic responses, Emerson searched for authority in others.[23]

In his youth, Emerson quite naturally idolized and then debunked his college professors. Yet the need to emulate persisted. Although he would later taunt him publicly for supporting the Fugitive Slave Law, at this time Emerson's estimation of Daniel Webster was so extravagant that Arthur M. Schlesinger, Jr., referred to it as "his invention of a statesman named Daniel Webster to whom he gave profound devotion and whom he carelessly confused with the popular Whig politician of the same name." But until meeting Alcott, Emerson's true "early oracle," as he called him, was Sampson Reed. Since hearing Reed's master's oration at Harvard in 1821, he had fallen under his spell. In 1827, he listed Reed as the single American representative of Transcendentalism, and later in his journals, quoting John 14:28, explicitly acknowledged him as a father figure: "I talk with Sampson & see it is not him but a greater than him, 'My Father is greater than I.' Truth speaks by him." As he would do with Alcott, Emerson linked Reed with giants: Burke and de Staël; Jesus, Dante, Chaucer, and Milton; and Webster and Wordsworth. Taking from Reed that genius is the enemy of genius by overinfluence and putting that sentiment into "The American Scholar," Emerson idolized Reed while admonishing against idolatry. Then came disillusionment. Emerson observed in 1836 that "as I become acquainted with S.R.'s books & teachers the miracle [of his genius] is somewhat lessened." A Swedenborgian by faith, Reed publicly took umbrage at Emerson's characterization of Swedenborg's thoughts in "The American Scholar." He later criticized Transcendentalism, and after that Emerson became estranged from him, even regretting that he had venerated Reed.[24]

But there were also friends of a lifetime to whom Emerson continued to give his all. During the 1830s, he so subordinated himself to Carlyle that the Scot even expressed embarrassment. Because he sought moral as well as intellectual guidance, Emerson cleaved especially to Alcott. Emerson, it was suggested by a contemporary, made Alcott into a "master" so that his friend "unconsciously reflected him to himself." We will see this demonstrated at a critical moment in his life.

Emerson's initial attraction to Alcott also came during a time of personal crisis. Emerson had been completely attached to his brother Charles, even planning to have him and his future wife, Elizabeth Hoar, live with him in his Concord home. Charles's sudden death in May, 1836, as we noted earlier, devastated Emerson. Following on the loss of Edward two years earlier, Emerson was then left with just William, who lived in New York and with whom he was warm but never intimate (Bulkeley was mentally challenged and rarely around). It was only a month after Charles died that Emerson began describing Alcott in wildly enthusiastic terms. Just as Aunt Mary played multiple roles in Emerson's life, so, too, did Alcott.

The two met about a year after Alcott came to Boston to start a school. Emerson's impressions began with modest appreciation, but quickly ascended to extravagant praise. In 1835, Emerson wrote in his journal: "[Alcott is a] wise man, simple, superior to display, and drops the best things as quietly as the least." By June, 1836, soon after Charles's death, Emerson confided to brother William: "Mr. Alcott . . . is a great genius. So thoroughly original that he seems to subvert all you know and leave only his own theories." Emerson then wrote Hedge, successfully urging him to include Alcott in the proposed Transcendental Club. Although all the other members were ordained ministers, Alcott was, to Emerson, "a God-made priest. . . . He is a world builder. . . . He is so resolute to force all thoughts & things to become rays from his centre, that, for the most part, they come." It was only a short time later that Emerson first began expressing doubts about Reed. In his journals Emerson compared Alcott to Jesus, Kant, Swedenborg, and Cousin as individuals to emulate. He would later place him in the company of Carlyle; Spinoza and Kant; George Fox; Montaigne and the young Thoreau. In observing that Alcott "seems to subvert all you know and leave only his own theories," Emerson gives an indication of his friend's influence. Immediately after an Alcott visit in 1836, Emerson recorded in his journals several insights that he soon used in *Nature*, and it is probable that at least some of them came directly from Alcott. While George Ripley gained most of the attention from other Transcendentalists, Emerson focused on and drew from Alcott.[25]

Emerson's feelings were fully reciprocated. After his first visit to Concord in 1835, Alcott recorded in his own journal: "I have not found a man in whose mind I felt more sympathy." By 1836, affection turned to adulation: "In beauty and finish of style, he is unrivalled among American writers. There is also more philosophic depth than in any other writer." In early 1837, Emerson became godlike: "[T]he day shall come when this man's Genius shall shine beyond the circle of his own city and nation. . . . Emerson is destined to be the high literary name of this age. . . . A race of more worthy artists shall supersede our present vulgar artisans. . . . Emerson's whip of small cords . . . shall do somewhat to drive the buyers and sellers of slang and profanity from this sacred place. . . .—Honorable notion—and sham-image killer, is he!"[26]

From the moment their relationship began in the fall of 1835, Emerson and Alcott engaged in mutual identity-building. Despite minor reservations on both sides, the mirroring of affection and the idealized estimation of one another created ever-increasing expectations. This is a vital point in understanding Emerson's mental state in the summer of 1837. The two friends constructed idealized images of one another, and ultimately Emerson had to decide how much of Alcott's high opinion of him he

Figure 15. Bronson Alcott, no date. Courtesy of the Houghton Library, Harvard University.

would live up to. Although reluctant to be in the forefront of action, he would now act more aggressively because he believed (rightly) that Alcott would have done the same.[27]

Long committed to working in experimental schools, Alcott was deeply influenced by Swiss educator Johann Heinrich Pestalozzi, whose philosophy was similar to Transcendentalist notions. In 1834, Alcott opened the small Temple School, supported by, among others, Emerson and William Ellery Channing. (It was housed in Boston's Masonic Temple, the frequent spot also of Emerson's lyceum talks.) Rigorously applying Transcendentalist thinking to the field of education and teaching pupils by the Socratic method, allegory, and vivid oral rendition, Alcott emphasized self-understanding over rote learning. Because he believed that "every book read should be an event for the child," one of the texts he used was the New Testament.[28]

In late 1836, at about the same time that Ripley and Norton were first sparring over the miracles question, against the advice of some friends and even Mary Moody Emerson (although not the enthusiastic Waldo Emerson), Alcott began publishing an account of his teaching methods as *Conversations with Children on the Gospels*. Expecting public acclaim for how his young students embraced the Gospels in a natural way, including the acts of pregnancy, birth, and circumcision, Alcott was instead harshly attacked for impiety or ridiculed as mad. Wrote the editor of one local paper: "Mr. Alcott is a very honest and sincere Christian for aught we know; but if he be either honest or sincere, he must be insane or half-witted, and his friends ought to take care of him without delay." Friends did express concern. Emerson's Aunt Mary, after reading the work, declared, "If ever [Alcott] preexisted it was in the Limbo of vanity beneathe some dreaming poppy." Henry Hedge was doubtful of the book, although he denied the rumor that he would review it harshly for the *Christian Examiner*. Even Alcott's own cousin and fellow educator William Andrus Alcott refused to endorse his efforts in print; and the great humanitarian Samuel Gridly Howe, who devoted his life to helping the handicapped, produced scathing satire.[29]

More than ridicule, Alcott feared violence. In April, he wrote in his journal: "I have been severely censured, I learn, even by friends to my enterprize, who respect my character, for the publication of this work. At one time, the excitement threatened a mob. The plan was to make the assault at my Friday evening conversation." In June he thought better of speaking publicly, even if the occasion was to inaugurate one of his favorite projects. As a friend claimed in the *Boston Quarterly Review*, "He has been . . . made to undergo as severe a persecution as the times allow." Although some parents expressed support, the end of the Temple School was a foregone conclusion, even to Alcott. (Admitting an African-American student did not help matters, either.) A year later, with virtually no remaining pupils and deeply in debt, Alcott closed its doors.[30]

Alcott's school represented more than an attempt to establish a career: it was also a commitment to a teaching and rearing philosophy that Emerson fully shared. In his days as minister, Emerson had urged congregants to relive and therefore reinvent for themselves the Sermon on the Mount. And even before meeting Alcott, Emerson set out in his journals a philosophy of education sympathetic to the methods of Pestalozzi, anticipating Alcott's own approach to teaching Scriptures. Emerson then actively supported the Temple School, even sending a deceased friend's child there at his own expense and announcing that his first child, the infant Waldo, would someday attend. He was similarly enthusiastic about *Conversa-*

tions with Children on the Gospels, strongly encouraging its publication. Emerson was so intimately involved in Alcott's undertaking that a decade later he still mourned the loss: "[Alcott] measures ages by teachers, & reckons history by Pythagoras, Plato, Jesus, & Pestalozzi. In his own school in Boston, when he had made the school-room beautiful, he looked on the work as half-done."[31]

When the public attacks came, how Emerson responded might not seem like much to us—it did not seem like much to himself. But to Alcott it meant the world. In March, 1837, Alcott reflected that a letter from Emerson was "the first sympathy that has stolen on my ear, from the *desolate & doubting present.* Only Emerson, of this age, know[s] me, of all that I have found. Well, one man,—*one very man, through and through,*—every one does not find." In the following weeks, Alcott expressed similar gratitude: "His manner and bearing toward me are noble and manly. More than any man of this metropolis, he has lent his influence in my favor. . . . His interest is grateful. It animates and strengthens me in my purpose and principles."[32]

Other Transcendentalists published letters and reviews in support of Alcott, some quite forceful. But it was Emerson's defense that Alcott especially prized. Although already linked to Alcott in February, when Harvard Divinity School students and faculty ridiculed them both, Emerson continued to associate himself publicly with his close friend. To two local newspapers which had published harsh reviews of *Conversations*, he submitted moderate letters, urging that Alcott's approach to education not be prejudged or read out of context. The *Boston Daily Courier* printed the defense, but he could not get Nathan Hale, editor of the *Boston Daily Advertiser* and Edward Everett's brother-in-law, to publish his letter. Emerson wrote Alcott that he despaired of the refusal. He feared that Hale's comments, left unrefuted, would bring about the close of the Temple School, but Alcott rightly thought the game was already lost. On May 9, *Courier* editor Joseph T. Buckingham quoted an unnamed clergy as having judged Alcott's *Conversations* "one third absurd, one third blasphemous, and one third obscene." In his journal, Alcott identified the anonymous minister as Andrews Norton.[33]

Alcott's journal, in fact, supplies an essential clue to Emerson's state of mind when composing "The American Scholar." In late March, Alcott lent Emerson his entries for the previous few months. Returning those pages a few weeks later, Emerson appended a note: "I never regretted more than in this case, my own helplessness in all practical contingencies. For a knowing and efficient friend can do a man with a mob, a better service than he himself. But I was created a seeing eye, and not a useful hand." Having read Alcott's journal, Emerson felt compelled to explain why he could not be of more help. And in his own journals he repeated

Figure 16. Alcott's Temple School, or School of Human Culture. Drawing by Francis Graeter, from *Record of Mr. Alcott's School Exemplifying the Principles and Methods of Moral Culture*, [by Elizabeth Palmer Peabody] (Boston: Roberts Brothers, 1874). Courtesy of the Concord Free Public Library.

the sentiment, beginning a process of self-recrimination that led to his explosive sentiments five months later at Harvard: "The Newspapers persecute Alcott. I have never more regretted my inefficiency to practical ends. I was born a seeing eye not a helping hand. I can only comfort my friends by thought, and not by love or aid. But they naturally look for this other also, and thereby vitiate our relationship, throughout."[34]

In referring to himself as a seeing eye, Emerson was here playing off his self-description proposed the previous year in *Nature*: "Standing on the bare ground—my head bathed by the blithe air, and uplifted into infinite space,—all mean egotism vanishes. I become a transparent eyeball; I am nothing; I see all." And when he was in that transparent state, people did not much matter to him: "The name of the nearest friend sounds then foreign and accidental. To be brothers, to be acquaintances,—master or servant, is then trifle and a disturbance." A year later, however, he privately regretted this affinity for pure perception. Having read Alcott's journal, he now worried that as a seeing eye he had failed his friend, even while Alcott thought otherwise. Soon after, he also expressed in his own journals that, as a result of his inaction, he was losing the respect of others. The anguish Emerson felt culminated in his powerful polemics in "The American Scholar." What in Alcott's diary caused Emerson such feelings?[35]

Under stress from public reactions to *Conversations*, Alcott looked closely at three public figures. William Ellery Channing, with whom Alcott had had a long and generally happy relationship, was no longer esteemed, since he cautiously distanced himself from Alcott during the crisis: "[Dr. Channing] never *makes an Idea*. But, after these have begun the work, and have put the public mind into action;—have already begun to work out the regenerating process,—then does he give his assent to them. . . . Dr. Channing always has the *last word* to say: never the *first*."[36]

Judged quite differently is Dr. Sylvester Graham, a physiologist who lectured on nutrition and temperance. Calling him "the prophet of physical renewal" and comparing him to John the Baptist, Alcott saw him as a martyr to truth: "His crusade exposes him to obloquy and scorn. Even now, he is mobbed, and the city authorities protect him. . . . He utters great and all-important doctrines. And these will, one day, win for him a name, worthy of all praise. . . . I shall defend him." Here are themes emerging in Alcott's own life: public abuse, the threat of mob violence, and the belief in eventual redemption.[37]

The third figure is Emerson. If Graham was John the Baptist, Emerson was the very embodiment of Christ. Although "[l]ittle men are puzzled by the subtlety of his conceptions, and complain of his mysticism . . . the day shall come when this man's Genius, shall shine beyond the circle of his own city and nation. . . . [E]re the superficial and pedantic are aware, he will be reigning monarch of our literature. . . . Thus shall the genius of Emerson, chase away, in its time, the small and arrogant intellects that now venture to stand between humanity and his orb."[38]

The lessons are obvious. Channing, cautious and anxious for approval, is ultimately undistinguished. The great man—such as Graham or Emerson—teaches what is initially unpopular but eventually triumphs. In fact, there is someone Alcott was measuring even more closely: himself. And his self-judgment accords closely with what he most admired in Graham and Emerson: "In the prosecution of my purpose, I anticipate no brilliant success. I expect no immediate praise. On the contrary, I look for censure, and perchance, at different periods of my labours, temporary defeat. . . . No opposition shall drive me from my settled and determinate purpose."[39]

These intimate thoughts were what Emerson read and returned to Alcott with an apology that he had not acted—could not act—more decisively in his defense. Alcott defined Emerson, at the time not nearly so highly esteemed by other Transcendentalists, as the courageous scholar, and Emerson regretted that, in being merely a seeing eye, he had not lived up to that opinion. Emerson, who as minister and lyceum speaker struggled with his own lack of complete candor, praised and defended Alcott whenever he could: in a sermon at Watertown, obliquely in a public address in Providence, and in a letter to Carlyle. But he never felt it was adequate.[40]

On May 19, a month after reading Alcott's journal and the day after Alcott left his house, Emerson began to gather himself. If there are such things as turning points in life, this was surely one of Emerson's, for Alcott's heroic constancy began moving him toward action. Expressing admiration for the unbowed Alcott, "the highest genius of the time," Emerson lamented in his journals that society was far readier to settle for what it already had than to strive for the ideal: "Harvard College, the Latin Schools, the Schools everywhere, the city life, the devotion of human life to trade—these are sorry things and are tenderly treated by us only because we see no better actual life. . . . We say it is impossible that we should realize our ideal and frigidly dismiss the Reformer." Only Alcott had the necessary courage and absolute candor: "Wonderful is his vision. The steadiness & scope of his eye at once rebukes all before it." The same day, Emerson wrote Margaret Fuller: "Mr. Alcott . . . has more of the godlike than any man I have ever seen and his presence rebukes & threatens & raises. He *is* a teacher . . . he is not only justified but necessitated to condemn & seek to upheave the vast Actual and cleanse the world."[41]

In his journal and in the letter, Emerson emphasized Alcott's aggressive responses of rebuking, threatening, condemning. But as yet, Emerson saw no course of action for himself. Other Transcendentalists had long spoken out on public issues, while Emerson, the restrained lyceum orator, could not even defend his friend properly. The week before, his garden had been his dictionary. Now, pained because of his inability to help Alcott, he dismissed that easy thought: "When I see an evil, it is unmanly to hide my head in the flowering bushes & say I will hunt the humble bee & behold the stars & leave this sorrow for those whom it concerns. I ought rather to live towards it." Emerson's impatience with his own character moved him enough to include that sentiment in the oration. It would become an essential quality of the American scholar not to hide "his head like an ostrich in the flowering bushes . . . [but to] look into the eye [of danger]."[42]

Three days later Emerson increased the pressure on himself. In a powerful and agonizing journal entry that formed his future agenda, this most confident and self-reliant of public speakers chastised himself for not speaking out on Wilhelm Meister, abolition, and Harvard College. Emerson once again expressed fear that in his reticence his friends had abandoned him: "You are measured by your silence & found wanting. You have no oracle to utter, & your fellowmen have learned that you cannot help them; for oracles speak."[43]

Emerson's allusion to Wilhelm Meister refers to Goethe's great and controversial works based on that character and to Carlyle's recent translation. The writings of Goethe and Carlyle were celebrated by Transcendentalists and ridiculed by Norton and other Unitarians. On the abolition controversy, Unitarians generally demurred in their support, while Alcott, at least, and perhaps some other Transcendentalists were becoming outspoken. Emerson, as we have seen, had in his lyceum lectures an extraordinary opportunity to address the question, but continued to struggle until his first public statement some six months after "The American Scholar" and even beyond.[44]

Finally, Emerson again named his alma mater, linked to these other Unitarian-Transcendentalist divides. Although he had resigned his position there three years earlier, Andrews Norton, who was leading the attack on the miracles question, was still closely identified with that institution and drew much of his support from those affiliated with it (he would later be offered another professorship there, which he would decline). He had as well just brought out his study of the Gospels to academic and popular acclaim, while Alcott's imaginative work resulted in public humiliation. Harvard not only produced the status quo; it stood as a bulwark against those who thought differently. Emerson would soon derisively refer to academics as "the book learned class" and "the Third Estate" and to Norton and friends as "Philistines." Emerson was preparing to speak out . . . but how and to whom?[45]

Just a month later, Emerson, who had until then remained largely silent—and perhaps precisely because of that silence—suddenly found himself invited to be orator at Harvard's most public and prestigious event. Yet, given the opportunity finally to prove his mettle, he continued to feel anxiety. Emerson was sick in June—another inflammation of the lung—and his lassitude lingered into July, for there are significantly fewer journal entries. Although invited on June 22, he only began to think about the speech in earnest near the end of July. Fearing that he would have nothing to say by the end of August, he turned to Alcott.[46]

Amid his public humiliation, Alcott had remained strong in the spring. But by July his spirits plummeted, and he suffered from what was, at the very least, nervous exhaustion. Then, on July 25, he wrote Emerson: "I am just up from a severe indisposition and find myself extremely weak and shiftless. I hear that you are regaining your former strength; and hope the demand upon your corporeal nature will enable you to compass the P.B.K. without detriment. Shall see you soon." Emerson responded to this obviously provocative missive in two ways. On July 27, clearly concerned, he invited Alcott to visit: "I grieve to hear you have been sick and are still feeble. . . . what better can you do than come out here instantly to spend a fort-night with me. . . . lounging is the first medicine for such as you." Emerson was so anxious that just four days later he issued a second invitation: "Do come, if possibly you can. I write or read in the morning after breakfast or in the evening after tea. At other hours, I can help you get well." Alcott made that visit in mid-August.[47]

But Emerson found another message in Alcott's letter. He would soon be following in the tradition of the greats: Kirkland, Quincy, Buckminster, Everett, Story—and, of course, his own father. And yet, he hadn't fully earned the opportunity, for the last-minute invitation was probably due to well-placed friends. More troublesome still, Emerson was summoning up the courage finally to speak on behalf of colleagues while simultaneously sensing hostility emanating from Cambridge. Then, Alcott's letter reminded him that there was barely a month before the talk. Whatever he was suffering from—and some scholars consider his adult illnesses psychosomatic—he needed to get to work.[48]

The day after Alcott's letter inquiring about the state of the oration, Emerson went to the Athenaeum, hoping "for wit, for excitement,—to awake in me the muse. In vain and in vain." He began searching for inspiration from within, for "books are but crutches, the resorts of the feeble & lame." The following day he invited Alcott to Concord, following up with another letter on August 1. Three days later, he recorded continued anxiety about his impending talk: "I sometimes fear that . . . I[,] careless of action, intent on composition, have exhausted already all my stock of experience, have fairly written out." On August 7, he complained to his brother William that "we cannot get any word from Olympus[,] any Periclean word for Φ.B.K." And two days later, he despaired in his jour-

nals: "I sit and have nothing to say. In the great calm my ship can do
nothing." The stakes were high and he needed something new to fire his
imagination.[49]

Just as Emerson intended to help Alcott, he also depended on his friend.
Alcott was, after all, Emerson's new oracle, and he had helped the previous year in the creation of *Nature*. Emerson's instincts proved true. Just
after Alcott, along with Hedge, came in August, Emerson found his voice
and immediately took to writing. A series of brief journal entries over
the summer reflects Emerson's growing anger that "the College becomes
idolatrous—a temple full of idols." But it was on August 18, the day after
Alcott concluded his visit, that Emerson exploded: "One thing is plain[:]
[the student] must have a training by himself—the training of another age
will not fit him. He himself & not others must judge what is good for
him. Now the young are oppressed by their instructors. . . . Meek young
men grow up in colleges & believe it is their duty to accept the views
which books have given & grow up slaves." Liberation of the young from
the confines of mindless education, a goal Emerson fully shared with his
humiliated friend Bronson Alcott, was to become the governing metaphor
of "The American Scholar." Three days later, he dreamed of a duel.[50]

Emerson could duel because, whatever Alcott's deficiencies in intellect
or common sense, his moral courage taught Emerson the scholar's essential duty. Previously, Emerson had supposed that the intelligentsia would
receive the scholar sympathetically. And so Emerson's initial vision conjured up the pacific intermediary standing between the cosmic divinity
and humanity. That scholar was "the great Man" who, as Emerson told
Alcott, "should occupy the whole space between God and the mob. . . .
Thus did Jesus, dwelling in mind with pure God, & dwelling in social
position & hearty love with fishers & women." In the oration, Emerson
continued to describe the scholar as such a sympathetic intermediary:
"Years are well spent in country labors; in town . . . in frank intercourse
with many men and women . . . to the one end of mastering in all their
facts a language by which to illustrate and embody our perceptions."[51]

But through his diary and by personal example, Alcott taught Emerson
about the combative scholar. Sylvester Graham, he wrote, "is mobbed,
and the city authorities protect him. . . . [One day his doctrines will] win
for him a name, worthy of all praise." Emerson's "influence will not, at
once, be felt on the age. [But his genius will] chase away, in its time, the
small and arrogant intellects that now venture to stand between humanity
and his orb." Alcott himself "look[s] for censure, and perchance, at different periods of my labours, temporary defeat. . . . No opposition shall
drive me from my settled and determinate purpose."

Although Emerson had been thinking about the scholar's attributes for
two years, it is only during that summer, when he was so involved in

Alcott's miseries, that he embraced the vision of the scholar scorned by, but ultimately triumphant over, the elite. This went directly into the oration: "[The scholar] takes the cross of making his own, and, of course, the self-accusation, the faint heart, the frequent uncertainty . . . and the state of virtual hostility in which he seems to stand to society, and especially to educated society." Alcott's lesson came easily, because the willingness of the scholar to be unpopular presented a perfect illustration of Emerson's most basic tenet: self-trust. And once he allowed his friend's beliefs and experience, so perfectly aligned, to guide his own understanding, the caustic tone of the address was determined. Because the American scholar is rejected by the educated, Emerson, too, must be rejected if he wished to be a scholar.[52]

Soon after the oration, Horace Mann reported that a lady of society considered Emerson "crazy," a judgment also heard far off in England by the gossipy Harriet Martineau. By April, Governor Everett would announce to dinner guests that his former student "destroys all the principles of thinking, judging, and acting—all evidence—all experience—all moral laws formed upon the observed relations of things." And after giving his Divinity School address that July, Emerson attended the 1838 Phi Beta Kappa ceremony and noted: "The young people & the mature hint at odium, & aversion of faces to be presently encountered in society. I say no: I fear it not." The hostility was not imagined. When taking tea a few days later at the home of "a family belonging to the straitest sect of Boston conservatism" (whose name is expunged in his journal), Convers Francis discovered that they "abhor & abominate R. W. Emerson as a sort of mad dog: & when I defended that pure and angelic spirit . . . they laughed at me with amazement,—for no such sounds had penetrated their *clique* before." No longer just a seeing eye, Emerson now took the inevitable blows of standing for principle. A year later he could write in "Self-Reliance" that "to be great is to be misunderstood."[53]

Yet Emerson was still not to himself the self-reliant scholar who formed his thoughts independently, for he continued to make Alcott the master: "Let the other party say what he will, Alcott unerringly takes the highest moral ground . . . & cannot be outgeneralled. . . . [H]is sympathies with the present company are not troublesome to him, never embarrass for a moment his perception. He is cool, bland, urbane, yet with his eye fixed on the highest fact." But it was different with Emerson, who conformed to his company: "If they are ordinary & mean, I am. If the company were great I should soar: in all mere mortal parties, I take the contagion of their views & lose my own." And so, "I see the facts as all cultivated men always have seen them, and am a great man alone." This he admitted to himself while at the same time writing in "Self-Reliance": "A great man is coming to eat at my house. I do not wish to please him: I wish that he should wish to please me."[54]

Privately, Emerson always saw Alcott, rather than himself, as having the quality he most admired. Yet how much of Emerson's idealized appreciation of his friend translated precisely into the scholar of his oration we can, of course, never know. Alcott's biographers certainly see a close connection. And the following year, in constructing an iconoclastic address for Harvard's Divinity School, Emerson indisputably drew heavily on an individual for inspiration, there negatively. Throughout the fall of 1837 and spring of 1838, Emerson was subjected to the dull sermons of the Reverend Barzillai Frost, and criticism filled his journals. These attacks on the unfortunate Frost were then turned nearly verbatim into inspired religious challenges to Divinity School students. As, for example, does Saul Bellow, who closely identifies with him philosophically, Emerson used acquaintances as sitting models.[55]

At the very moment in May when Emerson felt ashamed of his own silence, in one of his few expressions of disappointment in him Alcott reflected: "He holds men and things at a distance; pleases himself with using them for his own benefit, and as means of gathering material for his works." Alcott had appreciated how Emerson used him in writing *Nature*. Once again, during the creation of "The American Scholar," Alcott was willing to serve not only as muse but as model. This time, however, Emerson did not just observe. Inspired—perhaps compelled—by Alcott's example and expectations, he acted.[56]

Chapter Seven

FOREVER THE AMERICAN SCHOLAR

ON AUGUST 31, 1837, EMERSON STOOD BEFORE AN AUDIENCE
more demanding than any he had ever addressed. Facing two challenges,
he solved them simultaneously. First, fearing that by his silence on contemporary issues he was failing his friends, he overcame an inclination to
avoid controversy and, to clergy and faculty raised on Lockean materialism, boldly pronounced a soaring, idealistic affirmation of inner truth and
intuition. Not only must the American scholar resist European traditions,
but, driven on by personal experience and constant reinvention, that
scholar must be liberated from native ones as well. Second, to some extent
as minister and lyceum orator Emerson could command the moment. But
at Harvard, the constraints of tradition demanded conformity. Angry at
his alma mater for its current direction and naturally resistant to social
expectations, Emerson unleashed a blistering attack, infused with strains
of a vernacular that further insulted his Brahmin listeners. The polemics
ignited his idealism; the idealism tempered his polemics. And all the while
he worried that this engagement with people and principles might compromise his self-reliance.

A defiant rejection of convention and received wisdom, the speech remains a triumph of self-trust. But written in haste and with great emo-
tion, it is not carefully constructed or rigorously argued. Emerson had
neither the will nor possibly even the talent for that. Yet it has the ring
of truth because it unmistakably came from the heart. "The American
Scholar" succeeds precisely because its idealism arose out of historical
circumstances.

Understanding how Emerson mixed idealism with practical concerns
reveals a lot about his character. With a brilliantly idiosyncratic prose
style, a willingness to be self-contradictory, and dazzling insights of per-

sonal reflection hurled in all directions, Emerson would appear to be the intrepid explorer of his own existence, fully alive within his ideas. Observed Oscar W. Firkins in what is still one of the most discerning studies of the subject: "The secret of Emerson may be conveyed in one word, the superlative, even the superhuman, value which he found in the unit of experience, the direct, momentary, individual act of consciousness. This is the centre from which the man radiates: it begets all and explains all. He may be defined as an experiment made by nature in the raising of the single perception or impression to a hitherto unimaginable value."

There is a great deal of truth to this. But living in each moment of experience did not come any more easily to Emerson than to the rest of us. Before accepting the courageous, introspective candor of his essays as fully reflective of his consciousness, we should read Emerson in the same binary manner in which he wrote—first for himself and then for the public. What we could then appreciate is Emerson's attempt to achieve personal self-reliance, as announced in his published works, but also his need to win public acceptance, as revealed in his journals and correspondence. Any assessment of Emerson's journey into idealism must take account of his private struggle with ambition and commitment.

"The American Scholar" is the first great manifestation of that struggle. In trying to balance his desire to be self-reliant with his devotion to friends, principles, and even ambition, Emerson produced a revolution in thought and performance. Far more than he felt able to do in the lyceum, Emerson turned academia into a contested space. At Harvard, he departed from the academy's celebratory tradition and challenged, rather than confirmed, his audience. Just ten months earlier, he announced that his greatest desire was to deliver "what all must receive." But circumstances now demanded otherwise, as Emerson acknowledged: "I might not carry with me the feeling of my audience in stating my own belief. But I have already shown the ground of my hope, in adverting to the doctrine that man is one." No previous Phi Beta Kappa orator would have wished for the very reaction Emerson anticipated that day.[1]

The response within the society was, indeed, predictable, and four years later: "Considerable heat was manifested by certain Transcendentalists because the Rev. Theodore Parker, of Roxbury, could not be elected [as an alumnus member]," testified an eye-witness. "Severe threats were thrown out by some who aspired to have the pre-eminence. But when they saw that their vaporing and strutting was in vain, they at length desisted." The first election of an alumnus with obvious Transcendentalist affiliation, that of John Weiss, didn't occur until 1845, and the next, of John Sullivan Dwight, not until 1862. Emerson, who would judge his alma mater "a wafer in comparison with the solid land which my friends represent," decided to "avoid the Stygian anniversaries at Cambridge[,] those hurrahs among the ghosts, those yellow, bald, toothless meetings in memory of red checks, black hair, and departed health." It was not until after the Civil War that Emerson and Harvard reconciled, and then the honors accorded him came in a rush.[2]

As the alliance of money and religion imposed conformity and constrained discourse, higher education during the Federalist period suffered through, in the words of Richard Hofstadter, "the Great Retrogression." Emerson's oration, by arguing for the sanctity of individual creativity, "the doctrine that man is one," directly attacked that conformity and the intellectual fragmentation caused by institutionalized education. A century earlier, the faculty and president of then-Congregationalist Harvard had disputed the teachings of visiting British revivalist George Whitefield: "First then, we charge him, with *Enthusiasm*. . . . [W]e mean by an *Enthusiast*, one that acts, either according to Dreams, or some sudden Impulses and Impressions upon his Mind, which he fondly imagines to be from the Spirit of God . . . tho' he hath no Proof." Emerson's teacher and Unitarian leader George Ticknor might grant that the secret of German academic success was its "enthusiasm & learning, which immediately broke through all the barriers that opposed it." Yet Unitarians, like most of their Congregationalist ancestors, still mistrusted spiritual exuberance. Combining spiritual with intellectual enthusiasm, Emerson made self-trust of instinct, insight, and ideal a desirable academic quality. He valorized all human knowledge.[3]

As they began responding to the intellectual, as well as the economic, consequences of the Industrial Revolution, colleges would gradually expand their curricula. With under two dozen professors, many of whom were in charge of legal, medical, or theological training, the Harvard faculty of Emerson's day could not cover much beyond the basics. In the humanities, still framed by the seemingly fixed cultural truths of classical and biblical studies, it was only just before the Civil War that Harvard got around to offering courses even on English literature. But when Charles William Eliot soon after steered an expanded Harvard toward an elective system and emphasized student choice, he acknowledged Emerson's influence. By the end of the nineteenth century, Kantian idealism and the study of poetry and literature would contend with Bible studies as essential sources of insight and would remove the final barriers to humanistic speculation. Yet long before, with Transcendentalists asserting that the vernacular could be as inspirational as were sacerdotal writings, Emerson, beginning with "The American Scholar," urged the complete secularization of the academy and the recentering of learning.[4]

Although Lidian shared her husband's initial pessimism that his oration "has had its day," she predicted that "it may bloom like the aloe next century." Some contemporary orators acknowledged Emerson and Transcendentalism critically. But none met the new ideas head-on, and most simply ignored Emerson or continued to define the American scholar narrowly. Yet his vision did bloom again. Just six years after the turn of that next century, W.E.B. DuBois delivered a remarkable address, framed in the spirit of Emerson's paean to individual development. Standing at Hampton College—"a smug Hampton" he called it—DuBois recognized that he was talking to a hostile audience. Still, "in the world this alone is necessary—that if a man speak and act, he speak and act the truth and not a lie." Lashing out at Booker T. Washington's idea that African-American education ought to concentrate on vocational training, DuBois urged listeners to live up to "the powerful assertion of a self, conscious of its might." College cannot achieve its highest ideals when it is "training not with reference to what we can be, but with sole reference to what somebody wants us to be." For, "the aim of the higher training of the college is the development of power." At about the same time, John Dewey and Alexander Meiklejohn also claimed Emerson as their own. The interesting thing, of course, is that Dewey, who emphasized experiential and collaborative learning, and Meiklejohn, who drew on Kantian idealism, had essentially opposing views of education and fought throughout most of their careers. Both, however, could agree on Emerson's towering influence.[5]

If his talk would inspire others, Emerson could not see that in 1837. Journal entries for that period suggest he was driven by the fear that in his silence he had failed his friends. Emerson's concern was not far off. By the early 1840s, with the publication of *Essays: First Series*, Emerson became a well-known public figure, and there is a natural tendency to assume that even earlier he was the leader of the Transcendentalists. For the time around the Phi Beta Kappa address, his colleagues, we have seen, thought otherwise. Their diaries and correspondence suggest that, hardly in full accord on most issues, they never thought that Emerson stood for them—some even questioned what he stood for.

But because he depended on Alcott, because he cared what people thought of him—because, in other words, he wasn't the self-reliant scholar he described in his oration—Emerson rose to the occasion, delivering a passionate and enduring talk. Momentum from "The American Scholar" carried him through his erratic attacks against slavery, abuse of Native American rights, and regressive religious beliefs. He did not immediately sustain those efforts, because he could not yet fully balance his desire for self-reliance, as he then understood it, with the need to act with others. But he withdrew from the political arena as much out of fear that he might offend his lyceum audience. The inconsistencies troubled him, but not to the extent that he could yet successfully confront them.

Emerson, in fact, was not so in control of his destiny or even his intentions as many would credit. Closely connected to the modern contention that at the time of "The American Scholar" he was the leader of the Transcendentalists is the assertion that Emerson set out to create American ordinary-language philosophy. We have seen that nothing in his journals or correspondence suggests that he was consciously aware of such an effort. Emerson never saw himself as a philosopher of any sort, because he was not, literally speaking, "a lover of wisdom." Never one to build blocks on top of one another but desiring simply to live and observe, he was a lover of the spontaneous insight his own experience could provide. Emerson lived a philosophical life without determining philosophical truth.[6]

Henry Hedge, in reviewing *Essays: Second Series*, meditated on Emerson's identity. He was no Christian in the normal sense of the word; he was no philosopher, for he was too poetical; but he was not a great poet because of "a defect of temperament—an excess of purely intellectual life." What kind of work, then, did Emerson produce? "A true record of a true soul; the rarest of all literary phenomena! There occur to us, in the whole history of literature, but two or three instances of the kind." In the end, Hedge could name only one other: Montaigne. Hedge had it right: we must leave Emerson the way he presents himself.[7]

And how, precisely, is that? Charles Capper has described Emerson's lifework as bound up in "the necessity to liberate souls from spiritually confining institutions." Emerson in fact wanted to free the entire public. When he decided to end his professional affiliation with organized religion, he wrote his mother that he "shall not preach more except from the Lyceum." Calling himself a secular minister, his lyceum lectures became sermons of intended liberation for the audience and himself: "Here is a pulpit that makes other pulpits tame & ineffectual. . . . Here [the true orator] may lay himself out utterly, large, enormous, prodigal, on the subject of the hour. . . . Here he may dare to hope for ecstasy & eloquence."[8]

What did Emerson consider a secular preacher, but a poet? It was an identity that his enemies and even many of his friends were only too eager to confirm. It defined him as someone who did not engage in theological and philosophical debate by traditional discursive means. Emerson may well have believed that poetic expression was a higher form of truth, or at least a higher form of trying to see and express truth. To friend and foe alike, however, it was comforting to see him refusing to compete within their own intellectual arena. Greatly admired, to no small measure Emerson was also humored.[9]

For as of old, the poet could be an oracle or prophet. That is how he saw himself, and that is how he was seen, although not with the degree of respect he might have desired. Wrote Transcendentalist Samuel Osgood soon after the Divinity School address: "Let him utter his beautiful poetry & dreamings & pass for a prophet in the land. He will doubtless do good in his way." Like his spiritual ancestor Plotinus, whom he quoted at the very beginning of *Nature*, Emerson was known to fall into a trance of disembodied reverie. Most of the time, however, the aspiring oracle and prophet found himself in the lyceum, where, with its utilitarian expectations, he could not possibly fulfill his ambition. Prophets go where there is spiritual need. They do not limit themselves to the fifty-minute format and they don't charge for admission.[10]

Henry James, conceding Matthew Arnold's judgment that Emerson was not a man of letters, called him instead "a man of lectures." Yet until his talk at Harvard, the anonymity of the lyceum audience gave no fuel to his passions. Emerson thought confrontation compromised his self-reliance. But "The American Scholar" proves that confrontation heightened his idealism, forcing the candor and directness he never achieved in his lyceum talks and his essays.[11]

Slow to learn this lesson and still wrestling with his two warring demons, self-reliance and self-restraint, Emerson decided that he would say his piece at *his* college and *his* church, and then refrain from the subsequent debate. That might be appropriate for his idealized American scholar. But what Emerson said had consequences. Only later did he come to realize that, having made strong statements of principle, he had to remain active in order to support those who had drawn courage from his stand. He eventually appreciated that he could not be solely a seeing eye and that self-reliance needed to be tempered by attachment. Emerson's struggle around the time of "The American Scholar" shows that he was just beginning to understand that self-reliance was more than a mere ideal.

Wayne Booth reminds us, "Revolutionary critics are enslaved by a nasty law of nature; I can say only what I *can* say, and that will be largely what I have learned to say from the kings and queens I would depose." Booth's observation was actually anticipated by one of Emerson's contemporaries. An anonymous, self-styled "friend" published a stinging critique of Emerson's attack on orthodoxy and tradition, claiming that, in being oppositional, he remained largely unchanged. For, "when a man knocks down his own papa, he does not thereby cease to belong to the family. . . . It is not by going from thick to thin that you alter, but by becoming a new mind through both thick and thin." At the time of "The American Scholar," Emerson was not yet ready to embrace fully both thick and thin.[12]

And yet we should not judge Emerson's hesitations too harshly. Perry Miller asserted, "Nothing would be easier than to collect from the *Journals* enough [negative] passages about the Democratic party to form a manual of Boston snobbery." We must distinguish between Emerson's antipathy for Jacksonian politics and Boston snobbery. Emerson assuredly had the former, but not much of the latter. George Ripley, although ambivalent about his kinsman, wrote in his diary that "in his freedom from all affectation, in his attachment to reality, in his indignant rejection of all varnish, gilding, and foppery, whether in character or in literature, [Emerson] has scarcely an equal."[13]

Although enjoying the privileges of Boston society, Emerson made a strong effort to break free of its essential constraints. Among his great contributions to the American Renaissance, for example, was his attention to vernacular culture. "The American Scholar" shocked its audience, not so much because of the high idealism, but mostly because it introduced the intense cacophony of everyday life. In contrast, writing specifically about Brahmins George Ticknor and Edward Everett, a near contemporary characterized them and their ilk: "There is a tendency to make dignity an encumbrance, instead of a natural growth of character strong enough to support a little freedom. . . . [T]he Bostonian . . . is afraid of himself." Emerson repressed a great deal, but in his energetic investigation of life he eventually got around to confronting his ghosts. He never willingly settled for comfort at the price of intellectual freedom. Throughout his career, Emerson was viewed as the American Carlyle. But unlike his Scottish friend, Emerson was always engaged in what he considered to be the service of his country. If occasionally despondent, he used his moods as another voice to stir himself rather than as an expression of social despair.[14]

A pragmatic idealist, Emerson's great observation in "The Transcendentalist," published in *Essays: First Series*, was that Transcendentalism was simply one of many historical reactions to materialism. Because the world would never be perfect, individuals must make their stand in their own way. "Without [action], thought can never ripen into truth," he asserted in "The American Scholar." By anchoring ideals in experience, Emerson avoided the dangerous possibility of letting idealism run to ideological extremes—a tendency that's been the bane of modern times. And so, while other Phi Beta Kappa orators celebrated the cultural hegemony of the literary elite, Emerson offered instruction in how one comes to trust and use what one has learned independently. In trying to balance his engagement with colleagues and Harvard with a simultaneous desire to transcend those experiences, Emerson demanded action linked to principle, but principle that comes authentically from the individual. Reflecting back perhaps on that very event, he chose these words to conclude "Self-Reliance": "Nothing can bring you peace but yourself. Nothing can bring you peace but the triumph of principles." That is why many consider him "America's Philosopher of Democracy."[15]

Near the end of his life, Emerson believed that he had lived long enough to see his American scholar:

I please myself with the thought that our American mind is not now eccentric or rude in its strength, but is beginning to show a quiet power, drawn from wide and abundant sources, proper to a Continent and to an educated people. . . . I am not less aware of that excellent and increasing circle of masters in arts and in song and in science, who cheer the intellect of our cities and this country to-day,—whose genius is not a lucky accident, but normal, and with broad foundation of culture, and so inspires the hope of steady strength advancing on itself, and a day without night.[16]

Tied to traditional forms of expression and to the national enterprise, his retrospective scholar is not entirely the American scholar of 1837. Yet even in 1837, Emerson was himself hardly the scholar he commended to his audience. Then again, there he not only provided a powerful ideal; by naming individuals at the end of the oration, Emerson acknowledged practical attainments. In his aspirations Emerson aimed for the highest peaks, but he appreciated that life might deliver something less. "The American Scholar" was a transitory experience, a fragile mix of contradictory impulses that dissolved even as it formed. The best of what we do is often built on that internal tension masked by the illusion of permanence. No one has understood or expressed that better than Emerson.

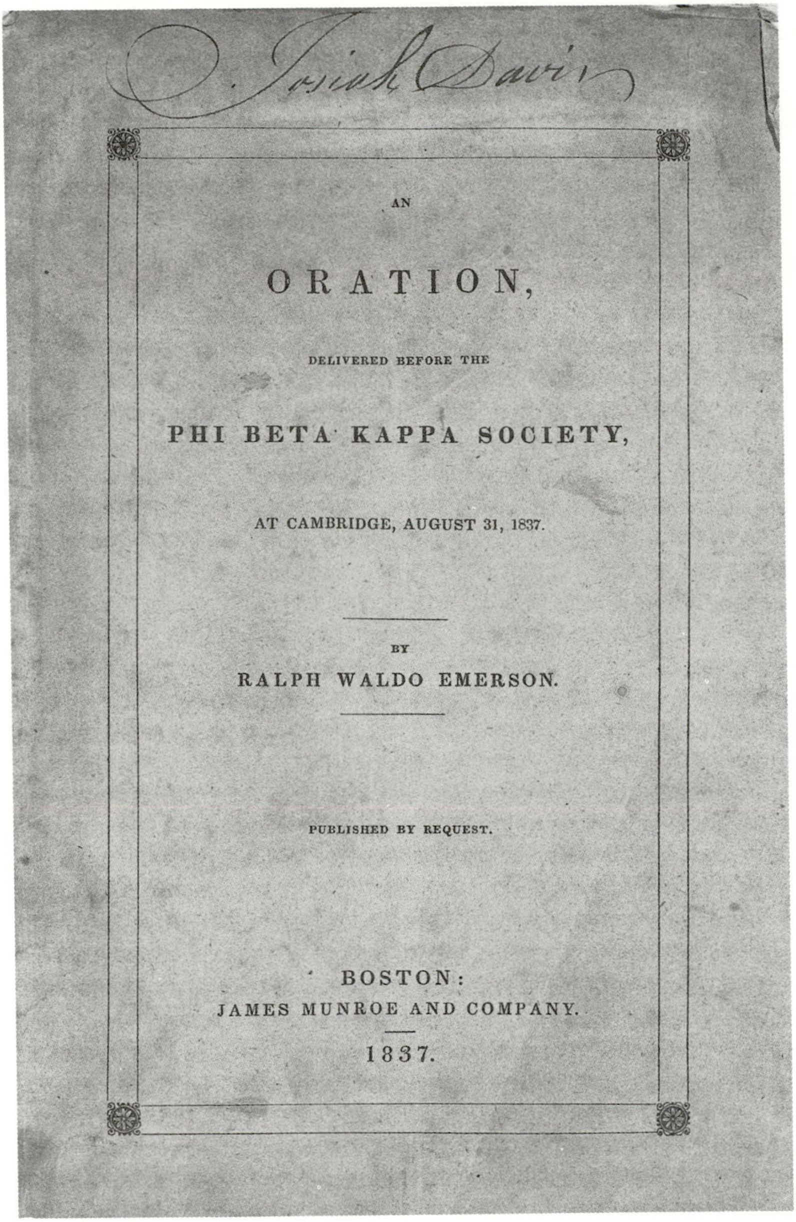

Josiah Davis

AN

ORATION,

DELIVERED BEFORE THE

PHI BETA KAPPA SOCIETY,

AT CAMBRIDGE, AUGUST 31, 1837.

BY

RALPH WALDO EMERSON.

PUBLISHED BY REQUEST.

BOSTON:
JAMES MUNROE AND COMPANY.

1837.

Figure 17. This copy may have belonged to the same Josiah Davis who owned both the property on which the Concord Academy now sits and a house in which Henry David Thoreau died and which the Alcott family later owned. Courtesy of the Houghton Library, Harvard University.

Appendix

TEXT OF "THE AMERICAN SCHOLAR"

MR. PRESIDENT, AND GENTLEMEN,

I greet you on the re-commencement of our literary year. Our anniversary is one of hope, and, perhaps, not enough of labor. We do not meet for games of strength or skill, for the recitation of histories, tragedies and odes, like the ancient Greeks; for parliaments of love and poesy, like the Troubadours; nor for the advancement of science, like our cotemporaries in the British and European capitals. Thus far, our holiday has been simply a friendly sign of the survival of the love of letters amongst a people too busy to give to letters any more. As such, it is precious as the sign of an indestructible instinct. Perhaps the time is already come, when it ought to be, and will be something else; when the sluggard intellect of this continent will look from under its iron lids and fill the postponed expectation of the world with something better than the exertions of mechanical skill. Our day of dependence, our long apprenticeship to the learning of other lands, draws to a close. The millions that around us are rushing into life, cannot always be fed on the sere remains of foreign harvests. Events, actions arise, that must be sung, that will sing themselves. Who can doubt that poetry will revive and lead in a new age, as the star in the constellation Harp which now flames in our zenith, astronomers announce, shall one day be the pole-star for a thousand years.

In the light of this hope, I accept the topic which not only usage, but the nature of our association, seem to prescribe to this day,—the AMERICAN

SCHOLAR. Year by year, we come up hither to read one more chapter of his biography. Let us inquire what new lights, new events and more days have thrown on his character, his duties and his hopes.

It is one of those fables, which out of an unknown antiquity, convey an unlooked for wisdom, that the gods, in the beginning, divided Man, into men, that he might be more helpful to himself; just as the hand was divided into fingers, the better to answer its end.

The old fable covers a doctrine ever new and sublime; that there is One Man,—present to all particular men only partially, or through one faculty; and that you must take the whole society to find the whole man. Man is not a farmer, or a professor, or an engineer, but he is all. Man is priest, and scholar, and statesman, and producer, and soldier. In the *divided* or social state, these functions are parcelled out to individuals, each of whom aims to do his stint of the joint work, whilst each other performs his. The fable implies that the individual to possess himself, must sometimes return from his own labor to embrace all the other laborers. But unfortunately, this original unit, this fountain of power, has been so distributed to multitudes, has been so minutely subdivided and peddled out, that it is spilled into drops, and cannot be gathered. The state of society is one in which the members have suffered amputation from the trunk, and strut about so many walking monsters,—a good finger, a neck, a stomach, an elbow, but never a man.

Man is thus metamorphosed into a thing, into many things. The planter, who is Man sent out into the field to gather food, is seldom cheered by any idea of the true dignity of his ministry. He sees his bushel and his cart, and nothing beyond, and sinks into the farmer, instead of Man on the farm. The tradesman scarcely ever gives an ideal worth to his work, but is ridden by the routine of his craft, and the soul is subject to dollars. The priest becomes a form; the attorney, a statute-book; the mechanic, a machine; the sailor, a rope of a ship.

In this distribution of functions, the scholar is the delegated intellect. In the right state, he is, *Man Thinking*. In the degenerate state, when the victim of society, he tends to become a mere thinker, or, still worse, the parrot of other men's thinking.

In this view of him, as Man Thinking, the whole theory of his office is contained. Him nature solicits, with all her placid, all her monitory pictures. Him the past instructs. Him the future invites. Is not, indeed, every man a student, and do not all things exist for the student's behoof? And, finally, is not the true scholar the only true master? But, as the old oracle said, "All things have two handles. Beware of the wrong one." In life, too often, the scholar errs with mankind and forfeits his privilege. Let us see him in his school, and consider him in reference to the main influences he receives.

I. The first in time and the first in importance of the influences upon the mind is that of nature. Every day, the sun; and, after sunset, night and her stars. Ever the winds blow; ever the grass grows. Every day, men and women, conversing, beholding and beholden. The scholar must needs stand wistful and admiring before this great spectacle. He must settle its value in his mind. What is nature to him? There is never a beginning, there is never an end to the inexplicable continuity of this web of God, but always circular power returning into itself. Therein it resembles his own spirit, whose beginning, whose ending he never can find—so entire, so boundless. Far, too, as her splendors shine, system on system shooting like rays, upward, downward, without centre, without circumference,—in the mass and in the particle nature hastens to render account of herself to the mind. Classification begins. To the young mind, every thing is individual, stands by itself. By and by, it finds how to join two things, and see in them one nature; then three, then three thousand; and so, tyrannized over by its own unifying instinct, it goes on tying things together, diminishing anomalies, discovering roots running underground, whereby contrary and remote things cohere, and flower out from one stem. It presently learns, that, since the dawn of history, there has been a constant accumulation and classifying of facts. But what is classification but the perceiving that these objects are not chaotic, and are not foreign, but have a law which is also a law of the human mind? The astronomer discovers that geometry, a pure abstraction of the human mind, is the measure of planetary motion. The chemist finds proportions and intelligible method throughout matter: and science is nothing but the finding of analogy, identity in the most remote parts. The ambitious soul sits down before each refractory fact; one after another, reduces all strange constitutions, all new powers, to their class and their law, and goes on forever to animate the last fibre of organization, the outskirts of nature, by insight.

Thus to him, to this school-boy under the bending dome of day, is suggested, that he and it proceed from one root; one is leaf and one is flower; relation, sympathy, stirring in every vein. And what is that Root? Is not that the soul of his soul?—A thought too bold—a dream too wild. Yet when this spiritual light shall have revealed the law of more earthly natures,—when he has learned to worship the soul, and to see that the natural philosophy that now is, is only the first gropings of its gigantic hand, he shall look forward to an ever expanding knowledge as to a becoming creator. He shall see that nature is the opposite of the soul, answering to it part for part. One is seal, and one is print. Its beauty is the beauty of his own mind. Its laws are the laws of his own mind. Nature then becomes to him the measure of his attainments. So much of nature as he is ignorant of, so much of his own mind does he not yet possess. And, in fine, the ancient precept, "Know thyself," and the modern precept, "Study nature," become at last one maxim.

II. The next great influence into the spirit of the scholar, is, the mind of the Past,—in whatever form, whether of literature, of art, of institutions, that mind is inscribed. Books are the best type of the influence of the past, and perhaps we shall get at the truth—learn the amount of this influence more conveniently—by considering their value alone.

The theory of books is noble. The scholar of the first age received into him the world around; brooded thereon; gave it the new arrangement of his own mind, and uttered it again. It came into him—life; it went out from him—truth. It came to him—short-lived actions; it went out from him—immortal thoughts. It came to him—business; it went from him— poetry. It was—dead fact; now, it is quick thought. It can stand, and it can go. It now endures, it now flies, it now inspires. Precisely in proportion to the depth of mind from which it issued, so high does it soar, so long does it sing.

Or, I might say, it depends on how far the process had gone, of transmuting life into truth. In proportion to the completeness of the distillation, so will the purity and imperishableness of the product be. But none is quite perfect. As no air-pump can by any means make a perfect vacuum, so neither can any artist entirely exclude the conventional, the local, the perishable from his book, or write a book of pure thought that shall be as efficient, in all respects, to a remote posterity, as to cotemporaries, or rather to the second age. Each age, it is found, must write its own books; or rather, each generation for the next succeeding. The books of an older period will not fit this.

Yet hence arises a grave mischief. The sacredness which attaches to the act of creation,— the act of thought,—is instantly transferred to the record. The poet chanting, was felt to be a divine man. Henceforth the chant is divine also. The writer was a just and wise spirit. Henceforward it is settled, the book is perfect; as love of the hero corrupts into worship of his statue. Instantly, the book becomes noxious, The guide is a tyrant. We sought a brother, and lo, a governor. The sluggish and perverted mind of the multitude, always slow to open to the incursions of Reason, having once so opened, having once received this book, stands upon it, and makes an outcry, if it is disparaged. Colleges are built on it. Books are written on it by thinkers, not by Man Thinking; by men of talent, that is, who start wrong, who set out from accepted dogmas, not from their own sight of principles. Meek young men grow up in libraries, believing it their duty to accept the views which Cicero, which Locke, which Bacon have given, forgetful that Cicero, Locke and Bacon were only young men in libraries when they wrote these books.

Hence, instead of Man Thinking, we have the bookworm. Hence, the book-learned class, who value books, as such; not as related to nature and the human constitution, but as making a sort of Third Estate with the world and the soul. Hence, the restorers of readings, the emendators, the bibliomaniacs of all degrees.

This is bad; this is worse than it seems. Books are the best of things, well used; abused, among the worst. What is the right use? What is the one end which all means go to effect? They are for nothing but to inspire. I had better never see a book than to be warped by its attraction clean out of my own orbit, and made a satellite instead of a system. The one thing in the world of value, is, the active soul,—the soul, free, sovereign, active. This every man is entitled to; this every man contains within him, although in almost all men, obstructed, and as yet unborn. The soul active sees absolute truth; and utters truth, or creates. In this action, it is genius; not the privilege of here and there a favorite, but the sound estate of every man. In its essence, it is progressive. The book, the college, the school of art, the institution of any kind, stop with some past utterance of genius. This is good, say they,—let us hold by this. They pin me down. They look backward and not forward. But genius always looks forward. The eyes of man are set in his forehead, not in his hindhead. Man hopes. Genius creates. To create, to create,—is the proof of a divine presence. Whatever talents may be, if the man create not, the pure efflux of the Deity is not his:—cinders and smoke, there may be, but not yet flame. There are creative manners, there are creative actions, and creative words; manners, actions, words, that is, indicative of no custom or authority, but springing spontaneous from the mind's own sense of good and fair.

On the other part, instead of being its own seer, let it receive always from another mind its truth, though it were in torrents of light, without periods of solitude, inquest and self-recovery, and a fatal disservice is done. Genius is always sufficiently the enemy of genius by overinfluence. The literature of every nation bear me witness. The English dramatic poets have Shakspearized now for two hundred years.

Undoubtedly there is a right way of reading,—so it be sternly subordinated. Man Thinking must not be subdued by his instruments. Books are for the scholar's idle times. When he can read God directly, the hour is too precious to be wasted in other men's transcripts of their readings. But when the intervals of darkness come, as come they must,—when the soul seeth not, when the sun is hid, and the stars withdraw their shining,—we repair to the lamps which were kindled by their ray to guide our steps to the East again, where the dawn is. We hear that we may speak. The Arabian proverb says, "A fig tree looking on a fig tree, becometh fruitful."

It is remarkable, the character of the pleasure we derive from the best books. They impress us ever with the conviction that one nature wrote and the same reads. We read the verses of one of the English poets, of Chaucer, of Marvell, of Dryden, with the most modern joy,—with a pleasure, I mean, which is in great part caused by the abstraction of all *time* from their verses. There is some awe mixed with the joy of our surprise, when this poet, who lived in some past world, two or three hundred years ago, says that which lies close to my own soul, that which I also had well nigh thought and said. But for the evidence thence afforded to the philosophical doctrine of the identity of all minds, we should suppose some pre-established harmony, some foresight of souls that were to be, and some preparation of stores for their future wants, like the fact observed in insects, who lay up food before death for the young grub they shall never see.

I would not be hurried by any love of system, by any exaggeration of instincts, to underrate the Book. We all know, that as the human body can be nourished on any food, though it were boiled grass and the broth of shoes, so the human mind can be fed by any knowledge. And great and heroic men have existed, who had almost no other information than by the printed page. I only would say, that it needs a strong head to bear that diet. One must be an inventor to read well. As the proverb says, "He that would bring home the wealth of the Indies, must carry out the wealth of the Indies." There is then creative reading, as well as creative writing. When the mind is braced by labor and invention, the page of whatever book we read becomes luminous with manifold allusion. Every sentence is doubly significant, and the sense of our author is as broad as the world. We then see, what is always true, that as the seer's hour of vision is short and rare among heavy days and months, so is its record, perchance, the least part of his volume. The discerning will read in his Plato or Shakspeare, only that least part,—only the authentic utterances of the oracle,—and all the rest he rejects, were it never so many times Plato's and Shakspeare's.

Of course, there is a portion of reading quite indispensable to a wise man. History and exact science he must learn by laborious reading. Colleges, in like manner, have their indispensable office,—to teach elements. But they can only highly serve us, when they aim not to drill, but to create; when they gather from far every ray of various genius to their hospitable halls, and, by the concentrated fires, set the hearts of their youth on flame. Thought and knowledge are natures in which apparatus and pretension avail nothing. Gowns, and pecuniary foundations, though of towns of gold, can never countervail the least sentence or syllable of wit. Forget this, and our American colleges will recede in their public importance whilst they grow richer every year.

III. There goes in the world a notion that the scholar should be a recluse, a valetudinarian,— as unfit for any handiwork or public labor, as a penknife for an axe. The so called "practical men" sneer at speculative men, as if, because they speculate or *see*, they could do nothing. I have heard it said that the clergy,—who are always more universally than any other class, the scholars of their day,—are addressed as women: that the rough, spontaneous conversation of men they do not hear, but only a mincing and diluted speech. They are often virtually disfranchised; and, indeed, there are advocates for their celibacy. As far as this is true of the studious classes, it is not just and wise. Action is with the scholar subordinate, but it is essential. Without it, he is not yet man. Without it, thought can never ripen into truth. Whilst the world hangs before the eye as a cloud of beauty, we cannot even see its beauty. Inaction is cowardice, but there can be no scholar without the heroic mind. The preamble of thought, the transition through which it passes from the unconscious to the conscious, is action. Only so much do I know, as I have lived. Instantly we know whose words are loaded with life, and whose not.

The world,—this shadow of the soul, or *other me*, lies wide around. Its attractions are the keys which unlock my thoughts and make me acquainted with myself. I launch eagerly into this resounding tumult. I grasp the hands of those next me, and take my place in the ring to suffer and to work, taught by an instinct that so shall the dumb abyss be vocal with speech. I pierce its order; I dissipate its fear; I dispose of it within the circuit of my expanding life. So much only of life as I know by experience, so much of the wilderness have I vanquished and planted, or so far have I extended my being, my dominion. I do not see how any man can afford, for the sake of his nerves and his nap, to spare any action in which he can partake. It is pearls and rubies to his discourse. Drudgery, calamity, exasperation, want, are instructers in eloquence and wisdom. The true scholar grudges every opportunity of action past by, as a loss of power.

It is the raw material out of which the intellect moulds her splendid products. A strange process too, this, by which experience is converted into thought, as a mulberry leaf is converted into satin. The manufacture goes forward at all hours.

The actions and events of our childhood and youth are now matters of calmest observation. They lie like fair pictures in the air. Not so with our recent actions,—with the business which we now have in hand. On this we are quite unable to speculate. Our affections as yet circulate through it. We no more feel or know it, than we feel the feet, or the hand, or the brain of our body. The new deed is yet a part of life,—remains for a time immersed in our unconscious life. In some contemplative hour, it detaches itself from the life like a ripe fruit, to become a thought of the mind. Instantly, it is raised, transfigured; the corruptible has put on incorruption. Always now it is an object of beauty, however base its origin and neighborhood. Observe, too, the impossibility of antedating this act. In its grub state, it cannot fly, it cannot shine,—it is a dull grub. But suddenly, without observation, the selfsame thing unfurls beautiful wings, and is an angel of wisdom. So is there no fact, no event, in our private history, which shall not, sooner or later, lose its adhesive inert form, and astonish us by soaring from our body into the empyrean. Cradle and infancy, school and playground, the fear of boys, and dogs, and ferules, the love of little maids and berries, and many another fact that once filled the whole sky, are gone already; friend and relative, profession and party, town and country, nation and world, must also soar and sing.

Of course, he who has put forth his total strength in fit actions, has the richest return of wisdom. I will not shut myself out of this globe of action and transplant an oak into a flower pot, there to hunger and pine; nor trust the revenue of some single faculty, and exhaust one vein of thought, much like those Savoyards, who, getting their livelihood by carving shepherds, shepherdesses, and smoking Dutchmen, for all Europe, went out one day to the mountain to find stock, and discovered that they had whittled up the last of their pine trees. Authors we have in numbers, who have written out their vein, and who, moved by a commendable prudence, sail for Greece or Palestine, follow the trapper into the prairie, or ramble round Algiers to replenish their merchantable stock.

If it were only for a vocabulary the scholar would be covetous of action. Life is our dictionary. Years are well spent in country labors; in town—in the insight into trades and manufactures; in frank intercourse with many men and women; in science; in art; to the one end of mastering in all their facts a language, by which to illustrate and embody our perceptions. I learn immediately from any speaker how much he has already lived, through the poverty or the splendor of his speech. Life lies behind us as the quarry from whence we get tiles and copestones for the masonry of to-day. This is the way to learn grammar. Colleges and books only copy the language which the field and the work-yard made.

But the final value of action, like that of books, and better than books, is, that it is a resource. That great principle of Undulation in nature, that shows itself in the inspiring and expiring of the breath; in desire and satiety; in the ebb and flow of the sea, in day and night, in heat and cold, and as yet more deeply ingrained in every atom and every fluid is known to us under the name of Polarity,—these "fits of easy transmission and reflection," as Newton called them, are the law of nature because they are the law of spirit.

The mind now thinks; now acts; and each fit reproduces the other. When the artist has exhausted his materials, when the fancy no longer paints, when thoughts are no longer apprehended, and books are a weariness,—he has always the resource *to live*. Character is higher than intellect. Thinking is the function. Living is the functionary. The stream retreats to its source. A great soul will be strong to live, as well as strong to think. Does he lack organ or medium to impart his truths? He can still fall back on this elemental force of living them. This is a total act. Thinking is a partial act. Let the grandeur of justice shine in his affairs. Let the beauty of affection cheer his lowly roof. Those "far from fame" who dwell and act with him, will feel the force of his constitution in the doings and passages of the day better than it can be measured by any public and designed display. Time shall teach him that the scholar loses no hour which the man lives. Herein he unfolds the sacred germ of his instinct, screened from influence. What is lost in seemliness is gained in strength. Not out of those on whom systems of education have exhausted their culture, comes the helpful giant to destroy the old or to build the new, but out of un-handselled savage nature, out of terrible Druids and Berserkirs, come at last Alfred and Shakspeare.

I hear therefore with joy whatever is beginning to be said of the dignity and necessity of labor to every citizen. There is virtue yet in the hoe and the spade, for learned as well as for unlearned hands. And labor is every where welcome; always we are invited to work; only be this limitation observed, that a man shall not for the sake of wider activity sacrifice any opinion to the popular judgments and modes of action.

I have now spoken of the education of the scholar by nature, by books, and by action. It remains to say somewhat of his duties.

They are such as become Man Thinking. They may all be comprised in self-trust. The office of the scholar is to cheer, to raise, and to guide men by showing them facts amidst appearances. He plies the slow, unhonored, and unpaid task of observation. Flamsteed and Herschel, in their glazed observatory, may catalogue the stars with the praise of all men, and, the results being splendid and useful, honor is sure. But he, in his private observatory, cataloguing obscure and nebulous stars of the human mind, which as yet no man has thought of as such,—watching days and months, sometimes, for a few facts; correcting still his old records;—must relinquish display and immediate fame. In the long period of his preparation, he must betray often an ignorance and shiftlessness in popular arts, incurring the disdain of the able who shoulder him aside. Long he must stammer in his speech; often forego the living for the dead. Worse yet, he must accept—how often! poverty and solitude. For the ease and pleasure of treading the old road, accepting the fashions, the education, the religion of society, he takes the cross of making his own, and, of course, the self-accusation, the faint heart, the frequent uncertainty and loss of time which are the nettles and tangling vines in the way of the self-relying and self-directed; and the state of virtual hostility in which he seems to stand to society, and especially to educated society. For all this loss and scorn, what offset? He is to find consolation in exercising the highest functions of human nature. He is one who raises himself from private considerations, and breathes and lives on public and illustrious thoughts. He is the world's eye. He is the world's heart. He is to resist the vulgar prosperity that retrogrades ever to barbarism, by preserving and communicating heroic sentiments, noble biographies, melodious verse, and the conclusions of history. Whatsoever oracles the human heart in all emergencies, in all solemn hours has uttered as its commentary on the world of actions,—these he shall receive and impart. And whatsoever new verdict Reason from her inviolable seat pronounces on the passing men and events of to-day,—this he shall hear and promulgate.

These being his functions, it becomes him to feel all confidence in himself, and to defer never to the popular cry. He and he only knows the world. The world of any moment is the merest appearance. Some great decorum, some fetish of a government, some ephemeral trade, or war, or man, is cried up by half mankind and cried down by the other half, as if all depended on this particular up or down. The odds are that the whole question is not worth the poorest thought which the scholar has lost in listening to the controversy. Let him not quit his belief that a popgun is a popgun, though the ancient and honorable of the earth affirm it to be the crack of doom. In silence, in steadiness, in severe abstraction, let him hold by himself; add observation to observation; patient of neglect, patient of reproach, and bide his own time,—happy enough if he can satisfy himself alone that this day he has seen something truly. Success treads on every right step. For the instinct is sure that prompts him to tell his brother what he thinks. He then learns that in going down into the secrets of his own mind, he has descended into the secrets of all minds. He learns that he who mastered any law in his private thoughts, is master to that extent of all men whose language he speaks, and of all into whose language his own can be translated. The poet in utter solitude remembering his spontaneous thoughts and recording them, is found to have recorded which men in "cities vast" find true for them also. The orator distrusts at first the fitness of his frank confessions,—his want of knowledge of the persons he addresses,—until he finds that he is the complement of his hearers;—that they drink his words because he fulfils for them their own nature; the deeper he dives into his privatest secretest presentiment,—to his wonder he finds, this is the most acceptable, most public, and universally true. The people delight in it; the better part of every man feels, This is my music: this is myself.

In self-trust, all the virtues are comprehended. Free should the scholar be,—free and brave. Free even to the definition of freedom, "without any hindrance that does not arise out of his own constitution." Brave; for fear is a thing which a scholar by his very function puts behind him. Fear always springs from ignorance. It is a shame to him if his tranquillity, amid dangerous times, arise from the presumption that like children and women, his is a protected class; or if he seek a temporary peace by the diversion of his thoughts from politics or vexed questions, hiding his head like an ostrich in the flowering bushes, peeping into microscopes, and turning rhymes, as a boy whistles to keep his courage up. So is the danger a danger still: so is the fear worse. Manlike let him turn and face it. Let him look into its eye and search its nature, inspect its origin,—see the whelping of this lion, which lies no great way back; he will then find in himself a perfect comprehension of its nature and extent; he will have made his hands meet on the other side, and can henceforth defy it, and pass on superior. The world is his who can see through its pretension. What deafness, what stone-blind custom, what overgrown error you behold, is there only by sufferance,—by your sufferance. See it to be a lie, and you have already dealt it its mortal blow.

Yes, we are the cowed,—we the trustless. It is a mischievous notion that we are come late into nature; that the world was finished a long time ago. As the world was plastic and fluid in the hands of God, so it is ever to so much of his attributes as we bring to it. To ignorance and sin, it is flint. They adapt themselves to it as they may; but in proportion as a man has anything in him divine, the firmament flows before him, and takes his signet and form. Not he is great who can alter matter, but he who can alter my state of mind. They are the kings of the world who give the color of their present thought to all nature and all art, and persuade men by the cheerful serenity of their carrying the matter, that this thing which they do, is the apple which the ages have desired to pluck, now at last ripe, and inviting nations to the harvest. The great man makes the great thing. Wherever Macdonald sits, there is the head of the table. Linnaeus makes botany the most alluring of studies and wins it from the farmer and the herb-woman. Davy, chemistry: and Cuvier, fossils. The day is always his, who works in it with serenity and great aims. The unstable estimates of men crowd to him whose mind is filled with a truth, as the heaped waves of the Atlantic follow the moon.

For this self-trust, the reason is deeper than can be fathomed,—darker than can be enlightened. I might not carry with me the feeling of my audience in stating my own belief. But I have already shown the ground of my hope, in adverting to the doctrine that man is one. I believe man has been wronged: he has wronged himself. He has almost lost the light that can lead him back to his prerogatives. Men are become of no account. Men in history, men in the world of to-day are bugs, are spawn, and are called "the mass" and "the herd." In a century, in a millenium, one or two men; that is to say—one or two approximations to the right state of every man. All the rest behold in the hero or the poet their own green and crude being—ripened; yes, and are content to be less, so *that* may attain to its full stature. What a testimony—full of grandeur, full of pity, is borne

to the demands of his own nature, by the poor clansman, the poor parti-
san, who rejoices in the glory of his chief. The poor and the low find
some amends to their immense moral capacity, for their acquiescence in
a political and social inferiority. They are content to be brushed like flies
from the path of a great person, so that justice shall be done by him to
that common nature which it is the dearest desire of all to see enlarged
and glorified. They sun themselves in the great man's light, and feel it to
be their own element. They cast the dignity of man from their downtrod
selves upon the shoulders of a hero, and will perish to add one drop of
blood to make that great heart beat, those giant sinews combat and con-
quer. He lives for us, and we live in him.

Men such as they are, very naturally seek money or power; and power
because it is as good as money,—the "spoils," so called, "of office." And
why not? for they aspire to the highest, and this, in their sleepwalking,
they dream is highest. Wake them, and they shall quit the false good and
leap to the true, and leave governments to clerks and desks. This revolution is to be wrought by the gradual domestication of the idea of Culture.
The main enterprise of the world for splendor, for extent, is the upbuilding
of a man. Here are the materials strown along the ground. The private
life of one man shall be a more illustrious monarchy,—more formidable
to its enemy, more sweet and serene in its influence to its friend, than
any kingdom in history. For a man, rightly viewed, comprehendeth the
particular natures of all men. Each philosopher, each bard, each actor,
has only done for me, as by delegate, what one day I can do for myself.
The books which once we valued more than the apple of the eye, we have
quite exhausted. What is that but saying that we have come up with the
point of view which the universal mind took through the eyes of that one
scribe; we have been that man, and have passed on. First, one; then, another; we drain all cisterns, and waxing greater by all these supplies, we
crave a better and more abundant food. The man has never lived that can
feed us ever. The human mind cannot be enshrined in a person who shall
set a barrier on any one side to this unbounded, unboundable empire. It
is one central fire which flaming now out of the lips of Etna, lightens the
capes of Sicily; and now out of the throat of Vesuvius, illuminates the
towers and vineyards of Naples. It is one light which beams out of a
thousand stars. It is one soul which animates all men.

But I have dwelt perhaps tediously upon this abstraction of the Scholar.
I ought not to delay longer to add what I have to say, of nearer reference
to the time and to this country.

Historically, there is thought to be a difference in the ideas which pre-
dominate over successive epochs, and there are data for making the genius
of the Classic, of the Romantic, and now of the Reflective or Philosophical
age. With the views I have intimated of the oneness or the identity of the

mind through all individuals, I do not much dwell on these differences. In fact, I believe each individual passes through all three. The boy is a Greek; the youth, romantic; the adult, reflective. I deny not, however, that a revolution in the leading idea may be distinctly enough traced.

Our age is bewailed as the age of Introversion. Must that needs be evil? We, it seems, are critical. We are embarrassed with second thoughts. We cannot enjoy any thing for hankering to know whereof the pleasure consists. We are lined with eyes. We see with our feet. The time is infected with Hamlet's unhappiness,—

"Sicklied o'er with the pale cast of thought."

Is it so bad then? Sight is the last thing to be pitied. Would we be blind? Do we fear lest we should outsee nature and God, and drink truth dry? I look upon the discontent of the literary class as a mere announcement of the fact that they find themselves not in the state of mind of their fathers, and regret the coming state as untried; as a boy dreads the water before he has learned that he can swim. If there is any period one would desire to be born in,—is it not the age of Revolution; when the old and the new stand side by side, and admit of being compared; when the energies of all men are searched by fear and by hope; when the historic glories of the old, can be compensated by the rich possibilities of the new era? This time, like all times, is a very good one, if we but know what to do with it.

I read with joy some of the auspicious signs of the coming days as they glimmer already through poetry and art, through philosophy and science, through church and state.

One of these signs is the fact that the same movement which effected the elevation of what was called the lowest class in the state, assumed in literature a very marked and as benign an aspect. Instead of the sublime and beautiful, the near, the low, the common, was explored and poetised. That which had been negligently trodden under foot by those who were harnessing and provisioning themselves for long journies into far countries, is suddenly found to be richer than all foreign parts. The literature of the poor, the feelings of the child, the philosophy of the street, the meaning of household life, are the topics of the time. It is a great stride. It is a sign—is it not? of new vigor, when the extremities are made active, when currents of warm life run into the hands and the feet. I ask not for the great, the remote, the romantic; what is doing in Italy or Arabia; what is Greek art, or Provencal Minstrelsy; I embrace the common, I explore and sit at the feet of the familiar, the low. Give me insight into to-day, and you may have the antique and future worlds. What would we really know the meaning of? The meal in the firkin; the milk in the pan; the ballad in the street; the news of the boat; the glance of the eye; the form and the gait of the body;—show me the ultimate reason of these matters;—show me the sublime presence of the highest spiritual cause lurking, as always it does lurk, in these suburbs and extremities of nature; let me see every trifle bristling with the polarity that ranges it instantly on an eternal law; and the shop, the plough, and the ledger, referred to the like cause by which light undulates and poets sing—and the world lies no longer a dull miscellany and lumber room, but has form and order; there is no trifle; there is no puzzle; but one design unites and animates the farthest pinnacle and the lowest trench.

This idea has inspired the genius of Goldsmith, Burns, Cowper, and, in a newer time, of Goethe, Wordsworth, and Carlyle. This idea they differently followed and with various success. In contrast with their writing, the style of Pope, of Johnson, of Gibbon, looks cold and pedantic. This writing is blood-warm. Man is surprised to find that things near are not less beautiful and wondrous than things remote. The near explains the far. The drop is a small ocean. A man is related to all nature. This perception of the worth of the vulgar, is fruitful in discoveries. Goethe, in this very thing the most modern of the moderns, has shown us, as none ever did, the genius of the ancients.

There is one man of genius who has done much for this philosophy of life, whose literary value has never yet been rightly estimated;—I mean Emanuel Swedenborg. The most imaginative of men, yet writing with the precision of a mathematician, he endeavored to engraft a purely philosophical Ethics on the popular Christianity of his time. Such an attempt, of course, must have difficulty which no genius could surmount. But he saw and showed the connexion between nature and the affections of the soul. He pierced the emblematic or spiritual character of the visible, audible, tangible world. Especially did his shade-loving muse hover over and interpret the lower parts of nature; he showed the mysterious bond that allies moral evil to the foul material forms, and has given in epical parables a theory of insanity, of beasts, of unclean and fearful things.

Another sign of our times, also marked by an analogous political movement is, the new importance given to the single person. Every thing that tends to insulate the individual,—to surround him with barriers of natural respect, so that each man shall feel the world is his, and man shall treat with man as a sovereign state with a sovereign state;—tends to true union as well as greatness. "I learned," said the melancholy Pestalozzi, "that no man in God's wide earth is either willing or able to help any other man." Help must come from the bosom alone. The scholar is that man who must take up into himself all the ability of the time, all the contributions of the past, all the hopes of the future. He must be an university of knowledges. If there be one lesson more than another which should pierce his ear, it is, The world is nothing, the man is all; in yourself is the law of all nature, and you know not yet how a globule of sap ascends; in yourself slumbers the whole of Reason; it is for you to know all, it is for you to dare all. Mr. President and Gentlemen, this confidence in the unsearched might of man, belongs by all motives, by all prophecy, by all preparation, to the American Scholar. We have listened too long to the courtly muses of Europe. The spirit of the American freeman is already suspected to be timid, imitative, tame. Public and private avarice make the air we breathe thick and fat. The scholar is decent, indolent, complaisant. See already the tragic consequence. The mind of this country taught to aim at low objects, eats upon itself. There is no work for any but the decorous and the complaisant. Young men of the fairest promise, who begin life upon our shores, inflated by the mountain winds, shined upon by all the stars of God, find the earth below not in unison with these,—but are hindered from action by the disgust which the principles on which business is managed inspire, and turn drudges, or die of disgust,—some of them suicides. What is the remedy? They did not yet see, and thousands of young men as hopeful now crowding to the barriers for the career, do not yet see, that if the single man plant himself indomitably on his instincts, and there abide, the huge world will come round to him. Patience—patience;—with the shades of all the good and great for company; and for solace, the perspective of your own infinite life; and for work, the study and the communication of principles, the making those instincts prevalent, the conversion of the world. Is it not the chief disgrace in the world, not to be an unit;—not to be reckoned one character;—not to yield that peculiar fruit which each man was created to bear, but to be reckoned in the gross, in the hundred, or the thousand, of the party, the section, to which we belong; and our opinion predicted geographically, as the north, or the south. Not so, brothers and friends,—please God, ours shall not be so. We will walk on our own feet; we will work with our own hands; we will speak our own minds. Then shall man be no longer a name for pity, for doubt, and for sensual indulgence. The dread of man and the love of man shall be a wall of defence and a wreath of love around all. A nation of men will for the first time exist, because each believes himself inspired by the Divine Soul which also inspires all men.

ABBREVIATIONS
USED IN THE NOTES

AS: "The American Scholar," in *Transcendentalism: A Reader*, ed. Joel Myerson (New York: Oxford University Press, 2000). Pagination conforms to the text as reproduced here in the appendix.

CEC: *The Correspondence of Emerson and Carlyle*, ed. Joseph Slater (New York: Columbia University Press, 1964).

CW: *The Collected Works of Ralph Waldo Emerson* ed. Alfred E. Ferguson et al. (Cambridge: Harvard University Press, 1971–1994), 5 volumes.

EL: *The Early Lectures of Ralph Waldo Emerson*, ed. Stephen E. Whicher et al. (Cambridge: Harvard University Press, 1959–1972), 3 volumes.

L: *The Letters of Ralph Waldo Emerson*, ed. Ralph L. Rusk and Eleanor M. Tilton (New York: Columbia University Press, 1939–1995), 10 volumes.

LJE: *The Selected Letters of Lidian Jackson Emerson*, ed. Delores Bird Carpenter (Columbia: University of Missouri Press, 1987).

JMN: *The Journals and Miscellaneous Notebooks of Ralph Waldo Emerson*, ed. William H. Gilman et al. (Cambridge: Harvard University Press, 1960–1982), 16 volumes.

MME: *The Select Letters of Mary Mood Emerson*, ed. Nancy Craig Simmons (Athens: University of Georgia Press, 1993).

W: *The Complete Works of Ralph Waldo Emerson*, ed. Edward Waldo Emerson (Boston: Houghton Mifflin, 1903–1904), 12 volumes.

N O T E S

PREFACE

1. *Emersonian Circles: Essays in Honor of Joel Myerson*, ed. Wesley T. Mott and Robert E. Burkholder (Rochester: University of Rochester Press, 1997), xi.

INTRODUCTION

1. AS 139; JMN 5:326. On the naming of the journal: Richard Nelson Current, *Phi Beta Kappa in American Life: The First Two Hundred Years* (New York: Oxford University Press, 1990), 131–136; on the motto: *American Scholar* 67, no. 2 (1998): 4.

2. Elective system: Hazen C. Carpenter, "Emerson, Eliot, and the Elective System," *New England Quarterly* (henceforth *NEQ*) 24 (1951): 13–34; opinion advancing: James Elliot Cabot, *A Memoir of Ralph Waldo Emerson* (Boston: Houghton Mifflin, 1887) 2:629. Revered expression: see, for example, Harold K. Bush, Jr., *American Declarations: Rebellion and Repentance in American Cultural History* (Urbana: University of Illinois Press, 1999), 110–112. Alfred Kazin, "The Father of Us All," *New York Review of Books* 28 (21 January 1982), 4, 6; and, idem, "Where Would Emerson Find His Scholar Now?" *American Heritage* 38 (1987): 93–96. Harold Bloom, "Mr. America," *New York Review of Books* 31 (22 November 1984): 19–24.

3. Merton M. Sealts, Jr., *Emerson on the Scholar* (Columbia: University of Missouri Press, 1992) examines Emerson's lifelong interest in the idea of the scholar, but does not focus particularly on "The American Scholar" address. Among the best intellectual biographies of Emerson are Stephen E. Whicher, *Freedom and Fate: An Inner Life of Ralph Waldo Emerson* (Philadelphia: University of Pennsylvania Press, 1953); Joel Porte, *Representative Man* (New York: Oxford University Press, 1979); Robert D. Richardson, Jr., *Emerson: The Mind on Fire* (Berkeley: University of California Press, 1995); and Barbara L. Packer, *The Cambridge History of American Literature* (henceforth *CHAL*), ed. Sacvan Bercovitch (Cambridge: Cambridge University Press, 1995) 2:329–604.

4. David Robinson, *Apostle of Culture: Emerson as Preacher and Lecturer* (Philadelphia: University of Pennsylvania Press, 1982), 4. At Dartmouth: "Literary Ethics," CW 1:99–116.

5. On the growing scholarly belief in the continual development of Emerson's commitment to reform, see most recently Len Gougeon, "'Fortune of the Republic': Emerson, Lincoln, and Transcendental Warfare," *ESQ: A Journal of the American Renaissance* (henceforth *ESQ*) 45 (1999): 259–324, and Michael Strysick, "Emerson, Slavery, and the Evolution of the Principle of Self-Reliance," in *The Emerson "Dilemma": Essays on Emerson and Society Reform*, ed. T. Gregory Garvey (Athens: University of Georgia Press, 2001), 139–168.

6. CEC 173.

7. Lawrence A. Cremin, *An American Education: Some Notes toward a New History* (Bloomington, Ill.: Phi Delta Kappa, 1969), 12.

CHAPTER 1
"THE AMERICAN SCHOLAR"

1. Contemporary: anonymous review of Orville Dewey's oration in *Christian Examiner* (henceforth *CE*) 9 (1830): 218–235; see also Maria Sophia Quincy, "The Harvard Commencement of 1829," *Harvard Graduates' Magazine* 26 (1918), 580. Powers in the chapter: *Catalogue of the Harvard Chapter of Phi Beta Kappa, Alpha Chapter of Massachusetts* (Cambridge: Riverside Press, 1933), 152; see, for example, Everett to Story, 10 September 1828, Edward Everett Papers, MHS. Channing: *Memoir of William Ellery Channing with Extracts from His Correspondence and Manuscripts*, ed. William Henry Channing (Boston: Wm. Crosby and H. P. Nichols, 1848), 1:241.

2. Emerson's intentions: JMN 5:84; also JMN 5:116–117, 164, 167, 187–188. Sealts, *Emerson on the Scholar*, 44–45, may well be correct in identifying JMN 4:371–372, from 1834, as the beginning of this formulation. Sealts, 52–59, gives further background to the oration, but none of those journal entries went into "The American Scholar," nor do they reflect the passion and conviction of the speech. Wainwright did attend commencement: John Pierce, Memoirs, vol. 7, p. 158, MHS.

3. Oliver Wendell Holmes, Sr., *Ralph Waldo Emerson* (Boston: Houghton Mifflin, 1885), 2; Charles W. Eliot, *Harvard Memories* (Cambridge: Harvard University Press, 1923), 54. Emerson had been the president's freshman (serving as factotum), winner of essay prizes, member of literary and discussion clubs, and class poet: Ralph L. Rusk, *The Life of Ralph Waldo Emerson* (New York: Columbia University Press, 1949), 63–88, and William Bancroft Hill, "Emerson's College Days" *Literary World* (22 May 1880), 180–181, reprinted in Kenneth Walter Cameron, ed., *Emerson the Essayist* (Hartford: Transcendental Books, 1945), 1:459–462. Maurice Gonnaud's portrait of Emerson as a despairing and self-doubting college student is far too extreme: *An Uneasy Solitude: Individual and Society in the Work of Ralph Waldo Emerson*, trans. Lawrence Rosenwald (Princeton: Princeton University Press, 1987), 21–34. See, for example, L 1:67 and JMN 1:129–30.

4. MH bMS Am 1280.220 (149). Reunions: JMN 5:194–195.

5. Life crisis: Henry Nash Smith, "Emerson's Problem of Vocation—A Note on 'The American Scholar'," *NEQ* 12 (1939): 52–67. Important new scholarship discussed in *Encyclopedia of Transcendentalism*, ed. Wesley T. Mott (Westport, Conn.: Greenwood Press, 1996), 110. Lyceum attendance: Clarence Gohdes, "Alcott's 'Conversation' on the Transcendental Club and the *Dial*," *American Literature* 3 (1931): 15; Packer, *CHAL*, 2:393–394.

6. Very unsatisfactory: Henry Hedge to Cabot in Cabot, *Memoir*, 1:244–245. "My coming from Bangor, where I then resided, was always the signal for a meeting." Hedge to Dall, 1 February 1877, in Caroline Wells Healey Dall, *Transcendentalism in New England: A Lecture Delivered before the Society of Philosophical Enquiry* (Boston: Roberts Brothers, 1897), 16; also Theodore Parker to George Ellis, 27 May 1838, Theodore Parker Papers, MHS. Members: Joel Myerson, "A Calendar of Transcendental Club Meetings," *American Literature* 44 (1972): 197–207.

7. Hedge to Convers Francis, 14 February 1843, published in Ronald Vale Wells, *Three Christian Transcendentalists* (New York: Columbia University Press, 1943), 205.

8. Immanuel Kant, *Critique of Pure Reason*, ed. and trans. Norman Kemp Smith (London: Macmillan & Co., 1933), 22. Clarke in "Cambridge," in James Freeman Clarke, *Autobiography, Diary and Correspondence*, ed. Edward Everett Hall (Boston: Houghton Mifflin, 1891), 39 (also in Joel Myerson, ed., *Transcendentalism: A Reader* [New York: Oxford University Press, 2000], 672).

9. Sydney E. Ahlstrom, *A Religious History of the American People* (New Haven: Yale University Press, 1973), 585–596.

10. Literary canon: Richard Rorty, "Genteel Syntheses, Professional Analyses, Transcendentalist Culture," in *Two Centuries of Philosophy in America*, ed. Peter Caws (Oxford: Basil Blackwell, 1980), 228–239. Transformed American intellectuals: Louis Menand, *The Metaphysical Club: A Story of Ideas in America* (New York: Farrar, Straus and Giroux, 2001).

11. Not a formal topic: Myerson, "A Calendar," 204, citing Alcott's Journal (8 May 1839 entry) for January–June 1839, pp. 745–748. Rule: Hedge to Emerson, 14 June 1836, bMS 183, Andover-Harvard Theological Library, Harvard Divinity School; JMN 5:194–195; see Rusk, *Life of Emerson*, 235–236, for discussion of Emerson's initial reluctance.

12. Participation: L 1:329–330. Emerson gave or at least recorded typical toasts offered at the dinner: JMN 6:146. A more skeptical view is at JMN 3:275. Emerson was elected for no particular accomplishment other than having several friends and relatives already members and willing to vote for him: brothers Charles and Edward, cousins George Emerson, Orville Dewey, and George Ripley; of friends, especially Convers Francis, George Bancroft, Sampson Reed, Caleb Stetson, George P. Bradford, and Frederic Henry Hedge.

13. Frothingham's feelings: letter to Emerson, 17 October 1844, MH bMS Am 1280 (1138): "I venture to believe that no one has a truer regard for your character & genius then I have." See also Parker to Ellis, 3 January 1839, Theodore Parker Papers, MHS. Emerson was his frequent dinner guest: O. B. Frothingham, *Recollections and Impressions, 1822–1890* (New York: G. P. Putnam's Sons,

1891), 21. Frothingham's sympathies toward the Transcendentalists: Hedge to Emerson, 14 June 1836, bMS 183, Andover-Harvard Theological Library, Harvard Divinity School; Frothingham to Emerson, 21 August 1837, MH bMS Am 1280 (1135); John Pierce, Memoirs, vol. 7, pp. 282–283, MHS; cf. vol. 7, pp. 64–65. Frothingham's complex relationship to Transcendentalism is discussed most recently by April Selley in *Biographical Dictionary of Transcendentalism*, ed. Wesley T. Mott (Westport, Conn.: Greenwood Press, 1996), 99–101. There is no evidence before the hearings on Theodore Parker in 1842 that Frothingham was oppositional. Good luck: Frothingham to Emerson, 9 August 1837, MH bMS Am 1280 (1134). Chair of the committee: in the 1845 minutes, the first person named as member of the committee was specified as chair; it's likely that the convention was practiced earlier as well. Bradford and Walker: Hedge to Emerson, 14 June 1836, bMS 183, Andover-Harvard Theological Library, Harvard Divinity School; JMN 5:195; L 3:114. The minutes and records of Harvard Phi Beta Kappa are at the Harvard University Archives, HUD 3684.554, box 64, "Minutes of Anniversary Meetings, 1826–1921."

14. Emerson's poem: Carl F. Strauch, "Emerson's Phi Beta Kappa Poem," *NEQ* 23 (1950): 65–90. Stetson's oration: John Pierce, Memoirs, vol. 7, pp. 359–361, MHS; Samuel Osgood to James Freeman Clarke, 4 September 1838, Perry-Clarke Collection, MHS; Cyrus A. Bartol to Ellis, 1 October 1838, George Ellis Papers, MHS. See also Theodore Parker Journal, vol. 1, p. 34, bMS 101, Andover-Harvard Theological Library, Harvard Divinity School; and Convers Francis to Henry Hedge, 12 November 1838, MeBaHi, printed in Guy R. Woodall, "The Record of a Friendship: The Letters of Convers Francis to Frederic Henry Hedge in Bangor and Providence, 1835–1850," *Studies in the American Renaissance* (henceforth SAR) 1991: 38.

15. Everett, "The Circumstances Favorable to the Progress of Literature in America," in *Orations and Speeches on Various Occasions* (Boston: Little, Brown and Co., 1850–1868), 1:9. Old idol: L 1:128, JMN 6:71; all must receive: JMN 4:324, 5:219; emulation: "Historic Notes of Life and Letters of New England," in W 10:330–335.

16. Edward acknowledging William: MME 189. Great applause: John Pierce, Memoirs vol. 1, p. 329, MHS; cf. William B. Sprague, *Annals of the American Pulpit; or Commemorative Notices of Distinguished American Clergymen of the Various Denominations* (New York: Robert Carter & Brothers, 1865), 8:241. The text of his speech is lost: William Hopkins Tillinghast, ed., *Bibliographical Contributions*, vol. 42, *The Orators and Poets of Phi Beta Kappa, Alpha of Massachusetts* (Cambridge: Harvard University Library, 1891), 3. Closely resembled William: Edward Emerson, *Emerson in Concord: A Memoir* (London: Sampson Low, 1889), 6.

17. Alcott on Emerson: Alcott Journal 47–52, 19 January 1837, in Larry A. Carlson, "Bronson Alcott's 'Journal for 1837' (Part One),'" *SAR*, 1981: 47. Attending: Convers Francis '15, George Bancroft '17, Sampson Reed '18, Caleb Stetson '22, George Ripley '23, George P. Bradford '25, Frederic Henry Hedge '25, William Henry Channing '29, James Freeman Clarke '29, Charles Timothy Brooks '32, Samuel Osgood '32, Jones Very '36, Richard Henry Dana '37, and Charles Stearns Wheeler '37. On Alcott, see also Gohdes, *American Literature* 1931: 18; on Emerson's friend Margaret Fuller, see L 2:94–95; on Nathaniel

Langdon Frothingham, see above and L 7:285, n. 49; and on several others, see LJE 58.

18. Palfrey to Ticknor, 28 September 1836, MB CH. A. 13.67. Francis Bowen, "Transcendentalism," *CE* 21 (1837): 371–385. Parker to Ellis, 20 February 1837, Theodore Parker Papers, MHS. Samuel Osgood to James Freeman Clarke, 20 July 1837, Perry-Clarke Collection, MHS.

19. Duel: JMN 5:371; hideous dream: JMN 3:317.

20. JMN 5:372.

21. AS 139.

22. AS 131, 135, 138, 134, 145.

23. Ronald Story, *The Forging of an Aristocracy: Harvard and the Boston Upper Class, 1800–1870* (Middletown, Conn., Wesleyan University Press, 1980), 24–25.

24. John Pierce, Memoirs, vol. 6, p. 440, MHS. Holmes, *Emerson*, 115.

25. Mild criticisms in the "Address on Education" in June, 1837 (EL 2:202), and "Education" in 1840 (EL 3:294); "The School" (1838: EL 3:34–50) has no criticism. At Dartmouth: "Literary Ethics," W 1:100, L 2:145–146.

26. AS 132.

27. Know thyself: AS 134; experience: AS 137.

28. Self-trust: AS 139; world's eye: AS 139–140.

29. AS 141, 143, 144, 145.

30. Gladstone: CEC 215; Harriet Martineau, *Retrospect of Western Travel* (London: Saunders and Otley, 1838), 2:106–107, 203–210; to Carlyle: CEC 174. On brisk sales of the talk, CW 1:51.

31. William Henry Channing, Review of "An Oration Delivered before the Phi Beta Kappa Society, at Cambridge, August 31, 1837, by Ralph Waldo Emerson. Boston. James Munroe & Co," *Boston Quarterly Review* 1 (1838): 106.

32. John Pierce, Memoirs, vol. 7, p. 155, MHS.

33. Alcott: Gohdes, *American Literature* 1931: 18; Lowell, "Thoreau's Letters," *North American Review* 101 (October 1865): 600; Holmes, *Emerson*, 115.

34. James Richardson to Thoreau, 7 September 1837, *The Correspondence of Henry David Thoreau*, ed. Walter Harding and Carl Bode (New York: New York University Press, 1958), 11. Edward E. Hale, ed., "A Harvard Undergraduate in the Thirties: From the Diary of Edward Everett Hale," *Harper's Monthly Magazine* 132 (1916): 694.

35. Horace Mann Journal, 31 August 1837, Horace Mann Papers, MHS. Brownson to Emerson, 10 November 1837, Harvard College Library in the University of Notre Dame Archives microfilm, ed. Thomas T. McAvoy and Lawrence J. Bradley (1966), reel 9.

36. Economic uncertainties: AS 140. B. L. Packer, *Emerson's Fall: A New Interpretation of the Major Essays* (New York: Continuum, 1982), 85–102; Robert T. Burkholder, "The Radical Emerson: Politics in 'The American Scholar'," *ESQ* 34 (1988): 37–58. But at JMN 5:336 (25 May 1837), Emerson calls the panic a "momentary mischance," and by August he had inherited from the estate of his first wife and his mood is more optimistic (Burkholder, 50–53). Emerson used economic hardship as a trope in *Nature* (CW 1:24), just as in "The American Scholar" and long afterwards, see Michael T. Gilmore, *American Romanticism and the Marketplace* (Chicago: University of Chicago Press, 1985), 19–20. Dull

sermon: Sealts, *Emerson on the Scholar*, 94–95; identity crisis: first proposed by Smith, *NEQ* (1939): 52–67.

CHAPTER 2
AMERICA IN "THE AMERICAN SCHOLAR"

1. Puritans: David Minter, "The Puritan Jeremiad as a Literary Form," in *The American Puritan Imagination: Essays in Revaluation*, ed. Sacvan Bercovitch (Cambridge: Cambridge University Press, 1974), 45. William and Mary: Current, *Phi Beta Kappa in American Life*, 5–7. Conventional meaning: Bliss Perry, "Emerson's Most Famous Speech," in his *The Praise of Folly and Other Papers* (Boston, Houghton Mifflin, 1923), 81–113, points out that it had "become a standard undergraduate theme." 1837: AS 132–133. Although clearly having in mind the American scholar (as noted by a contemporary reviewer, William Henry Channing, *Boston Quarterly Review* [1838]: 110), he entitled the initial version "An Oration, Delivered before the Phi Beta Kappa Society at Cambridge, August 31, 1837." He renamed it in 1849; see Joel Myerson, "Practical Editions: Ralph Waldo Emerson's 'The American Scholar'," *Proof* 3 (1973): 380.

2. Lowell, *North American Review* 1865: 600. AS 142, 144. Theophilus Parsons and Sampson Reed may have been the only Swedenborgians in the audience. John Pierce, Memoirs, vol. 7, 162, MHS, believed there was one Swedenborgian minister among Harvard alumni.

3. Harvard history: William R. Hutchinson, *The Transcendentalist Ministers: Church Reform in the New England Renaissance* (New Haven: Yale University Press, 1959), 6–12. We do not deny: "Review of Dr. Codman's Speech in the Board of Overseers of Harvard College, February 3, 1831," *CE* 10 (1831), 144.

4. [Lyman Beecher], *The Autobiography of Lyman Beecher*, ed. B. Cross (Cambridge, Mass.: Belknap Press, 1961), 2:82. Octavius Brooks Frothingham, *George Ripley* (Boston: Houghton Mifflin, 1883), 42–43. On taking hold, see Packer, *CHAL* 2:331–336.

5. Moral cause: see especially Lawrence Buell, "Unitarianism Aesthetics and Emerson's Poet-priest," *American Quarterly* 20 (1968): 3–20; and idem, *Literary Transcendentalism: Style and Vision in the American Renaissance* (Ithaca: Cornell University Press, 1973), 23–54. Hutchinson, *Transcendentalist Ministers*, provides an insightful interpretation of Unitarian beliefs. *Review* quoted by Benjamin T. Spencer, *The Quest for Nationality: An American Literary Campaign* (Syracuse: Syracuse University Press, 1957), 63.

6. Henry Adams, *The Education of Henry Adams*, ed. Ira B. Nadel (Oxford: Oxford University Press, 1999), 31, 32; Merle Curti, *The Growth of American Thought*, 3rd ed. (New York: Harper & Row, 1964), 343; Emerson's letter: L 1:128; *Life, Letters, and Journals of George Ticknor*, ed. George Stillman Hillard and Anna Eliot Ticknor (Boston: James R. Osgood and Company, 1876), 2:188–189.

7. "Moore's Poems," *Monthly Anthology and Boston Review* 4 (1807): 44; *Review of Mrs. Herman's Forest Sanctuary* 6, quoted by David B. Tyack, *George Ticknor and the Boston Brahmins* (Cambridge: Harvard University Press, 1967), 149–150; "Report on the Inauguration of President Kirkland of Harvard," *Monthly Anthology and Boston Review* 9 (1810): 350.

8. Moses: *CE* 55 (1853): 445. Curti, *Growth of American Thought*, 225–249; Channing ecumenical: Buell, *American Quarterly* 1968: 3–20; "Remarks on National Literature," reprinted in *The Works of William E. Channing, D.D.* (Boston: James Munroe and Company, 1841), quotations are from pp. 248 and 251.

9. Andrew Delbanco, *William Ellery Channing: An Essay on the Liberal Spirit in America* (Cambridge: Harvard University Press, 1981), 85. Still smarting: "Unitarianism Vindicated against the Charges of Skeptical and Infidel Tendencies," *CE* 11 (1831): 179; the anonymous reviewer was likely Andrew P. Peabody. Revivalists and Princeton: Perry Miller, *Life of the Mind in America from the Revolution to the Civil War* (New York: Harcourt Brace Jovanovich, 1965), 193.

10. Current, *Phi Beta Kappa in American Life*, 27–36, 51–57.

11. "On The Dangers and Duties of Men of Letters; An Address, Pronounced before the Society of ΦΒΚ, on Thursday, August 31st, 1809," *Monthly Anthology and Boston Review* 7 (1809): 146, 157–158. See also Robert Milder, "'The American Scholar' as Cultural Event," *Prospects* 16 (1991): 119–147. In its warnings about the isolation of scholars, however, Buckminister's oration is perhaps closest to Emerson's.

12. Richard Beale Davis, "Edward Tyrrel Channing's American Scholar of 1818," *Key Reporter* 26 (Spring, 1961): 1–4. Biblical criticism: Story, *Forging of an Aristocracy*, 214. On Walker: Daniel Walker Howe, *The Unitarian Conscience: Harvard Moral Philosophy, 1805–1861* (Middletown, Conn.: Wesleyan University Press, 1988), 2nd ed., 181.

13. "Characteristics of the Age. A Discourse Pronounced at Cambridge, before the Phi Beta Kappa Society of Harvard University, August 31, 1826," in *The Miscellaneous Writings of Joseph Story*, ed. William W. Story (Boston: Charles C. Little and James Brown, 1852), 358–359.

14. Jackson: Andrew P. Peabody, *Harvard Reminiscences* (Boston: Ticknor and Co., 1888), 35–36; and Frederick Rudolph, *The American College and University: A History* (New York: Alfred Knopf, 1962), 201. Whiggish argument: Miller, *Life of the Mind*, 223–230. Parsons, *On the Duties of Educated Men in a Republic* (Boston: Russell, Odiorne & Co: 1835), 12–13.

15. Martineau, *Retrospect of Western Travel*, 2:106.

16. Wayland's talk: John Pierce, Memoirs, vol. 6, p. 440, MHS. Wayland's oration was upon "the practical uses of the principles of faith" (James O. Murray, *Francis Wayland* [Boston: Houghton Mifflin, 1891, 79]), and Alcott thought it "a very sound and eloquent oration" (Alcott Journal 179, 1 September 1836, in Joel Myerson, "Bronson Alcott, 'Journal for 1836,'" *SAR* 1978: 69). Everett's talk: Current, *Phi Beta Kappa in American Life*, 35.

17. Knowledge of previous orations: JMN 1:399, 3:38, 3:275; 4:315; 5:86–87, 418; L 1:74; 1:210; aware of discussion of a national literature: JMN 1:260, 287, 289; 2:393; accepted Federalist view: Daniel S. Malachuk, "The Republican Philosophy of Emerson's Early Lectures," *NEQ* 71 (1998): 404–428. Emerson's poem: Strauch, *NEQ* 23 (1950), 65–90; with JMN 4:315–316; Charles Emerson to Elizabeth Hoar, 30 August 1834, MH bMS Am 1280.220 (52), folder 18; Edward Waldo Emerson, *Emerson's Concord. A Memoir* (Boston: Houghton Mifflin, 1889), 223–224.

18. Surpass Europe: Curti, *Growth of American Thought*, 140–148; Packer, *Emerson's Fall*, 85–95. Meagre: JMN 2:90 (cf. 39, 218); 5:428; dearth: JMN 4:296; 5:210–211.

19. Titanic Continent: Alcott Journal 213, 3 October 1836, in Joel Myerson, "Bronson Alcott, 'Journal for 1836'," *SAR* 1978: 80. Emerson recorded only that the meeting was a "pleasant" experience and was particularly impressed by the contribution of Bronson Alcott (JMN 5:194, 218). Influence of friends: see chapter 5; not called out: JMN 5:210–211; Stanley Cavell, *Conditions Handsome and Unhandsome: The Constitution of Emersonian Perfectionism* (La Salle, Ill.: Open Court, 1990), 35; roots: JMN 5:303–4, 306.

20. One of these signs: AS 143–144; to create: JMN 5:341, AS 135; see also Buell, *Literary Transcendentalism*, 29–30.

21. Henry F. Pommer, "The Contents and Basis of Emerson's Belief in Compensation," *PMLA: Publications of the Modern Language Association of America* 77 (1962): 248–253. Each philosopher: AS 142; see also AS 140; Emerson had tried these thoughts out earlier in lyceum lectures: EL 2:99; also EL 2:9, 17, 62. Feed us: AS 142.

22. Later essays: especially in *Representative Men*; see Judith Shklar, "Emerson and the Inhibitions of Democracy," *Political Theory* 18 (1990): 601–614. Whicher, *Freedom and Fate*, 36. Defiant existence: W 1:113–115 AS .

23. On the extent of European training of Harvard faculty, see Robert A. McCaughey, *Josiah Quincy, 1772–1864: The Last Federalist* (Cambridge: Harvard University Press, 1974), 136–139; and Elizabeth Hurth, "Sowing the Seeds of 'Subservience': Harvard's Early Göttingen Students," *SAR* 1992, 91–106. Delbanco, *William Ellery Channing*, 55–82, explores specifically Channing's European frame of reference. Quotation is from "Remarks on National Literature," reprinted in *The Works of William E. Channing, D.D.*, 271. Union College speaker: Gulian C. Verplanck, *The Advantages and the Dangers of the American Scholar. A Discourse Delivered on the Day Preceding the Annual Commencement of Union College, July 26, 1836* (New York: Wiley and Long, 1836).

24. Mischievous notion: AS 141; kinsman: CEC 173–174. This is the truest scholar Emerson was ever to conjure, returning by 1839 to a scholar linked to the national enterprise: "Self-Reliance": CW 2:47–48.

25. Orestes A. Brownson, "American Literature," *Boston Quarterly Review* 2 (1839): 25; also in Miller, *Transcendentalists*, 433. William Henry Channing, *Boston Quarterly Review* (1838): 107, 113–114, 119–120.

26. Refusal at Brook Farm: for example, Miller, *Transcendentalists*, 464–465. If a single man: AS 145; other orators: Alfred Laurence Brophy, "The Intersection of Property and Slavery in Southern Legal Thought: From Missouri Compromise through Civil War" (Ph.D. diss., Harvard University, 2001), 88–123.

CHAPTER 3
THE SCHOLAR TRANSFORMED

1. Able to be a polemic: L 7:322; advising young men: JMN 5:365–365; L 2:144–145, 146.

2. Old friends: JMN 5:192–193; see also 1:129–30; 2:231; 5:87, 190; 7:60, 61; L 2:34. Milton: JMN 2:300, 377; more circumspect at JMN 2:79–80 and L 1:128. After John Kirkland's resignation in 1828, Emerson had hoped that the presidency of Harvard would fall to Everett: L 1:232. Maugre: Emerson was still enthralled with Everett in 1831 (L 1:328), but not by 1835 (JMN 5:32–33); see also JMN 3:295; 4:42–43; 5:22, 92. Ticknor: JMN 1:35, 47; 3:184; see also Rusk, *Life of Emerson*, 79–80.

3. Popularity: Sprague, *Annals of the American Pulpit*, 8:276–281, 506; Peabody, *Harvard Reminiscences*, 10–11; Samuel Eliot Morison, "The Great Rebellion of Harvard and the Resignation of President Kirkland," *The Colonial Society of Massachusetts, Transactions* 27 (1927–1930), 58. Friendship: Alexander Young in *American Unitarian Biography. Memoirs of Individuals Who Have Been Distinguished by Their Writings, Character, and Efforts in the Cause of Liberal Christianity*, ed. William Ware (Boston: James Munroe, and Co., 1850), 1:286–288. See the endearing letter from Kirkland to William Emerson, 24 December 1793, MH bMS Am 1280.226 (3743). Financially possible: Rusk, *Life of Emerson*, 9, 62, 65. Remembrance: Kirkland to Edward Emerson, MH bMS Am 1280.226 (3741), 21 May 1827; also bMS Am 1280.226 (3742), 7 July 1827.

4. Emerson on Kirkland: L 1:76–78. For Kirkland's kindness to Emerson: Lawrence Buell, *New England Literary Culture: From Revolution through Renaissance* (Cambridge: Cambridge University Press, 1986), 143; Rusk, *Life of Emerson*, 74–75. Harvard's shift: Conrad Wright, "The Election of Henry Ware: Two Contemporary Accounts Edited with Commentary," *Harvard Library Bulletin* 17 (1969): 245–278. Lower house: Peter Dobkin Hall, "What the Merchants Did with Their Money: Charitable and Testamentary Trusts in Massachusetts, 1780–1880," in *Entrepreneurs: The Boston Business Community, 1700–1850*, ed. Conrad Edick Wright and Kathryn P. Viens (Boston: Massachusetts Historical Society, 1997), 399–400; see also Mary Kupiec Cayton, "Who Were the Evangelicals?: Conservative and Liberal Identity in the Unitarian Controversy in Boston, 1804–1833," *Journal of Social History* 31 (1997): 85–107. Fund-raiser: Sprague, *Annals of the American Pulpit*, 8:264.

5. Unpopularity: Morison, *The Colonial Society of Massachusetts, Transactions* 27 (1927–1930), 54–112; drifting: Howe, *The Unitarian Conscience*, 266–267, and Story, *Forging of an Aristocracy*, 46; faculty fight: most recently, Robert Habich, "Emerson's Reluctant Foe: Andrews Norton and the Transcendental Controversy," *NEQ* 65 (1992): 212–216; Eliot: quoted by Turner, *Charles Eliot Norton*, 28; strategies: Tyack, *George Ticknor*, 109–123.

6. Sun of Harvard: Alexander Young in William Ware, ed., *American Unitarian Biography*, 1:320; see also Story, *Forging of an Aristocracy*, 44–51; Norton to Palfrey, 8 June 1840, MH bMS Am 1704 (637), letter 59 in packet no. 6. See also John Pierce, Memoirs, vol. 8, p. 442, MHS.

7. Loss personally: L 1:210, 230, and 232; Emerson initially understood that the stroke would end Kirkland's presidency, but then allowed himself, as did others, to blame the corporation. Charles Chauncy Emerson "Class Oration": MH bMS Am 1280.220 (118).

8. Emerson quotation: JMN 12:204; Ripley quotation: Samuel Eliot Morison, *Three Centuries of Harvard, 1636–1936* (Cambridge: Harvard University Press, 1936), 197.

9. Course on moral philosophy: James Turner, "Secularization and Sacralization: Speculations of Some Religious Origins of the Secular Humanities Curriculum, 1850–1900," in *The Secularization of the Academy*, ed. George M. Marsden and Bradley J. Longfield (New York: Oxford University Press, 1992), 75. Morison, *Dictionary of American Biography*, 15:309; slavery: McCaughey, *Josiah Quincy*.

10. Everett to Palfrey, 20 January, 1829, MH bMS Am 1704 (301) 41–50. See also Everett to Bancroft, 11 September 1838, and Everett to Story, 3 October 1828, for his promoting his own brother's candidacy, Edward Everett Papers, MHS. Norton to Palfrey, 8 June 1840, MH bMS Am 1704 (637), letter 59 in packet no. 6.

11. Spill: L 1:230; Everett: Morison, *Three Centuries of Harvard*, 233–234; Bigelow: George E. Ellis, *Memoir of Jacob Bigelow, M.D., LL.D.* (Cambridge: John Wilson and Son, 1880), 48, drawing on Bigelow's diary; Parker: Arthur E. Sutherland, *The Law at Harvard: A History of Ideas and Men, 1817–1967* (Cambridge, Mass.: Belknap Press, 1967), 80–81.

12. Junta: Peabody, *Harvard Reminiscences*, 24; characterization of Bowditch: Morison, *Three Centuries of Harvard*, 220; on the report, still excellent is Allen R. Clark, "Andrews Norton: A Conservative Unitarian" (Harvard College honors thesis, 1943), 80–91. Switching support from Ticknor: Story to George Ticknor, 11 February 1829, in William W. Story, *Life and Letters of Joseph Story* (Boston: C. C. Little and J. Brown, 1851), 1:565. Bowditch had also originally supported Ticknor for the presidency: Edward Everett to Alexander Everett: 15 September 1828, Edward Everett Papers, MHS. Ticknor likely helped Bowditch undermine Kirkland: Ticknor to Bowditch 31 May 1826, MB Ms.A. 2346 (1). Ridiculed remarks: L 1:280. Special friend: Amos Perry, "Old Days at Harvard 2," *Boston Transcript*, 21 June 1899. See also Story to Quincy, 30 January 1830, Quincy Family Papers Manuscripts, QP 69, MHS, a telling example of special interest peddling and personal ingratiation.

13. Endowment: Story, *Forging of an Aristocracy*, 24–56.

14. Faculty resigning: Story, *Forging of an Aristocracy*, 72. Classics: McCaughey, *Josiah Quincy*, 147–148; Howe, *Unitarian Conscience*, 263. Ticknor to Charles Davies, 25 October 1834: *Life, Letters, and Journals of George Ticknor*, 1:399–400. On Ticknor's last attempt at reform: Ticknor to Bowditch, 24 February 1834, MB Ms.E.210.19 v.2 (105–106). Norton on governance: to Palfrey, 27 January 1831, MH bMS Am 1704 (637) letter no. 46 in packet 5. Parsons in *Boston Daily Advertiser* 42, no. 14254 (28 November 1837), p. 2; Woodall, *SAR* 1991: 31. See also Robert A. McCaughey, "The Transformation of American Academic Life: Harvard University, 1821–1892," *Perspectives in American History* 8 (1974): 255–263.

15. Social advantage: Story, *Forging of an Aristocracy*, 97, quoting Adams. See also David F. Allmendinger, Jr., *Paupers and Scholars: The Transformation of Student Life in Nineteenth-Century New England* (New York: St. Martin's Press, 1975), 130. High-minded: Edmund Quincy, *Life of Josiah Quincy* (Boston: Tick-

nor and Fields, 1868), 438. See, generally, Story, *Forging of an Aristocracy*, 61–64, 89–134. Economic elite: James McLachlan, "The American College in the Nineteenth Century: Toward a Reappraisal," *Teachers College Record* 80 (1978): 287–297.

16. Martineau, *Retrospect of Western Travel*, 2:94. The book wasn't published until 1838, but Martineau met twice with Emerson on her visit, even staying with him in Concord, so shared feelings are likely.

17. Cabot, *Memoir*, 1:54.

18. Long dominated: James Freeman Clarke, *Autobiography, Diary and Correspondence*, 38. Quincy oversaw process: Morison, *Three Centuries of Harvard*, 260; detailed in McCaughey, *Josiah Quincy*, 148–149. Longfellow to Ticknor, 28 September 1837, Dartmouth College Library, quoted by Tyack, *George Ticknor*, 127. The same happened when Quincy attended Story's class: Eliot, *Harvard Memories*, 49.

19. Richard Henry Dana, Jr., *An Autobiographical Sketch (1815–1842)*, ed. Robert F. Metzdorf (Hamden, Conn.: Shoe String Press, 1953), 59; see also Clarke, *Autobiography, Diary and Correspondence*, 38 (also in Myerson, *Transcendentalism: A Reader*, 671).

20. Step-mother: Harvard University Archives, HUD 3684.555 box 68, Phi Beta Kappa Records 4, 1825–1841, 13 June 1834; John Quincy Adams: McCaughey, *Josiah Quincy*, 152–162, supplies important archival information; Martineau, "The Claims of Harvard College upon Its Sons," *CE* 17 (1834), 93–127; idem, *Retrospect of Western Travel* 2:95; library: Convers Francis to Henry Hedge, 10–12 December 1837, MeBaHi (published by Woodall, *SAR* 1991: 31).

21. Teacher: Peabody, *Harvard Reminiscences*, 116–123; abolitionist: *The Works of Charles Follen, with a Memoir of His Life*, ed. Eliza Lee Follen (Boston: Hilliard, Gray, and Co., 1842), 1:343, and Story, *Forging of an Aristocracy*, 78. Quincy certainly warned his good friend, Dean of the Divinity School John Gorham Palfrey, against the same: McCaughey, *Josiah Quincy*, 189; Quincy to Palfrey, 25 May 1838, Josiah Quincy Papers, Harvard University Archives. Repression of abolitionist talk on campus was common: see *American Higher Education: A Documentary History*, ed. Richard Hofstadter and Wilson Smith (Chicago: University of Chicago Press, 1961), 1:429.

22. George Ripley, "Inaugural Discourse, Delivered before the University in Cambridge, Massachusetts, September, 1831, by Charles Follen," *CE* 11 (1832): 374. Follen sympathetic: Frederic Henry Hedge to Margaret Fuller, 20 February 1835, bMS 384, Andover-Harvard Theological Library, Harvard Divinity School; Theodore Parker Journal, vol. 1, p. 35, bMS 101/1, Andover-Harvard Theological Library, Harvard Divinity School; and note how Follen wiggled out of a request by Andrews Norton to support him in the miracles controversy (Follen to Norton, 15 October 1838, MH Norton Collection bMS Am 1089, box 6). Subsequent decision: Theodore Parker complained that the Divinity School library had "almost none of the new theologic thought of the German masters" (Miller, *Transcendentalists*, 484).

23. JMN 4:276–77.

24. Worcester: Ripley to Bancroft, 6 November 1837, George Bancroft Papers, MHS; Orestes Brownson, "Norton's Evidence," *Boston Quarterly Review* 2

(1839): 86–113 (also in Miller, *Transcendentalists*, 205–209); F. B. Sanborn, *The Personality of Emerson* (Boston: Charles E. Goodspeed, 1903), 9. Emerson's famous, devastating observation of Harvard of 1846 provides good, if ex post facto, perspective: JMN 9:379–381.

25. Holmes, *Emerson*, 115, quoting "The American Scholar" AS 143.

26. Realism in previous talks: EL 2:88, 145. Finger, neck: AS 132; dull grub: AS 137–138; clergy: AS 137; see R. Jackson Wilson, "Emerson as Lecturer: Man Thinking, Man Saying," in *The Cambridge Guide to Ralph Waldo Emerson*, ed. Joel Porte and Saundra Morris (Cambridge: Cambridge University Press, 1999), 90–95. William Henry Channing, *Boston Quarterly Review* 1838: 109–110.

27. Influence: for example, F. O. Matthiessen, *American Renaissance: Art and Expression in the Age of Emerson and Whitman* (New York: Oxford University, 1941), 1–75; and David S. Reynolds, *Beneath the American Renaissance: The Subversive Imagination in the Age of Emerson and Melville* (New York: Alfred Knopf, 1988), 15–24, 92–103, 448–496. Reed: Miller, *Transcendentalists*, 49ff. Emerson, "Carlyle's French Revolution," *CE* 23 (1838): 386. Princeton Seminary: Miller, *Transcendentalists*, 238; JMN 5:431.

28. JMN 5:176, 465. See Reynolds, *Beneath the American Renaissance*, 16–24, 92–97. But Emerson also criticized Taylor: JMN 5:255, 287, 324–325.

29. Old fable: AS 132; bookworm: AS 134–135; towns of gold: AS 136; prophet redeemed: AS 139–140; our saints: JMN 5:358. On the jeremiad: Sacvan Bercovitch, *The American Jeremiad* (Madison: University of Wisconsin Press, 1978), 3–30; Susan L. Roberson, *Emerson in His Sermons: A Man-Made Self* (Columbia: University of Missouri Press, 1995), 54–60.

30. Charles Grandison Finney, *Lectures on Revivals of Religions* (New York: Leavitt, Lord & Co, 1835) 2nd ed., 174, compared with AS 134. Policing: Keith J. Hardman, *Charles Grandison Finney, 1792–1875: Revivalist and Reformer* (Syracuse: Syracuse University Press, 1987), 223; power: JMN 3:324.

31. Churches: Nathan O. Hale, *The Democratization of American Christianity* (New Haven: Yale University Press, 1989), 3–4; and references in Anne C. Rose, *Transcendentalism as a Social Movement, 1830–1850* (New Haven: Yale University Press, 1981), 16. Revivalism: Hutchinson, *Transcendentalist Ministers*, 17–18. Finney quotations: William Gerald McLoughlin, *Modern Revivalism: Charles Grandison Finney to Billy Graham* (New York: Ronald Press Co., 1959), 88; Finney, *Lectures on Revivals of Religions*, 208. Unitarians: Rose, *Transcendentalism as a Social Movement*, 1–37; Reynolds, *Beneath the American Renaissance*, 54–91.

32. Miller, *Life of the Mind*, 18; Ephriam Perkins, "The Oneida and Troy Revivals," *CE* 4 (1827): 248; Frothingham, *George Ripley*, 43; Locke: Packer, *CHAL*, 2:338–339.

33. Lilian Handlin, "*Babylon est delenda*: the Young Andrews Norton," in *American Unitarianism: 1805–1865*, ed. Conrad Edick Wright (Boston: Massachusetts Historical Society, 1989), 53–85; and Ahlstrom, *Religious History of the American People*, passim.

34. Phrenzy: "A History of Harvard University from Its Foundation, in the Year 1636, to the Period of the American Revolution," *CE* 15 (1835): 330; matriculation: Sydney E. Ahlstrom, "The Middle Period, 1840–1880," in *The Harvard Divinity School*, ed. George Huntson Williams (Boston: Beacon Press, 1954), 78–103.

35. Mob violence: Leonard L. Richards, *"Gentlemen of Property and Standing": Anti-Abolition Mobs in Jacksonian America* (New York: Oxford University Press, 1970), 15.

36. Classical oratory: Sealts, *Emerson on the Scholar*, 104; colleges to create: AS 136.

CHAPTER 4

SELF-RELIANCE

1. In sermons: Roberson, *Emerson in His Sermons*, 121–122; EL 2:173. All confidence: AS 140; for this self-trust: AS 141.

2. LJE 58. Ripley, Stetson, and Bradford were all at the club's meeting: Albert J. von Frank, *An Emerson Chronology* (New York: G. K. Hall & Co. 1994), 126.

3. JMN 5:372, 373, 387.

4. Everett to Emerson, 22 November 1837, MH bMS Am 1280; Paul Revere Frothingham, *Edward Everett: Orator and Statesman* (Boston: Houghton Mifflin, 1925), 367. To himself, Everett merely noted that the speech was "in the new Platonic style" (Everett Journal, 31 August 1837, Edward Everett Papers, MHS). Ruth Emerson to RWE, 28 September 1837, with addendum from William: MH bMS Am 1280.226 (2701). Emerson did get the remarks from Everett two months later.

5. JMN 5:376.

6. Hedge to Emerson, 4 September 1837, bMS 183/1 (8), Andover-Harvard Theological Library, Harvard Divinity School; about and just: JMN 5:411.

7. Lidian's letter: LJE 67; sending off text: JMN 5:448; concern for the Divinity School address: JMN 7:65, 89, 95, 96; for *Essays: First Series*: CEC 291, 303, 308, L 2:444; getting the Divinity School address ready for commencement: L 2:148, 152.

8. Active in village: bibliography in Joel Myerson, ed., *The Transcendentalists* (New York: MLAA, 1984), 141. See, for example, JMN 5:422 and 429. Visitors: for example, JMN 7:213–221; see also Richardson, *Mind on Fire*, 313–317. Carlyle: CEC 255; solitude: JMN 5:454 (see also JMN 7:259); John Updike, "Emersonianism," *New Yorker*, 4 June 1984, 115.

9. "Self-Reliance": CW 2:31; detachment: Cabot, *Memoir*, 1:348–382; Richard Poirier, *The Renewal of Literature: Emersonian Reflections* (New York: Random House, 1987), 31–34, 141–143. About Charles: L 7:259–260; CEC 148; L 2:20, 24–25; see also JMN 5:150–153; *The Letters of Elizabeth Palmer Peabody: American Renaissance Woman*, ed. by Bruce A. Ronda (Middletown, Conn.: Wesleyan University Press, 1984), 164.

10. Demolish me: JMN 5:387; on his father: see chapter 6; guilt: Porte, *Representative Man*, 73; more than beautiful: Dall, *Transcendentalism in New England*, 35; fretted: *The Letters of Margaret Fuller*, ed. Robert N. Hudspeth (Ithaca: Cornell University Press, 1983), 1:294; also Marie Mitchell Olesen Urbanski, "The Ambivalence of Ralph Waldo Emerson towards Margaret Fuller," *Thoreau Journal Quarterly* 10 (1978): 26–36; and Jeffrey Steele, "Transcendental Friendship: Emerson, Fuller, and Thoreau," in *The Cambridge Guide to Ralph Waldo Emerson*, ed. Joel Porte and Saundra Morris (Cambridge: Cambridge University Press, 1999), 121–139; audience: JMN 11:258.

11. On Hedge: L 2:270; to Aunt Mary: L 1:328; estate: especially Joel Porte, *Representative Man*, 70–78; profit from lectures: CEC 88–89; JMN 7:136; household: for example, L 2:370–371.

12. CW 2:30–31, 41.

13. Various rhetorical strategies are discussed by Richard Poirier, "'Are They My Poor?': Emerson's Steinian Question," in his *Trying It Out in America* (New York: Farrar, Straus and Giroux, 1999), 203–217. On redacting, see CW 2:xxv–xxx, 331–335. Bloom: *Modern Critical Views: Ralph Waldo Emerson* (New York: Chelsea House, 1985), 5.

14. Great man alone: JMN 7:346–347; "Fate": W 6:47; see also *The Complete Sermons of Ralph Waldo Emerson*, ed. Albert J. von Frank, Teresa Toulouse, Ronald A. Bosco, and Wesley T. Mott, with an introduction by David M. Robinson (Columbia: University of Missouri Press, 1989–1992), 4:215; and "The Transcendentalist," CW 1:213. W.E.B. DuBois, *The Souls of Black Folk*, ed. David W. Blight and Robert Gooding-Williams (Boston: Bedford Books, 1997), 38. DuBois's use of double consciousness is best and most recently discussed by Dickson D. Bruce, Jr., "W.E.B. Du Bois and the Idea of Double Conscious," *American Literature* 64 (1992): 299–309, who does not, however, consider the echo of Plato, *Phaedrus* 253 d-e.

15. History as biography: JMN 7:202; "History," CW 2:6.

16. JMN 5:333–334.

17. Netting $360: JMN 12:177; renting space: Mary Kupiec Cayton, *Emerson's Emergence: Self and Society in the Transformation of New England, 1800–1845* (Chapel Hill: University of North Carolina Press, 1989), 140–143; Packer, *CHAL*, 2:393–394; preach no more: L 2:120; cf. 2:113.

18. Oliver Wendell Holmes, Sr., *The Autocrat at the Breakfast Table* (New York: E. P. Dutton, 1906), 193; announcement of 1828: "American Lyceum," *Independent Chronicle and Boston Patriot*, 13 September 1828; invitation of 1837: L 7:286.

19. Upward mobility: Donald M. Scott, "The Popular Lecture and the Creation of a Public in Mid-Nineteenth Century America," *Journal of American History* 66 (1980): 791–809; Mary Kupiec Cayton, "The Making of an American Prophet: Emerson, His Audiences, and the Rise of the Culture Industry in Nineteenth-Century America," *American Historical Review* 92 (1987): 606. Hedge, "An Address Delivered before the Phi Beta Kappa Society in Yale College, New Haven, 20 August 1833, by Edward Everett," *CE* 16 (1834): 17; do dear: JMN 4:372; hail: JMN 4:335; 7:300.

20. "New England": *The Later Lectures of Ralph Waldo Emerson, 1843–1871* (Athens: University of Georgia Press, 2001), ed. Ronald A. Bosco and Joel Myerson, 1:39–56. New drudgery: JMN 1:404; our weird: L 2:99; millions: JMN 5:461; free poor man: JMN 7:136.

21. To William: L 2:218; submit to sell: JMN 7:270; to Fuller: L 2:246; hate myself less: JMN 7:339; thunderbolt: L 2:256; Ripley to Dwight, 9 February 1840, MB Ms.E.4.1; to Carlyle: CEC 255; to William: L 2:272.

22. *Daily Cincinnati Gazette*, 24 May 1850; John J. McAleer, *Ralph Waldo Emerson: Days of Encounter* (Boston: Little, Brown and Co. 1984), 484–493, has collected contemporary reaction to Emerson's lecturing. Eulogy: Myerson,

Transcendentalism: A Reader, 656; a better text than W 10:456–457. On revenue from lecturing, see *Later Lectures*, 1:xix.

23. Least notice: Sarah Wider, "What Did the Minister Mean: Emerson's Sermons and Their Audience," *ESQ* 34 (1988): 1–21. Self-recrimination: JMN 3:312; other references discussed in Roberson, *Emerson in His Sermons*, 150. Why toil: JMN 3:325.

24. Compared: JMN 5:423 and EL 2:274; Charles's commencement address: L 1:239. In his published work, Emerson was quite capable of inserting himself as "I," including during an excursion in the woods ("History," CW 2:11).

25. Approaching the subject: EL 2:341; Alcott Journal 101, 28 January–3 February 1838, in Carlson, "Bronson Alcott's 'Journal for 1838' (Part One)," *SAR*, 1993: 199. Contemporaries: Guy Woodall, "The Journals of Convers Francis," *SAR* 1982: 251–252; Len Gougeon, "Ellis Gray Loring and a Journal for the Times," *SAR* 1990, 42; and George Ripley's criticism in Frothingham, *George Ripley*, 55–56. Modern scholars: Stephen Railton, *Authorship and Audience: Literary Performance in the American Renaissance* (Princeton: Princeton University Press, 1991), 36. Chastised: JMN 5:459.

26. CW 1:81. Railton, *Authorship and Audience*, 23–49, gives a nuanced and creative interpretation of the Divinity School address. But in arguing that Emerson never sought a direct rhetorical confrontation with his audience, he does not treat this explosive passage, the reaction to which Emerson surely was able to predict; see also JMN 7:41–42.

27. More to say: JMN 7:105; Lidian: JMN 7:112; farmer: JMN 7:71; to William: L 2:162, 177.

28. Lay population: JMN 5:477.

29. Preached in 1832: *Complete Sermons*, 4:115; see also 3:38, 43, 47, 59, 205, 206; 4:79, 214. Would not commit: JMN 5:90–91. On abolitionism among Emerson's friends and family at the time, see Phyllis Cole, *Mary Moody Emerson and the Origins of Transcendentalism: A Family History* (New York, Oxford University Press, 1998), 233–238; and idem, "Pain and Protest in the Emerson Family," in Garvey, *The Emerson* Dilemma, 67–92.

30. Milton: EL 1:158.

31. Notebook: JMN 12:151–154, 157–158; potential theme: JMN 12:163, 184; many of the ideas may have come from Channing's 1835 *Slavery*, which Emerson called "one of the perfectly genuine works of the times" (JMN 5:150).

32. Not to praise: EL 2:167–168; domestic labor: EL 2:160–161, an echo of the earlier *Complete Sermons*, 4:241. Three brief references to slavery do not specify American slaves: EL 2:73, 154, 176.

33. Cotton mills: Howe, *Unitarian Conscience*, 284–285, 313; December 8: Leonard L. Richards, *"Gentleman of Property and Standing": Anti-Abolition Mobs in Jacksonian America* (New York: Oxford University Press, 1970), 69; other sources in Woodall, *SAR* 1991: 33, n. 14. A recent analysis of Channing's work is in Alfred L. Brophy, "Reason and Sentiment: The Moral Worlds and Modes of Reasoning of Antebellum Jurists (Review of *Heart versus Head: Judge-Made Law in Nineteenth Century America* by Peter Karsten)," *Boston University Law Review* 79 (1999): 1185–1187.

34. Every third man: JMN 5:505. Date of talk: Eleanor Tilton, "Emerson's Lecture Schedule—1837–1838—Revised," *Harvard Library Bulletin* 21 (1973): 384. Cabot, *Memoir*, 2:425–430. On the belief even within Emerson's circle that the issue was one of free speech, see Francis to Hedge, 10–12 December 1837, in Woodall, *SAR* 1991: 31. Few Transcendentalists at the time were abolitionists: Gohdes, *American Literature* 3 (1931): 26–27.

35. Cabot's portrayal: Garvey, *The Emerson* Dilemma, xvii–xix; Everett attempt: John L. Thomas, *The Liberator: William Lloyd Garrison* (Boston: Little, Brown and Co., 1963), 215.

36. *Complete Sermons*, 3:47.

37. JMN 5:428.

38. JMN 5:437.

39. Lyceum speech: CW 2:155; although this is from "Heroism," which survives only as he later published it in *Essays: First Series*, a journal entry of some weeks prior to the lyceum talk confirms the precise language of the essay, as does Cabot (who got it right this time), JMN 5:437; Cabot, *Memoir*, 2:423. To open our halls: JMN 12:152.

40. Richardson, *Mind on Fire*, 275–279, is good on the details; see also LJE 74; JMN 5:475, 477, 479. Letter: *Emerson's Antislavery Writings*, ed. Len Gougeon and Joel Myerson (New Haven: Yale University Press, 1995), 3; let the republic: JMN 5:479.

41. Friends: Nathaniel Langdon Frothingham to RWE, 5 June 1838, MH bMS Am 1280 (1136): "Let me thank you for your noble & beautiful letter to the president of the United States. I cannot but think it will make a sensation in the country." Theodore Parker to George Ellis, 27 May 1838, Theodore Parker Papers, MHS: "R. W. Emerson has written a letter to the President about the *Cherokees*, a wonderful letter truly." See also, T. Gregory Garvey, "Mediating Citizenship: Emerson, the Cherokee Removals, and the Rhetoric of Nationalism," *Centennial Review* 41 (1997): 461–469. Against me: JMN 7:95.

42. See the important new research by Len Gougeon in *Virtue's Hero: Emerson, Antislavery, and Reform* (Athens: University of Georgia Press, 1990); Gougeon and Myerson, eds., *Emerson's Antislavery Writings*, xxviii–li; and Gougeon, *ESQ* 1999: 259–324. Consider also Amy E. Earhart, "Representative Men, Slave Revolt, and Emerson's 'Conversion' to Abolitionism," *American Transcendental Quarterly* 13 (1999): 287–303. A balanced discussion is by T. Gregory Garvey in *The Emerson* Dilemma, xi–xxviii. On simultaneous changes in Emersonian language toward greater pragmatism, see David M. Robinson, *Emerson and the Conduct of Life: Pragmatism and Ethical Purpose in the Later Work* (Cambridge: Cambridge University Press, 1993), 89–110.

43. Free should the scholar be: AS 140; why need you rail: JMN 7:200.

44. JMN 5:371–372; see generally Poirier, *Renewal of Literature*.

CHAPTER 5
FRIENDS

1. Emerson: JMN 8:31; cf. L 2:444 (to William). Fuller: Julia Ward Howe, *Reminiscences: 1819–1899* (New York: New American Library, 1969), 296. Fran-

cis to Parker, 9 September 1841, Washburn Autograph Collection, MHS, quoted in Woodall, *SAR* 1991: 3. Stetson to Hedge, 28 October 1841, Schlesinger Library, Poor Family Collection, box 5, folder 78. Francis to Hedge, 25 October 1841, in Woodall, *SAR* 1991: 42.

2. Frederic Henry Hedge, "Conservatism and Reform," in *Martin Luther and Other Essays* (Boston: Roberts Brothers, 1888), pp. 134, 145, and 157.

3. On a new reading of "Fate," see Lawrence Buell, "Emerson's Fate," in Mott and Burkholder, *Emersonian Circles*, 11–28. Alexander H. Everett to George Bancroft, 11 January 1842, George Bancroft Papers, MHS. Having recorded in his journal at least brief details of dozens of previous speeches, this time John Pierce noted only, "Oration by Rev. Frederic Henry Hedge, of Bangor, 1 hour & 20 minutes, On Conservation & Reform" (Memoirs, vol. 9, p. 220, 25 August 1841, MHS). In writing a diary clearly intended for posterity ("our clerical Pepys," Oliver Wendell Holmes called him [*Emerson*, 12]), this conservative Unitarian minister may have thought it best to keep his own counsel. He was, after all, Henry Hedge's father-in-law. On the society's polarization: see chapter 7.

4. Rejected oration: L 3:84.

5. Earlier concerns that Hedge not happy: Parker Journal, vol. 1, pp. 13, 144, and 422, bMS 101/1, Andover-Harvard Theological Library, Harvard Divinity School. See also Elizabeth Palmer Peabody to John Sullivan Dwight, 20 September 1840, in *Letters of Elizabeth Palmer Peabody*, 245–247. Hedge to Francis, 26 January 1842, Washburn Autograph Collection, MHS.

6. Packer, *CHAL*, 2:495; Miller, *Transcendentalists*, 472.

7. 1836: Packer, *CHAL*, 2:391; Miller, *Transcendentalists*, 67. The likes of: JMN 5:195. Brownson: Dall, *Transcendentalism in New England*, 16. Caleb Stetson to Henry Hedge, 9 November 1836, Schlesinger Library, Poor Family Collection, box 5, folder 78: "I have just read Furness' book, and . . . it afforded me new & fresh delight." Also George Ripley to James Freeman Clarke, 16 January 1837, Perry-Clarke Collection, MHS. On the debate: Hutchinson, *Transcendentalist Ministers*, 55–57; and Joel Myerson, ed., *The Transcendentalists: A Review of Research and Criticism* (New York: Modern Language Association of America, 1984), 51–52. On Furness's consideration for the club: Hedge to Emerson, 14 June 1836, bMS 183, Andover-Harvard Theological Library, Harvard Divinity School. Henry Hedge on the club in Cabot, *Memoir*, 1:245–246; see also Hutchinson, *Transcendentalist Ministers*, 22–30.

8. Letters discussed in Joel Myerson, "Frederic Henry Hedge and the Failure of Transcendentalism," *Harvard Library Bulletin* 23 (1975): 404; Doreen Hunter, "Frederic Henry Hedge: What Say You?" *American Quarterly* 32 (1980): 196–198.

9. L 2:270–71. Fuller closer to Emerson: Fuller to Caroline Sturgis, 7 October 1839, including Emerson but not Hedge in her most intimate circle of friends (*Letters of Margaret Fuller*, 2:93).

10. Hedge to Emerson: LJE 58; Hedge to Emerson, 4 September 1837, bMS 183/1 (8), Andover-Harvard Theological Library, Harvard Divinity School. Emerson to Hedge: L 2:121. Uncharacteristic harshness: Hunter, *American Quarterly* 1980: 199; Woodall, *SAR* 1991: 3; also the important and first article on the subject, Myerson, *Harvard Library Bulletin*, 1975: 396–410.

11. Exhilarated: L 1:402; Hedge, "Everett's Phi Beta Kappa Oration" *CE* 16 (1834): 1–21; old & new: JMN 5:111; dots: 10–12 December 1837, in Woodall, *SAR* 1991: 30; also Alfred G. Litton, "The Development of the Mind and the Role of the Scholar in the Early Works of Frederic Henry Hedge," *SAR* 1989: 95–114.

12. Absolute laws: JMN 7:200; cf. 400; genius: JMN 7:236. Emerson and Hedge had been at that question earlier: JMN 5:338.

13. "Two Articles from the Princeton Review," *Boston Quarterly Review* 3 (1840): 270 (also in Miller, *Transcendentalists*, 242).

14. "Historic Notes on Life and Letters in New England," W 10:342; see also JMN 11:294.

15. Wanton experiment: see, for example, the anonymous review of "A Letter to William E. Channing, D.D. on the Subject of Religious Liberty, by Moses Stuart, Professor of Sacred Literature in the Theological Seminar, Andover," *CE* 10 (1831): 87–128. Retaliation: for example, "Calvinistic Ethics," in *CE* 19 (1835): 1–40. Gilman, "Unitarian Christianity Free from Objectional Extremes," *CE* 8 (1830): 133.

16. Black eyes: Hutchinson, *Transcendentalist Ministers*, 39; father: Charles Crowe, *George Ripley: Transcendentalist and Utopian Socialist* (Athens: University of Georgia Press, 1967), 25.

17. Bulwark: Joseph Allen to Henry Ware, Jr., 7 January 1821, Allen-Ware Family Papers, MHS. Spreading the gospel: Hutchinson, *Transcendentalist Ministers*, 16–17. On Walker: Alfred Guy Litton, "'Speaking the Truth with Love': A History of the *Christian Examiner* and Its Relation to New England Transcendentalism" (Ph.D. diss., University of South Carolina, 1993), 29–100.

18. "Degerando on Self-education and Development," *CE* 9 (1830), quotations from pp. 73, 104, and 79, respectively.

19. By 1826, Emerson had intuited the intellectual currents, without associating them with Coleridge: L 1:174. See also Cabot, *Memoir*, 1:139, where Emerson rebuffs Hedge's willingness in 1828 to introduce him to German literature. In December, 1829, Emerson admitted struggling with Coleridge: L 7:189. Emerson's letter to brother Edward, 31 May 1834, is the first evidence of his full embrace of Kantian and Coleridgean epistemology (L 1:412–413). Dewey, *Oration Delivered at Cambridge before the Society of Phi Beta Kappa: August 26, 1830* (Boston: Gray and Bowen, 1830), 17; cf. 23–24.

20. *CE* 11 (1832): 375 (also in Miller, *Transcendentalists*, 61).

21. Martineau, *Society in America* (London: Saunders and Otley, 1837), 3:211; Hedge, "Coleridge's Literary Character," *CE* 14 (1833): 119 (also in Miller, *Transcendentalists*, 69); on the attack on Locke, see Alfred Guy Litton, "'Speaking the Truth with Love,'" 48–50.

22. Duel: Manfred Kuehn, *Kant: A Biography* (Cambridge: Cambridge University Press, 2001), 319.

23. Open question: Doreen Hunter, *American Quarterly* 1980: 189–190; unfolding man: L 1:402; tenets from Kant: W 1:339–340.

24. Orestes A. Bronson, "Benjamin Constant," *CE* 17 (1834): 70 (also in Miller, *Transcendentalists*, 86); "Cousin's *Philosophy*," *CE* 21 (1836): 34–35 (also in Miller, *Transcendentalists*, 108).

25. Sprague, *Annals of the American Pulpit*, 8:433.

26. O. B. Frothingham, *Theodore Parker: A Biography* (Boston: J. R. Osgood, 1874), 78–79.

27. "Martineau's Rationale of Religious Enquiry," *CE* 21 (1836): 226–254 (also in Miller, *Transcendentalists*, 129–132). The best studies of the extraordinary subsequent events are: Hutchinson, *Transcendentalist Ministers*, 52–97; Howe, *Unitarian Conscience*, 82–92; and Packer, *CHAL*, 2:331–349. Miller, *Transcendentalists*, 130.

28. As early as 1827, Andrews Norton viewed theological liberalism as more threatening than Congregationalist orthodoxy; see Clark, "Andrews Norton: A Conservative Unitarian," 57–58. Ripley, *Boston Daily Advertiser*, 5 and 9 November 1836, vol. 42, nos. 13933 and 13936. Ripley's letter to his mother: Frothingham, *Ripley*, 13.

29. George Edward Ellis to Theodore Parker: 11 November 1836, MH autograph file. The initial inquiry from Parker is found in F. B. Sanborn and William T. Harris, *A. Bronson Alcott: His Life and Philosophy* (Boston: Roberts Brothers, 1893), 1:278. Ellis was far from a sympathizer: Samuel Osgood to James Freeman Clarke: 18 March 1840, Perry-Clarke Collection, MHS. Elizabeth Palmer Peabody to Mary Peabody, 23 November 1836, published in *Letters of Elizabeth Palmer Peabody*, 183–184. Samuel Osgood to James Freeman Clarke, 20 July 1837, Perry-Clarke Collection, MHS, discussed below.

30. Looking to Ripley: for example, Woodall, *SAR* 1991: 21–29; and Ripley to Clarke, 16 January 1837, Perry-Clarke Collection, MHS. Parker: Frothingham, *George Ripley*, 55–56.

31. Attempting in vain: Convers Francis to Frederic Henry Hedge, 14 November 1836, MeBaHi, in Woodall, *SAR* 1991: 22; Peabody to Mary Peabody: 23 November 1836, published in *Letters of Elizabeth Palmer Peabody*, 185–186; earlier attempts: Rose, *Transcendentalism as a Social Movement*, 53–55; William Ellery Channing to Norton, 25 March 1835, MH Norton Collection bMS Am 1089, box 5. Undermining: Brazer to Norton, 7 November, 1836, MH Norton Collection, MS Am 1089 box 4; Habich, *NEQ* 1992: 217–219; Buell, *Literary Transcendentalism*, 39; Merle Curti in *Dictionary of American Biography*, 2:612–613; Bruce A. Ronda, *Elizabeth Palmer Peabody: A Reformer on Her Own Terms* (Cambridge: Harvard University Press, 1999), 151–152. Made public: Peabody to Mary Peabody: 23 November 1836, published in *Letters of Elizabeth Palmer Peabody*, 187. Ruin: Norton to William Ware, 26 February 1840, Norton materials, MH bMS AM 1089 box 3. Philippic: Samuel Osgood to James Freeman Clarke, 8 October 1838, Perry-Clarke Collection, MHS. Brownson quotation: "Norton and the Transcendentalists," *Boston Quarterly Review* 3 (1840): 269 (also in Miller, *Transcendentalists*, 241); also Convers Francis wrote Henry Hedge about "their whole *clique* in Boston & Cambridge" (Francis to Hedge, 10 August 1838, MeBaHi, in Woodall, *SAR* 1991: 1–57). Dinner table: James W. Mathews, "Fallen Angel: Emerson and the Apostasy of Edward Everett," *SAR* 1990: 27–28, and David Tyack, *George Ticknor*, 151–152.

32. "Transcendentalism," *CE* 21 (1837): 371–385. Bowen later reacted harshly to "The American Scholar" in "Locke and Transcendentalism," *CE* 21 (1837): 170–194, and carried on the fight in *Critical Essays on a Few Subjects Connected with the History and Present Condition of Speculative Philosophy*

(Boston: H. B. Williams, 1842). On Bowen's relationship with Norton: Turner, *Charles Eliot Norton*, 35.

33. Greeted warmly: A. L., in *CE* 22 (1837): 321–343; E.N.T in *Christian Register and Boston Observer*, vol. 16, 15 April 1837, p. 58; *Salem Gazette*, vol. 51, 31 March 1837, p. 2. The best analysis of Norton's work remains Allen R. Clark, "Andrews Norton: A Conservative Unitarian," 61–62. Definitive: Turner, *Charles Eliot Norton*, 419, n. 41. Furness to Norton, 24 April 1837, MH Norton Collection, bMS Am 1089, box 6; Story to Norton, 28 December 1843, MH Norton Collection, bMS Am 1089, box 9, addressing specifically vols. 2 and 3, but referring as well to vol. 1. Stuart to Norton, 12 February 1838, MH Autograph File.

34. Brownson, *Boston Quarterly Review* 1839, 86–113. Frothingham to Norton, 10 and 13 April 1837, MH bMS Am 1089, box 6. Drafts of replies from Norton to Frothingham: MH bMS Am 1089, box 1 (the first dated 11 April 1837, the second undated). Alcott Journal 196, 19–25 March 1837 (in Carlson, *SAR* 1981: 90); cf. Miller, *Transcendentalists*, 152. Mary Moody Emerson writing in her Almanack at Concord also criticized Norton for his excessive intellectualism (George Tolman transcription, MH bMS Am 1280.235 (579), folder 22, 8 February 1836).

35. CEC 164, 126–127; L 2:81; George Ripley to John Sullivan Dwight, 6 August 1840, MB MS. E. 4.1 no. 27; Alexander H. Everett to George Bancroft, 11 January 1842, George Bancroft Papers, MHS.

36. Stetson to Hedge, 19 November 1839, Schlesinger Library, Poor Family Collection, box 5, folder 78; cf. letter of 28 February 1840. Francis to Parker, 26 December 1839, Theodore Parker Papers, MHS. Frothingham, *George Ripley*, 94–107, is still most informative on Ripley's prominence. Holmes, *Emerson*, 116. For Emerson's hesitations, see also CEC 185; Martineau, *Retrospect of Western Travel*, 2:106–197; LJE 78.

37. Emerson to Clarke: L 7:229–230; bully: JMN 2:57; Clarke to Emerson: L 1:425–426.

38. Reasoning weak: JMN 2:238. His control of German higher criticism was equally fragile: see Barbara Packer, "Origin and Authority: Emerson and the Higher Criticism," *Reconstructing American Literature*, ed. Sacvan Bercovitch (Cambridge: Harvard University Press, 1986), 67–92. Mr. Bowie: Hedge to Emerson, 10 June 1835, bMS 183/1 (4), Andover-Harvard Theological Library, Harvard Divinity School. Emerson's work is listed in Joel Myerson, ed., *Ralph Waldo Emerson: A Descriptive Bibliography* (Pittsburgh: University of Pittsburgh Press, 1982), 7 and 661; they include especially *A Historical Discourse, Delivered before the Citizens of Concord, 12th September, 1835* (Boston: I. R. Butts, 1835), and "Michael Angelo," *North American Review* 44 (January, 1837): 1–16. He also contracted for an essay on Milton, but it did not appear in the *North American Review* until July, 1838. *Nature* a poem: Convers Francis to Henry Hedge, 14 November 1836, in Woodall, *SAR* 1991: 23.

39. Starting a journal: L 1:358, 402; Hedge and Ripley: Hedge to Fuller, 20 February 1835, bMS 384/1 (17), Andover-Harvard Theological Library, Harvard Divinity School (see also CEC 119); Carlyle as editor: CEC 125; interesting Emerson in German literature: Cabot, *Memoir*, 1:139; in December, 1834, Hedge instructed Emerson on Schleiermacher (JMN 4:360).

40. Interesting Emerson in Carlyle: Rusk, *Life of Emerson*, 129–130; Carlyle's influence: Dickens, *American Notes* (New York: St. Martin's Press, 1995), 51; *Sartor*: Leon Jackson, "The Social Construction of Thomas Carlyle's New England Reputation, 1834–1836," *Proceedings of the American Antiquarian Society* 106 (1996): 165–189; stronger market: Thomas Carlyle, *Sartor Resartus: The Life and Opinions of Herr Teufelsdröckh in Three Books*, ed. Rodger L. Tarr (Berkeley: University of California Press, 2000), xxxi–xxxiv, lxxx–xciv; accountant: CEC 238; CEC 16–29 for details of Emerson's support of Carlyle's publications.

41. Bible of the movement: Thomas Carlyle, *Sartor Resartus*, ed. Rodger L. Tarr, lxxx. Ripley: Clarke to Channing, 13 October 1835, MH Am 1569 (290); Ripley to Emerson, June 1835, MH bMS Am 1280 (2716); L 1:432–433; Joseph Slater, "George Ripley and Thomas Carlyle," *PMLA* 67 (1952): 341–349. Ripley to Emerson, 5 October 1835, MH bMS Am 1280 (2717); and Ripley to Carlyle, 29 December 1836, MH autograph collection. Longfellow, Bancroft, Channing: CEC 119, 137–138; M. A. DeWolfe Howe, *The Life and Letters of George Bancroft* (New York: Charles Scribner's Sons, 1908), 1:222–227; CEC 119. Tremble: CEC 139–140. *First Essays*: Cayton, *American Historical Review* 1987: 602.

42. Modern criticism is summarized by Evelyn Barish, *Emerson: The Roots of Prophecy* (Princeton: Princeton University Press, 1989), 252–253. Still one of the best appreciations of Emerson's prose is Oscar W. Firkins, *Ralph Waldo Emerson* (Boston: Houghton Mifflin, 1915), 227–273.

43. Letter to Lidian: L 1:435. Longfellow Journal, 8 March 1838, MH Ms Am 1340 (194). Similarly, John Ware to John Gorham Palfrey, 14 January 1838, MH bMS Am 1704 (949).

44. Mary T. Peabody to Horace Mann, 27 March 1837, Horace Mann Papers, MHS. Parker: "Emerson," in *The Works of Theodore Parker*, ed. George Willis Cooke (Boston: American Unitarian Association, 1907), 8:104, and Julia Ward Howe, *Reminiscences: 1819–1899*, 291. Slippery: Woodall, *SAR* 1982: 247–248, on 16 February 1837. Dots and atoms: 10–12 December 1837, published in Woodall, *SAR* 1991: 30. See also Francis's journal entry for 6 December 1837 in Woodall, *SAR* 1982: 249–250; Parker to Francis, 6 December 1839, MB MS.C.1.6. Channing, *Boston Quarterly Review* 1838: 109; Brownson, "American Literature," *Boston Quarterly Review* 2 (1839): 4. Hedge, "Writings of R. W. Emerson," *CE* 38 (1845), 100; Ripley: Frothingham, *George Ripley*, 266–267.

45. Osgood to Clarke, 4 September 1838, Perry-Clarke Collection, MHS; see also 8 October 1838, Perry-Clarke Collection, MHS; Bartol to Ellis, 1 October 1838, George Ellis Papers, MHS; Francis to Parker, 28 January 1840, Theodore Parker Papers, MHS.

46. Parker to Francis: 6 December 1839, MB MS.C.1.6; Francis to Parker, 26 December 1839, Theodore Parker Papers, MHS; Francis to Parker, 18 January 1839, Theodore Parker Papers, MHS. Similarly, Sophia Ripley to John Sullivan Dwight, 9 February 1840, MB Ms.E.4.1. Heretic: L 7:323.

47. Peabody to Sophia Peabody: 23 June 1839, published in *Letters of Elizabeth Palmer Peabody*, 226; C. C. Felton, "Emerson's Essays," *CE* 30 (1841): 253. See also Francis to Hedge, 12 November 1838, in Woodall, *SAR* 1991: 27.

48. Praise and criticism: for example, Townsend Scudder, "Emerson's British Lecture Tour, 1847–1848," *American Literature* 7 (1935): 166–180.

49. Stanley Cavell, *In Quest of the Ordinary: Lines of Skepticism and Romanticism* (Chicago: University of Chicago Press, 1988), 3–49; idem, *This New Yet Unapproachable America: Lectures after Emerson, after Wittgenstein* (Albuquerque: Living Batch Press, 1989), 77–118; idem, *Conditions Handsome and Unhandsome*, 33–63. On Emerson's strategies, see Packer, *Emerson's Fall*, 1–21; Poirier, *The Renewal of Literature*, 192–202; and idem, *Poetry and Pragmatism* (Cambridge: Harvard University Press, 1992), 134–136; Joan Richardson, "Emerson's Sound Effects," *Raritan* 16 (1997): 83–101. Philosopher of democracy: Richard Rorty, "Education without Dogma: Truth, Freedom, and Our Universities," *Dissent* 36 (1989): 198–204.

50. JMN 7:402.

51. Public speaking: Edward Waldo Emerson, *Emerson's Concord*, 15–16; professorship: Emerson also admitted that he had waited all his life for an offer to teach at Harvard—again, in rhetoric (Cabot, *Memoir*, 1:72)—and thought rhetorical training was neglected there (Sanborn, *Personality of Emerson*, 38). Everything admissible: JMN 7:265, 7:402; echoed in *Later Lectures*, 1:48.

52. Newspapers: JMN 2:95, 278–279; 3:26, 277; 4:222; 5:284; EL 2:68; Ralph Waldo Emerson, "New Poetry," in *Essays and Lectures*, ed. Joel Porte (New York: Library of America, 1983), 1169. Martineau, *Society in America*, 3:265; two dozen lectures: Turner, *Charles Eliot Norton*, 38; fretted about attendance: L 2:9, 171; fifty-minute format: JMN 5:286.

53. AS 139.

54. George P. Lathrop, "Literary and Social Boston," *Harper's New Monthly Magazine* 62 (February, 1881), 383.

55. Quoted by Packer, *CHAL*, 2:381.

56. Extend New School: Ripley to Brownson, 15 January 1833, University of Notre Dame Archives, microfilm edition (1966), reel 1, ed. Thomas T. McAvoy and Lawrence J. Bradley. Finer piece: Ripley to Clarke, 15 March 1837, MH 1569.7 (560); Ripley to Dwight, 7 July 1840, MB MS. E. 4.1, no. 24. Within reach: Brownson to Bancroft, 25 September 1836, George Bancroft Papers, MHS; Brownson, "Norton and the Transcendentalists," *Boston Quarterly Review* 3 (1840): 279–280 (also in Miller, *Transcendentalists*, 246). Qualified support: "Alcott on Human Culture," *Boston Quarterly Review* 1 (1838): 431; "Mr. Emerson's *Address*," *Boston Quarterly Review* 1 (1838): 513. Ripley, "Letter to the Church in Purchase Street," in Miller, *Transcendentalists*, 256.

57. Criticizing Emerson: Crowe, *George Ripley*, 77. Criticizing *Dial*: Ripley to Dwight, 7 July 1840, MB MS. E. 4.1, no. 24; cf. Ripley to Dwight, 6 August 1840, MB MS. E. 4.1, no. 27. Never comfortable: Joel Myerson, *The New England Transcendentalists and the Dial: A History of the Magazine and Its Contributors* (Rutherford, N.J.: Fairleigh Dickinson University Press, 1980), 200–201.

58. Russell B. Nye, *George Bancroft* (New York: Washington Square Press, 1964), 149–150.

59. Good friends: Thomas R. Ryan, *Orestes A. Brownson, a Definitive Biography* (Huntington, Ind.: Our Sunday Visitor, 1976), 110–123. Monster spirit: Bancroft to Brownson, 9 July 1837, in University of Notre Dame Archives, microfilm edition (1966), reel 1, ed. Thomas T. McAvoy and Lawrence J. Bradley. Cf. Samuel Osgood to James Freeman Clarke, 20 July 1837, Perry-Clarke Collection, MHS.

Brownson on Ripley: Brownson to Bancroft, 10 November 1837, Cornell University, George Bancroft Papers from the Collection of Regional History and University Archives in the University of Notre Dame Archives microfilm, reel 9.

60. Ripley to Bancroft, 20 September 1837, George Bancroft Papers, MHS; Ripley to Bancroft, 6 November 1837, George Bancroft Papers, MHS. Ripley complimented Bancroft for a "lucid and satisfactory exposition of the causes of our present embarrassments. . . . Your appeal to the R [torn page] of the University is noble; your description of the abode of democracy at the heart of the country is a gem of pathos & melody. . . . [torn page] our conservative circles, which with his Reverence, the Dean of the Cambridge School at their head, lord it a little too despotically over our American Literature." Bancroft's address is noted, but not detailed, in the *Worcester Republican*, 27 September 1837, vol. 9, no. 39.

61. Not as intimate: Lillian Handlin, *George Bancroft: The Intellectual as Democrat* (New York: Harper & Row, 1984), 155–157. Bancroft: "On the Progress of Civilization," *Boston Quarterly Review* 1 (1838): 397, 404 (in Miller, *Transcendentalists*, 426, 428). Brownson: "Emerson," *Boston Quarterly Review* 2 (1839): 20, 26 (in Miller, *Transcendentalists*, 432–434).

62. Cayton, *Emerson's Emergence*, 51 n. 37, for bibliography; and Rusk, *Life of Emerson*, 258–260, for the Democratic Party. Also, Railton, *Authorship and Audience*, 23–49. John Jay Chapman, *Selected Writings* (New York: Farrar, Straus and Cudahy, 1957), 223. On whether Emerson's brand of Transcendentalism was naturally accommodating to social reform, see Robert Milder, "The Radical Emerson?" in *The Cambridge Guide to Ralph Waldo Emerson*, ed. Joel Porte and Saundra Morris (Cambridge: Cambridge University Press, 1999), 49–75; Gougeon, *ESQ* 1999: 259–324; and Strysick in *The Emerson* Dilemma, 139–168. Readily established: see, for example, Packer, *CHAL*, 2:399.

63. Alcott Journal 53–56 and 69–72, 7–13 January 1838 (in Carlson, *SAR* 1993: 188–189 and 192–193). Alcott is more conciliatory toward all Transcendentalists and especially Ripley in entry 255, 14–20 October 1838, (in Carlson, "Bronson Alcott's 'Journal for 1838' [Part Two]," *SAR*, 1994: 147). For a good example of how his friends misunderstood Emerson's political views: compare Parker to Francis, 6 December 1839, MB Ms.C.1.6, with Francis to Parker, 26 December 1839, Theodore Parker Papers, MHS.

64. Faint praise: Bartol to Ellis, 1 October 1838, George Ellis Papers, MHS. Clarke and Cranch, "R.W. Emerson and the New School," *Western Messenger* 6 (1838): 47 (in Miller, *Transcendentalists*, 203–204). See also Ripley to Clarke, 15 March 1837, MH 1569.7 (560).

65. Samuel Osgood to James Freeman Clarke, 28 February 1838, Perry-Clarke Collection, MHS; Parker to Ellis, 3 January 1839, Theodore Parker Papers, MHS.

66. Channing object of concern: Gohdes, *American Literature* 3 (1931): 17. Summary of modern opinion on Channing by David Robinson in *Transcendentalists: A Review of Research and Criticism*, 310–316.

67. Club attendance: Parker to John Sullivan Dwight, 10 January 1839, MB MS.E. 4.1, no. 16; David P. Edgell, *William Ellery Channing: An Intellectual Portrait* (Boston: Beacon Press, 1955), 143. Horace Mann Journal, 15 December 1837: Horace Mann Papers, MHS, provides important details about the club's formation. Child of Channing: Frothingham, *George Ripley*, 51; Parker drawn to

Channing: Edgell, *William Ellery Channing*, 143–149; Ripley's criticism: Frothingham, *George Ripley*, 55–56; oysters: W 10:340–341.

68. Undated letter, Norton to William Ware, probably 1839 or 1840, Norton materials, MH bMS AM 1089, box 3; Norton to Channing, 11 April 1840, published by David Palmer Edgell, "A Note on Channing's Transcendentalism," *NEQ* 22 (1949): 394–397. Norton to Palfrey, 22 April 1840, MH bMS Am 1704 (637), letter 58 in packet no. 6.

69. Channing abandoning Alcott: see chapter 6; repair relations: L 2:62; amputate: JMN 5:329; slavery: JMN 5:90, 150; Channing lobbied for reform: Ticknor to Bowditch, 24 February 1834, MB Ms.E.210.19 v.2 (105–106); oracle: JMN 5:333–334.

70. Distinguished ability: JMN 7:330; ideal university: JMN 7:198.

71. *CE* 1831: 160.

72. Ministry and law noted by Lawrence Buell, *Literary Transcendentalism*, 49–50; Story, *Forging of an Aristocracy*, 95. Motto: McCaughey, *Josiah Quincy*, 187.

Chapter 6
Alcott

1. Alcott JMN: 16:66; 5:409.

2. Parker Journal, vol. 1, p. 75, bMS 101/1, Andover-Harvard Theological Library, Harvard Divinity School; the undated entry is from late fall, 1838. William Emerson to RWE: "Susan & I are glad that your orphic protégé is putting the ocean between him & you, & hope he will learn a little practical wisdom before he comes back" (13 May 1842, Emerson Family Papers, MHS). Elizabeth Maxfield-Miller, "Elizabeth of Concord: Selected Letters of Elizabeth Sherman Hoar (1814–1878) to the Emersons, Family, and the Emerson Circle (Part Three)," *SAR* 1986: 134. See also Stetson to Hedge, 17 August 1840, Schlesinger Library, Poor Family Collection, box 5, folder 78. Emerson's defense of genius over talent (JMN 7:236) may be a defense of Alcott: Hedge to Cabot, in Cabot, *Memoir*, 1:281. Carlyle letter: CEC 337–338; see also 326, 329–330, 331, 333.

3. Emerson to Fuller: L 2:294; *Dial* 1 (1840): 85 (in Miller, *Transcendentalists*, 303). The contemporary judgment is part of a letter to the editor of the *Boston Post*, 1 January 1842; see Joel Myerson, "'In the Transcendental Emporium': Bronson Alcott's 'Orphic Sayings' in the *Dial*," *English Language Notes* 19 (1972): 31–38. Not named Alcott: Dall, *Transcendentalism in New England*, 22. Plato: "Historic Notes on Life and Letters in New England," W 10:341; hoping to outlive: Sanborn, *Personality of Emerson*, 73.

4. George William Curtis to James Elliot Cabot, MH AM 1280.235 (711), box 79.

5. Most liberal: John Pierce, Memoirs, vol. 1, p. 334, MHS.

6. Point telescope: William Emerson to Waldo, 1 February 1850, MH bMS Am 1280.226 (3041). William included Quincy's letter in his own missive to Waldo. Waldo to William: L 4:178–179; Porte, *Representative Man*, 168; see also Poirier, *Renewal of Literature*, 143–145.

7. JMN 4:141; CW (*Nature*) 1:45 (also JMN 5:182–183; JMN 7:270–271).

8. Symbol-hunter: Porte, *Representative Man*, 8.

9. Cole, *Mary Moody Emerson*, 10–11, 139; JMN 16:66; relying on Mary for information about his great-grandfather, Joseph Emerson of Malden: JMN 5:323; and likely for his earlier interest in family genealogy: JMN 3:351–353.

10. Henry James, "Emerson," in Brian M. Barbour, *American Transcendentalism: An Anthology of Criticism* (Notre Dame: University of Notre Dame Press, 1973), 264. With more sympathy: David R. Williams, "The Wilderness Rapture of Mary Moody Emerson: One Calvinist Link to Transcendentalism," *SAR* 1986: 1–16; Cole, *Mary Moody Emerson*; and Packer, *CHAL*, 2:365–368. Funeral shroud: for example, JMN 1:61, 199; Poirier, *Poetry and Pragmatism*, 207, n. 10. See also Evelyn Barish, "Emerson and 'The Magician': An Early Prose Fantasy," *American Transcendental Quarterly* 31 (1976): 13–18. Positive genius: quoted by George Tolman, "Life of Mary Moody Emerson" (1902), MH bMS Am 1280.235 (720), 2 of 2 (the typescript version), 46—unattributed, but Tolman knew Mary and other Emersons personally.

11. Mary loved William: MME 36, 148, 221; on their religious differences, see Cole, *Mary Moody Emerson*, 123–125. Mary to Waldo: MME 189. The reference does not appear in the extant speech, transcribed two years later: Emerson Family Papers, MHS. Perhaps Edward made the remark extemporaneously.

12. MME 221; cf. MME 20. William's ambition was also noticed by friend and colleague John Pierce (Memoirs, vol. 1, pp. 329–334; vol. 8, pp. 435–426, MHS).

13. MME 199, 213, 229–230.

14. MH bMS Am 1280.226 (879); cf. MME 194, with slight modification.

15. Parrisidical: MME 313–315; see discussion in Cole, *Mary Moody Emerson*, 214–219. Far sadder: MME 331; Concord fight: MME 428–431. Among the dead: Almanack (21f.); cf. Cole, *Mary Moody Emerson*, 249, and her fierce judgments in Rusk, *Life of Emerson*, 283–284. Letter to Hoar: MME 426–427; Cole, *Mary Moody Emerson*, 257–258. Friends shared her concern: Sarah Alden Bradford Ripley to Mary Moody Emerson, 4 September 1833, Sarah Alden Bradford Ripley Papers, Schlesinger Library, MC 180 folder 29.

16. Asking forgiveness: MME 367–369; ingenious lecture: George Tolman transcription of MME's Almanack, MH bMS Am 1280.235 (579), folder 18, 24 May 1842. Emerson's admiration: see especially JMN 8:391; also, for example, JMN 4:275, 300, 371; 5:102, 244, 409–410, 446, 8:178; 10:385; the *Journals* are also full of wise observations by his aunt. Emerson to Mary in 1841: L 2:396–98. Mary to Hoar: Maxfield-Miller, *SAR* 1986: 163.

17. Today 16 years: George Tolman transcription, MH bMS Am 1280.235 (579), folder 6, 12 May 1827; that Waldo read it: Cole, *Mary Moody Emerson* 201–207. Different roads: Emerson's MME journals, bMS 1280 H (146–149), vol. 2, p. 226; other anniversaries: George Tolman transcription, MH bMS Am 1280.235 (579), folder 12, for 1831, and folder 16, for 1839. She also wrote a remarkable letter to her sister-in-law in 1813, on the second anniversary of William's death (MME 73–75).

18. 1804 letter: Emerson's MME journals March, 1804, bMS 1280 H (146–149), vol. 1, p. 49. This letter has apparently escaped notice, as it is not listed in

Nancy Craig Simmons, "A Calendar of the Letters of Mary Moody Emerson," *SAR*, 1993: 1–41. 1821 letter: MH bMS 1280 H (146–149), vol. 1, pp. 88–90.

19. Have mercy: George Tolman transcription of the Almanack (4 January 1811), MH bMS Am 1280.235 (579), folder 4. Family destitute: Rusk, *Life of Emerson*, 54–62; if parents rich: JMN 4:263. Ezra Ripley: Cole, *Mary Moody Emerson*, 92, 120–122; memories painful: JMN 5:456.

20. Fair pictures: AS 137; see also JMN 4:309–310, 318; 5:428; 7:170; EL 2:254; CW 2:198. Letter to Howitt: L 3:417–418; father's sermons: JMN 2:272, 396; 16:325; controversial statement: "Experience," CW 4:29. Just after the death of young Waldo, he wrote Caroline Sturgis: "Alas! I chiefly grieve that I cannot grieve; that this fact takes no more deep hold than other facts, is as dream-like as they, a lambent flame that will not burn playing on the surface of my river. Must every experience—those that promised to be dearest & most penetrative,—only kiss my cheek like the wind & pass away?" (L 3:9–10).

21. Stories about his father: JMN 5:30; Edward Waldo Emerson, *Emerson's Concord*, 7; Ellen Tucker Emerson, "What I Can Remember about Father," MH. Reminders: for example, his father was friends with Webster (Webster to Edward Emerson, 5 December 1824, MH: bMS Am 1280.226 [4170]), and with Josiah Quincy (Quincy to William Emerson, 26 January 1807 and 17 June 1810, MH bMS Am 1280.226 [3945] and [3946]). Dined with Adams: JMN 3:279; election: L 2:357–358; Adams, diary entry for 2 August 1840, in *Memoirs of John Quincy Adams, Comprising Portions of His Diary from 1795 to 1848*, ed. Charles Francis Adams (Philadelphia: J. B. Lippincott & Co.,1876) 10:345.

22. Emerson's denial of his father became part of the public record. He did not contribute to (and so William received almost no notice in) Josiah Quincy's *History of the Boston Athenaeum with Biographical Notices of Its Deceased Founders* (Cambridge: Metcalf and Co., 1851), and, because Waldo again refused to participate, William does not even appear in William Ware's *American Unitarian Biography*. To William B. Sprague's *Annals of the American Pulpit* (published in 1865, but the material was solicited in 1849) Emerson contributed only a paragraph attacking Unitarianism (Sprague, *Annals*, 8:244–245, L 8:225–226).

Waldo's inquiries about his father began soon after; see MME 519–521, for Lidian's intervention, and MME to Elizabeth Hoar, 4 and 6 August, 1850, MH Am 1280.226 (1197): "Yet this sad sudden wrench of them & those papers. . . ." About then and for the first time in his life, Waldo made an honest assessment of his aunt (JMN 11:259), and a few weeks later sent her a (now lost) letter, asking about his father. Mary was so agitated that she couldn't sleep and, in replying the next day, added to the address "*Only* for Mr Emerson to open" and offered some loving insights about her late brother (MME 522–524). A second letter from Mary contains the same plea for confidentiality and acknowledges that he had pressed her further (MME 526–527). A third letter, although undated, is clearly also a response to a prior inquiry—"I resolve to send as you will expect"—and probably part of the 1850 correspondence (MME 402–403). On the folded address part of the letter, there is written "*Only* and *alone* to RWE." Similar warnings in the published edition of her correspondence occur only beginning with the two 1850 letters to Waldo about his father, and then thereafter (MME 528–530, 582, 586–

587). And the rich, deep blue paper is the same as Mary used for most of her 1850 correspondence.

Rejection of the father: Porte, *Representative Man*, 112–118; see also David Robinson, "The Road Not Taken: From Edwards, through Chauncy, to Emerson," *Arizona Quarterly* 48 (1992): 45–61. William Emerson, "An Oration, Delivered September 5th 1789 in the Chapel of Harvard College, at the Request of the PBK Society," Harvard University Archives, HUD 3684.775, box VT, pp. 40–48. Successfully: John Pierce, Memoirs vol. 1, p. 329, MHS; cf. John Pierce, in Sprague, *Annals*, 8:241.

23. Disenchantment: see also Ronald A. Bosco, "'Blessed Are They Who Have no Talent': Emerson's Unwritten Life of Amos Bronson Alcott," *ESQ* 26 (1990): 1–36.

24. Arthur M. Schlesinger, Jr., *The Age of Jackson* (Boston: Little, Brown and Co., 1945), 385–386. See Leonard Neufeldt, *The House of Emerson* (Lincoln: University of Nebraska Press, 1982), 104–107, for documentation on Emerson's views of Webster. Early oracle: JMN 5:181; representative of Transcendentalism: JMN 2:70; father greater: JMN 4:44; linked to giants: JMN 3:360; 5:54, 5:60; enemy of genius: AS 135; also, for example, JMN 5:197, 210–211. See Sampson Reed, "Oration on Genius," in Kenneth Walter Cameron, ed., *Emerson the Essayist. An Outline of His Philosophical Development through 1836* (Hartford: Transcendental Books, 1945), 2:9. S. R.'s books: JMN 5:232; took umbrage: *New Jerusalem Magazine* 11 (1837–38): 72 ("[Emerson's] remarks show that he has read him little;—or rather to little purpose"). Regretting: JMN 7:31; Carl F. Strauch, "Emerson Rejects Reed and Hails Thoreau," *Harvard Library Bulletin* 16 (1968): 257–273. Their entire relationship is detailed by Clarence Paul Hotson, "Sampson Reed, A Teacher of Emerson," *NEQ* 2 (1929): 249–277; see also Joel Myerson, ed., *Transcendentalists: A Review of Research and Criticism*, 149, 372–374.

25. Evidence on the early relationship in Kenneth Walter Cameron, "Bronson Alcott—A 'Welcome Influence'," in *Emerson the Essayist: An Outline of His Philosophical Development through 1836 with Special Emphasis on the Sources and Interpretation of Nature* (Transcendental Books: Hartford, 1945), 1:325–328. Simple, superior: JMN 5:98–99; June, 1836: JMN 5:167–168, 70; L 2:26–27, 27–28; letter to Hedge: L 2:29–30; comparisons: JMN 5:178–179, 293, 390, 457, 460; insights used in *Nature*: JMN 5:180–184, nn. 549, 551, 553, 554, 555, 559, 562, 563, 564. *Nature*, published anonymously, was mistaken by one reviewer as the work of Alcott: Merton M. Sealts, Jr., and Alfred R. Ferguson, eds., *Emerson's Nature—Origin, Growth, Meaning* [New York: Dodd, Mead & Co., 1969], 178). The Orphic Poet of *Nature* is often thought to be Alcott, and even Alcott, in his journal, acknowledged his own influence (entry 188, 11 September 1836; [in Myerson, "Bronson Alcott, 'Journal for 1836,'" *SAR*, 1978: 72], saying the same in a letter (*Letters of A. Bronson Alcott*, 28). Carlos Baker, *Emerson among the Eccentrics: A Group Portrait* (New York: Penguin Books, 1997), 52, provides an excellent example of likely influence.

26. Alcott Journal, 18 October 1835, in Sanborn and Harris, *A. Bronson Alcott*, 1:240. Alcott Journal 141 for 2 August 1836 (in Myerson, "Bronson Alcott, 'Journal for 1836'," *SAR* 1978: 65). Alcott Journal 47–52, 19 January 1837 (in

Carlson, *SAR* 1981: 47); cf. Alcott 152–153 (Carlson, *SAR* 1981: 74), Alcott 106 (Carlson, *SAR* 1981: 61).

27. Minor reservations: Alcott's criticism of Emerson: Journal 367–370, week of 14–20 May (in Carlson, "Bronson Alcott's 'Journal for 1837' [Part Two]," *SAR*, 1982: 75–76); echoed during the week of 10–16 December in Journal 589 (Carlson, *SAR* 1982: 139). Yet see the reassessment at Journal 17, 1–6 January 1838 (Carlson, *SAR* 1993: 180); see also 1837 Journal entry 372 (Carlson, *SAR* 1982: 76) and Journal 499–500 (Carlson, *SAR* 1982: 115). Emerson's criticisms of Alcott: JMN 5:328; "Historic Notes on Life and Letters in New England," W 10:341; JMN 5:178–179, 188, 218, 363. See also Frederick C. Dahlstrand, *Amos Bronson Alcott: An Intellectual Biography* (Rutherford, N.J.: Fairleigh Dickinson University Press, 1982), 145.

28. Although there were some differences in the approaches of Alcott and Pestalozzi (Dorothy McCuskey, *Bronson Alcott, Teacher* [New York: Macmillan Company, 1940], 33–37), Alcott's most recent biographer believes Alcott constructed a "Pestalozzian school" (Dahlstrand, *Amos Bronson Alcott*, 40–43). See also Alcott's Journal for 1837, 495–497 (Carlson, *SAR* 1982: 113–114). Every book: Baker, *Emerson among the Eccentrics*, 46.

29. Advice of friends: Ronda, *Elizabeth Palmer Peabody: A Reformer on Her Own Terms*, 129–131; JMN 5:248–249. On Mary Moody Emerson: Sanborn, *Personality of Emerson*, 23. *Conversations* is in Myerson, *Transcendentalism: A Reader*, 167–195. A good discussion of the *Conversations*, including Elizabeth Peabody's role, is in Packer, *CHAL*, 2:385–391. Mary Moody Emerson: MME 376. Hedge to Margaret Fuller, 23 May 1837, bMS 384/1 (18), Andover-Harvard Theological Library, Harvard Divinity School. Hedge: Carlson, *SAR* 1982, 149, n. 23; Alcott: *Annuals of Education* 7 (1837): 233–234; Howe: Alcott Journal 407–408 (Carlson, *SAR* 1982: 86–87). For the attacks, see Dahlstrand, *Amos Bronson Alcott*, 141–143, and Carlson, *SAR* 1981: 27–32, and *SAR* 1982, 53–57. See Rose, *Transcendentalism as a Social Movement*, 22–24, for a discussion of the *Boston Daily Courier*.

30. Assault: Journal 269, week of 9–15 April 1836 (Carlson, *SAR* 1981: 107). Alcott withdrew as inaugural speaker of Hiram Fuller's experimental Greene Street School in Providence, and Emerson reluctantly agreed to speak in his stead. See Dahlstrand, *Amos Bronson Alcott*, 141–142, for other threats. Brownson, *Boston Quarterly Review* 1838: 417–432. Foregone conclusion: Alcott Journal 99, week of 12–18 February 1837 (Carlson, *SAR* 1981: 59–60); Alcott 115, 17 February 1836 (Carlson, *SAR* 1981: 63); Alcott 208–211, 27 March 1836 (Carlson, *SAR* 1981: 92–93); Alcott 387, 18 May 1837 (Carlson, *SAR* 1982: 81). Closed doors: Dorothy McCuskey, *Bronson Alcott, Teacher*, 82–113, and Dahlstrand, *Amos Bronson Alcott*, 135–155, for details.

31. Sermon on Mount: Roberson, *Emerson in His Sermons*, 17–21; anticipating Emerson: JMN 4:93–94. See also Josephine E. Roberts, "Elizabeth Peabody and the Temple School," *NEQ* 15 (1942): 505, for their compatibility of educational principle. Young Waldo: JMN 5:63, 175; L 2:27–28; MME 376. Encouraging publication: JMN 5:181–182, 248–249, with n. 764. Work half-done: JMN 10:347.

32. Alcott Journal 204–205, 19–25 March 1837 (Carlson, *SAR* 1981: 91–92); Alcott 265–267, 9–15 April (Carlson, *SAR* 1981: 106–107); Alcott 291–292, 23–29 April (Carlson, *SAR* 1981: 112–113).

33. Other letters of support: Rose, *Transcendentalism as a Social Movement*, 82–83. Clarke's support: Alcott's Journal 181, 12–18 March 1837 (Carlson, *SAR* 1981: 81), but it comes earlier than Alcott needs it, and Clarke is not nearly as esteemed as Emerson. Emerson and Alcott ridiculed: Theodore Parker to George Ellis, 20 February 1837, Theodore Parker Papers, MHS. Emerson letter to Nathan Hale and the *Daily Advertiser*, 23? March 1837 (L 7:275–277); cf. Letter to the Editor of the *Boston Courier*, 2 or 3 April 1837 (L 7:277–279). *Daily Courier*: L 7:277, n. 15, and Alcott Journal 231 of 1837 (Carlson, *SAR* 1981: 97–98). *Daily Advertiser*: L 2:60–62; on Hale, see Rose, *Transcendentalism as a Social Movement*, 75–76. Despaired: Alcott 204–205, week of 19–28 March 1837 (Carlson, *SAR* 1981: 91–92); Alcott 208–211, 27 March 1837 (Carlson, *SAR* 1981: 92–93). Game lost: L 2:61–62; Norton: Carlson, *SAR* 1982: 152, n. 50.

34. JMN 5:298; lent Emerson his journal: Alcott Journal 265–267, 9–15 April (Carlson, *SAR* 1981, 106–107, with n. 166 [L 7:279–80]).

35. *Nature*: CW 1:10.

36. Alcott Journal 149 (Carlson, *SAR* 1981: 73); cf. 133–134 (Carlson, *SAR* 1981: 68–69); 154 (Carlson, *SAR* 1981: 74–75); 168–169 (Carlson, *SAR* 1981: 78); 194–195 (Carlson, *SAR* 1981: 89–90). Even after a rapprochement the following year, the bitterness lingered; see Journal 45–52, 7–13 January 1838 (Carlson, *SAR* 1993: 186–188): Channing was "neither wise, nor great." On their previous relationship: Dahlstrand, *Amos Bronson Alcott*, 104–110; Howe, *Unitarian Conscience*, 262–263.

37. Alcott Journal 35–44 (Carlson, *SAR* 1981: 43–46); cf. 145–146 (Carlson, *SAR* 1981: 72–73) 158–161 (Carlson, *SAR* 1981: 76).

38. Alcott Journal 47–52 (Carlson, *SAR* 1981: 46–48); 152–153 (Carlson, *SAR* 1981: 74); cf. 124 (Carlson, *SAR* 1981: 66).

39. Alcott Journal 98–100 for week of 12 February (Carlson, *SAR* 1981: 59–60).

40. Watertown: Alcott Journal 329–331, 30 April–6 May 1837 (Carlson, *SAR* 1982: 63–64); Providence: EL 2:195, echoing Emerson's request to Boston papers on Alcott's behalf, asking readers to suspend judgment until Alcott's school had a chance to prove itself; Carlyle: CEC 163; cf. 218.

41. JMN 5:328–331; Emerson to Fuller: L 2:76–77; see also L 2:288. For Alcott's passionate determination to remain a reformer despite his current difficulties, see his remarkable journal entry 234 for 2–8 April 1837 (Carlson, *SAR* 1981: 98–99); also, 337 for 30 April–6 May (Carlson, *SAR* 1982: 65–66), and 375–380 for 21–27 May (Carlson, *SAR* 1982: 77–78).

42. Garden: JMN 5:326; humble bee: JMN 5:330; ostrich: AS 140–141.

43. JMN 5:333–334.

44. Transcendentalists and abolition: Gohdes, *American Literature* 3 (1931): 26–27.

45. JMN 5:347; on Philistines, see chapter 5.

46. Inflammation: L 2:81.

47. Strong in spring: JMN 5:328. In early June, Alcott busied himself with restarting the Transcendental Club (*Letters of A. Bronson Alcott*, 31–33) and by attending meetings of several organizations he belonged to (Alcott Journal 403–406 [Carlson, *SAR* 1982: 85–86]). Exhaustion: Alcott 437 (Carlson, *SAR* 1982: 96). Just prior to that, Alcott's journal is full of despair, and he acknowledges his isolation. Severe indisposition: *Letters of A. Bronson Alcott*, 34–35. Do come: L 7:285, 27 July 1837; L 2:92, 1 August 1837.

48. On the hostility from Cambridge, see chapter 1. For the real illnesses, see Evelyn Barish, "The Moonless Night: Emerson's Crisis of Health, 1825–1827," in *Emerson Centenary Essays*, ed. Joel Myerson (Carbondale: Southern Illinois University Press, 1982), 1–16.

49. Crutches: JMN 5:345–346; careless of action: JMN 5:353, which goes into "The American Scholar": AS 138; Periclean word: L 2:94; great calm: JMN 5:358.

50. Results of Alcott's visit: JMN 5:363 and LJE 58. Series of brief entries: JMN 5:330–331, 347–348, 356–357, 361 (cf. AS 138); one thing plain: JMN 5:364–365; duel: JMN 5:371.

51. Receive sympathetically: JMN 5:164, 251; great Man: JMN 5:249, 19 November 1836; echoed in a lecture of January 1837: EL 2:62. Country labors: AS 138.

52. Earlier vision of scholar: JMN 5:84, 164, 167, 187–188; now: JMN 5:359–360; cross of making: AS 139.

53. Mann to Sally J. Gardner, 29 December 1837, Horace Mann Papers, MHS; Martineau: CEC 174. Everett: Longfellow Journal, 8 March 1838, MH Ms Am 1340 (194). Hint at odium: JMN 7:60–61; Francis diary: Woodall, *SAR* 1982: 252 (10 September 1838); also p. 254 (12 February 1840); and Francis to Hedge, 12 November 1838, in Woodall, *SAR* 1991: 27; see also the recollection of Emerson's son Edward Waldo Emerson, *Emerson's Concord*, 75. To be great: CW 2:34.

54. JMN 7:346–347; CW 2:35.

55. Close connection: McCuskey, *Bronson Alcott, Teacher*, 120: Baker, *Emerson among the Eccentrics*, 94–95; Hubert H. Hoeltje, *Sheltering Tree: A Story of the Friendship of Ralph Waldo Emerson and Amos Bronson Alcott* (Durham: Duke University Press, 1943), 60. Conrad Wright, "Emerson, Barzillai Frost, and the Divinity School Address," in his *The Liberal Christians: Essays on American Unitarian History* (Boston: Beacon Press, 1970), 41–61 [originally published in *Harvard Theological Review* 49 (1965): 19–43].

56. Alcott Journal 368 (Carlson, *SAR* 1982: 75).

CHAPTER 7
FOREVER THE AMERICAN SCHOLAR

1. Secret of Emerson: Firkins, *Ralph Waldo Emerson*, 297; truth to what Firkins wrote: see, for example, Loring's reflections in Len Gougeon, "Ellis Gray Loring and a Journal for the Times," *SAR* 1990: 42. On self-reliance and identification with the godhead, see Roberson, *Emerson in His Sermons*, 138–140; all must receive: JMN 4:324 and 5:219; man is one: AS 141. Rather than, as was then the usual expectation, the orator conform to the expectations of the audience:

James A. Berlin, *Writing Instruction in Nineteenth-Century American Colleges* (Carbondale: Southern Illinois University Press, 1984), 54; Railton, *Authorship and Audience*, 23–49.

2. Parker's rebuff: John Pierce, Memoirs, vol. 9, p. 220, MHS. Caleb Stetson wrote Henry Hedge, congratulating him on his oration that day but noting, "I was in no condition to enjoy it when delivered . . . being so painfully excited by the controversy of the morning" (Stetson to Hedge, 28 October 1841, Schlesinger Library, Poor Family Collection, box 5, folder 78). The official minutes of that morning's meeting state that Joseph Story "declared his intention of withdrawing from the Presidency," likely a premature resignation, as his term of three years was half that of each of his two predecessors and because the phrase is different from those used to describe how other presidents decided not to seek reelection.

The 1838 meeting was also especially tense. Observing Caleb Stetson's oration, John Pierce (Memoirs, vol. 7, p. 359–361, MHS) noted that "some, from his high admiration of [Emerson's] oration last year, anticipated something more in the affected & obscure style of thinking and writing made popular among some of our literati by Carlyle, & kindred authors." But "[f]or the most part, it was clearly intelligible." At its conclusion, Everett ridiculed the Carlylean style of writing (Everett Journal, Edward Everett Papers, MHS; and Cyrus Bartol to George Ellis, 1 October 1838, George Ellis Papers, MHS). Earlier that day, the entire seven-man Committee on Appointments, which had selected Transcendentalists Emerson and Stetson as orators, "declined a reappointment." Also "resigning" was C. C. Felton, who, as corresponding secretary, served ex officio on the Committee on Appointments and had significant influence in determining the choice of speaker. He was replaced by Francis Bowen, the Norton protégé who had published two articles harshly attacking Emerson and Transcendentalism. The orators for the following two years, Caleb Cushing and Leonard Woods, were close friends of Phi Beta Kappa president Joseph Story (HUD 3684.554, box 64, "Minutes of Anniversary [of Harvard Phi Beta Kappa] Meetings, 1826–1921").

Emerson: L 7:622; JMN 9:221. See also JMN 7:459: his contempt was likely aimed especially at Josiah Quincy and Joseph Story (Sanborn, *Personality of Emerson*, 61).

3. Retrogression: Hofstadter and Smith, eds., *American Higher Education: A Documentary History*, 1:257–259, 297–300, 308–311; and Hofstadter, *Academic Freedom in the Age of the College* (New Brunswick, N.J.: Transaction Publishers, 1996), 209. Quotations: *American Higher Education: A Documentary History*, 1:62, 258.

4. Expand curricula: Cremin, *American Education*, 270–281, 406–409. Emerson's influence: Carpenter, *NEQ* 1951: 13–34; for the argument that "The American Scholar" is the foundation text for the college elective system, see John Seiler Brubacher and Rudy Willis, *Higher Education in Transition; An American History, 1636–1956* (New York: Harper & Row 1958), 101–115. Kantian idealism: Bradley J. Longfield, "From Evangelicalism to Liberalism: Public Midwestern Universities in Nineteenth Century America," in *The Secularization of the University*, ed. George Marsden and Bradley J. Longfield (New York: Oxford University Press, 1992), 66, n. 2.

5. Bloom again: LJE 67. Contemporary orators: Alden Bradford, *Human Learning Favorable to True Religion: But the Transcendental Theory Hostile to the Christian Revelation. An Address Delivered before the Society of Φ.B.K. in Bowdoin College, September 2, 1841* (Boston: S. G. Simpkins, 1841); Heman Humphrey, *Discourse Delivered before the Connecticut Alpha of Phi Beta Kappa at New Haven, August 14, 1838* (New Haven: Hitchcock & Stafford, 1839), 14; Leonard Bacon, *Oration before the Phi Beta Kappa Society of Dartmouth College Delivered July 30, 1845* (Hanover: Dartmouth Press, 1845), 10; Increase Taxbox, *An Address on the Origin, Progress & Present Condition of Philosophy: Delivered before the Hamilton Chapter of the Alpha Delta Society on its Eleventh Anniversary at Clinton, N.Y.* (Utica: R. W. Roberts, 1843), 23. For the traditional treatment of the American scholar, see, for example, William T. Dwight, *An Address Delivered before the Phi Beta Kappa Society, Alpha of Maine, in Bowdoin College, Brunswick, September 6, 1849* (Portland: Mirror Office, 1849). "The Hampton Idea": W.E.B. DuBois, *The Education of Black People: Ten Critiques 1906–1960*, ed. Herbert Aptheker (Amherst: University of Massachusetts Press, 1973), 5–15; quotations are from pp. 7, 8, 9, and 13. Adam R. Nelson, *Education and Democracy: The Meaning of Alexander Meiklejohn, 1872–1964* (Madison: University of Wisconsin Press, 2001), especially 233–260.

6. On the distinction: Pierre Hadot, *Philosophy as a Way of Life: Spiritual Exercises from Socrates to Foucault*, by Arnold I. Davidson (Malden, England: Blackwell Published Ltd., 1995).

7. "Writings of R. W. Emerson," *CE* 38 (1845): 87–106.

8. Capper, *Margaret Fuller, An American Romantic Life*, 1:310. Preach no more: L 2:120; see also *Later Lectures*, 1:48 ("I look on the Lecture Room as the true Church of the coming time"). Ecstasy: JMN 7:265.

9. As poet: EL 2:274; L 1:435; W 7:90.

10. Saw himself: JMN 5:333–334. Osgood to Clarke, 4 September 1838, Perry-Clarke Collection, MHS; also Alcott Journal 47–52, 19 January 1837 (Carlson, *SAR* 1981: 47), and JMN 5:333–334; Horace Mann called Emerson an oracle, perhaps sarcastically (Mann to Peabody, 9 December 1838, Horace Mann Papers, MHS). Plotinus: Sanborn, *Personality of Emerson*, 9–10.

11. Henry James, "Emerson," in Barbour, *American Transcendentalism: An Anthology of Criticism*, 261.

12. Wayne C. Booth, *The Company We Keep* (Berkeley: University of California Press, 1988), 387. *Salem Register*, 3 June 1850, p. 2; reprinted in *Literary Comment in American Renaissance Newspapers*, ed. Kenneth Walter Cameron (Hartford: Transcendental Books, 1977), 19.

13. Miller, "Emersonian Genius and the American Democracy," *NEQ* 26 (1953): 29. Ripley in Frothingham, *George Ripley*, 270.

14. The Bostonian: George P. Lathrop, "Literary and Social Boston," *Harper's New Monthly Magazine* 62 (February, 1881), 386. Service of his country: Shklar, *Political Theory* 1990: 601–614.

15. Without [action]: AS 137; nothing can bring you peace: CW 2:51.

16. "Historic Notes of Life and Letters in New England": W 10:369–370.

BIBLIOGRAPHY

Adams, Henry, *The Education of Henry Adams*. Edited by Ira B. Nadel. Oxford: Oxford University Press, 1999.

Adams, John Quincy. *Memoirs of John Quincy Adams, Comprising Portions of His Diary from 1795 to 1848*. Edited by Charles Francis Adams. 12 vols. Philadelphia: J. B. Lippincott & Co., 1876.

Ahlstrom, Sydney E. *A Religious History of the American People*. New Haven: Yale University Press, 1973.

Alcott, A. Bronson. "Orphic Sayings," *The Dial* 1 (1840): 85–98.

———. *The Letters of A. Bronson Alcott*. Edited by Richard L. Herrnstadt. Ames: Iowa State University Press, 1969.

Allmendinger, David F., Jr. *Paupers and Scholars: The Transformation of Student Life in Nineteenth-Century New England*. New York: St. Martin's Press, 1975.

Bacon, Leonard. *Oration before the Phi Beta Kappa Society of Dartmouth College Delivered July 30, 1845*. Hanover: Dartmouth Press, 1845.

Baker, Carlos. *Emerson among the Eccentrics: A Group Portrait*. New York: Penguin Books, 1997.

Bancroft, George. "On the Progress of Civilization." *Boston Quarterly Review* 1 (1838): 389–407.

Barish, Evelyn. "Emerson and 'The Magician': An Early Prose Fantasy." *American Transcendental Quarterly* 31 (1976): 13–18.

———. "The Moonless Night: Emerson's Crisis of Health, 1825–1827." In *Emerson Centenary Essays*, edited by Joel Myerson. Carbondale: Southern Illinois University Press, 1982.

———. *Emerson: The Roots of Prophecy*. Princeton: Princeton University Press, 1989.

[Beecher, Lyman]. *The Autobiography of Lyman Beecher*. Edited by B. Cross. 2 vols. Cambridge, Mass.: Belknap Press, 1961.

Bercovitch, Sacvan. *The American Jeremiad*. Madison: University of Wisconsin Press, 1978.

———, ed. *The Cambridge History of American Literature*. Vol. 2. Cambridge: Cambridge University Press, 1995.

Berlin, James A. *Writing Instruction in Nineteenth-Century American Colleges.* Carbondale: Southern Illinois University Press, 1984.

Bloom, Harold. "Mr. America." *New York Review of Books* 3 (22 November 1984): 19–24.

———, ed. *Modern Critical Views: Ralph Waldo Emerson.* New York: Chelsea House, 1985.

Booth, Wayne C. *The Company We Keep.* Berkeley: University of California Press, 1988.

Bosco, Ronald A. "'Blessed Are They Who Have no Talent': Emerson's Unwritten Life of Amos Bronson Alcott." *ESQ: A Journal of the American Renaissance* 26 (1990): 1–36.

Bowen, Francis. "Locke and Transcendentalism," *Christian Examiner* 21 (1837): 170–194. *Christian Examiner* henceforth cited as *CE.*

———. "Transcendentalism." *CE* 21 (1837): 371–385.

———. *Critical Essays on a Few Subjects Connected with the History and Present Condition of Speculative Philosophy.* Boston: H. B. Williams, 1842.

Bradford, Alden. *An Address Delivered before the Society of Φ.B.K. in Bowdoin College, September 2, 1841.* Boston: S. G. Simpkins, 1841.

Brophy, Alfred L. "Reason and Sentiment: The Moral Worlds and Modes of Reasoning of Antebellum Jurists (Review of *Heart versus Head: Judge-Made Law in Nineteenth Century America* by Peter Karsten)." *Boston University Law Review* 79 (1999): 1161–1213.

———. "The Intersection of Property and Slavery in Southern Legal Thought: From Missouri Compromise through Civil War." Ph.D. diss., Harvard University, 2001.

Brownson, Orestes A. "Benjamin Constant." *CE* 17 (1834): 63–77.

———. "Cousin's *Philosophy.*" *CE* 21 (1836): 33–64.

———. "Alcott on Human Culture." *Boston Quarterly Review* 1 (1838): 417–433.

———. "Mr. Emerson's *Address.*" *Boston Quarterly Review* 1 (1838): 500–514.

———. "American Literature." *Boston Quarterly Review* 2 (1839): 1–27.

———. "Norton on *the Evidences of Christianity.*" *Boston Quarterly Review* 2 (1839): 86–113.

———. "Norton and the Transcendentalists." *Boston Quarterly Review* 3 (1840): 265–323.

Bruce, Dickson D., Jr., "W.E.B. Du Bois and the Idea of Double Conscious." *American Literature* 64 (1962): 299–309.

Brubacher, John Seiler, and Rudy Willis. *Higher Education in Transition; An American History, 1636–1956.* New York: Harper & Row, 1958.

Buckminster, Joseph S. "On The Dangers and Duties of Men of Letters; An Address, Pronounced before the Society of ΦBK, on Thursday, August 31st, 1809." *Monthly Anthology and Boston Review* 7 (1809): 145–158.

Buell, Lawrence. "Unitarianism Aesthetics and Emerson's Poet-Priest." *American Quarterly* 20 (1968): 3–20.

———. *Literary Transcendentalism: Style and Vision in the American Renaissance.* Ithaca: Cornell University Press, 1973.

———. *New England Literary Culture: From Revolution through Renaissance*. Cambridge: Cambridge University Press, 1986.

———. "Emerson's Fate." In *Emersonian Circles: Essays in Honor of Joel Myerson*, edited by Wesley T. Mott and Robert E. Burkholder. Rochester: University of Rochester Press, 1997, 11–28.

Burkholder, Robert E. "Emerson, Kneeland, and the Divinity School Address." *American Literature* 58 (1986): 1–14.

———. "The Radical Emerson: Politics in 'The American Scholar.'" *ESQ: A Journal of the American Renaissance* 34 (1988): 37–58.

Bush, Harold K., Jr. *American Declarations: Rebellion and Repentance in American Cultural History*. Urbana: University of Illinois Press, 1999.

Cabot, James Elliot. *A Memoir of Ralph Waldo Emerson*. 2 vols. Boston: Houghton Mifflin, 1887.

"Calvinist Ethics." *CE* 19 (1835): 1–40.

Cameron, Kenneth Walter, ed. *Emerson the Essayist: An Outline of His Philosophical Development through 1836 with Special Emphasis on the Sources and Interpretation of Nature*. 2 vols. Transcendental Books: Hartford, 1945.

Capper, Charles. *Margaret Fuller: An American Romantic Life*. vol 1, *The Private Years*. Oxford: Oxford University Press, 1992 (vol. 2, forthcoming).

Carlson, Larry A. "Bronson Alcott's 'Journal for 1837' (Part One)." *Studies in the American Renaissance* 1981: 27–132.

———. "Bronson Alcott's 'Journal for 1837' (Part Two)." *Studies in the American Renaissance*. 1982: 53–168.

———. "Bronson Alcott's 'Journal for 1838' (Part One)." *Studies in the American Renaissance*. 1993: 161–244.

———. "Bronson Alcott's 'Journal for 1838' (Part Two)." *Studies in the American Renaissance*. 1994: 123–194.

Carlyle, Thomas. *Sartor Resartus: The Life and Opinions of Herr Teufelsdröckh in Three Books*. Edited by Rodger L. Tarr. Berkeley: University of California Press, 2000.

Carpenter, Hazen C. "Emerson, Eliot, and the Elective System." *New England Quarterly* 24 (1951): 13–34.

Catalogue of the Harvard Chapter of Phi Beta Kappa, Alpha Chapter of Massachusetts. Cambridge, Mass.: Riverside Press, 1933.

Cavell, Stanley. *In Quest of the Ordinary: Lines of Skepticism and Romanticism*. Chicago: University of Chicago Press, 1988.

———. *This New Yet Unapproachable America: Lectures after Emerson, after Wittgenstein*. Albuquerque: Living Batch Press, 1989.

———. *Conditions Handsome and Unhandsome: The Constitution of Emersonian Perfectionism*. La Salle, Ill.: Open Court, 1990.

Cayton, Mary Kupiec. "The Making of an American Prophet: Emerson, His Audiences, and the Rise of the Culture Industry in Nineteenth-Century America," *American Historical Review* 92 (1987): 597–620.

———. *Emerson's Emergence: Self and Society in the Transformation of New England, 1800–1845*. Chapel Hill: University of North Carolina Press, 1989.

Cayton, Mary Kupiec. "Who Were the Evangelicals?: Conservative and Liberal Identity in the Unitarian Controversy in Boston, 1804–1833." *Journal of Social History* 31 (1997): 85–107.

Channing, William Ellery. *The Works of William E. Channing, D.D.* Boston: James Munroe and Company, 1841.

———. *Memoir of William Ellery Channing with Extracts from His Correspondence and Manuscripts.* Edited by William Henry Channing. 3 vols. Boston: Wm. Crosby and H. P. Nichols, 1848.

Channing, William Henry. Review of "An Oration Delivered before the Phi Beta Kappa Society, at Cambridge, August 31, 1837, by Ralph Waldo Emerson. Boston. James Munroe & Co." *Boston Quarterly Review* 1 (1838): 106–120.

Chapman, John Jay. *Selected Writings.* New York: Farrar, Straus and Cudahy, 1957.

Clark, Allen R. "Andrews Norton: A Conservative Unitarian." Harvard College honors thesis, 1943.

Clarke, James Freeman. *Autobiography, Diary and Correspondence.* Edited by Edward Everett Hale. Boston: Houghton Mifflin, 1891.

Clarke, James Freeman and Christopher Pearse Crunch. "The New School in Literature and Religion." *Western Messenger* 6 (1838): 42–47.

Cole, Phyllis. *Mary Moody Emerson and the Origins of Transcendentalism: A Family History.* New York: Oxford University Press, 1998.

———. "Pain and Protest in the Emerson Family." In *The Emerson "Dilemma": Essays on Emerson and Social Reform*, edited by T. Gregory Garvey. Athens: University of Georgia Press, 2001.

Cremin, Lawrence A. *An American Education: Some Notes toward a New History.* Bloomington, Ill.: Phi Delta Kappa, 1969.

———. *American Education: The National Experience, 1783–1876.* New York: Harper & Row, 1980.

Crowe, Charles. *George Ripley: Transcendentalist and Utopian Socialist.* Athens: University of Georgia Press, 1967.

Current, Richard Nelson. *Phi Beta Kappa in American Life: The First Two Hundred Years.* New York: Oxford University Press, 1990.

Curti, Merle. *The Growth of American Thought.* 3rd ed. New York: Harper & Row, 1964.

Dahlstrand, Frederick C. *Amos Bronson Alcott: An Intellectual Biography.* Rutherford, N.J.: Fairleigh Dickinson University Press, 1982.

Dall, Caroline Wells Healey. *Transcendentalism in New England: A Lecture Delivered before the Society of Philosophical Enquiry.* Boston: Roberts Brothers, 1897.

Dana, Richard Henry, Jr. *An Autobiographical Sketch (1815–1842).* Edited by Robert F. Metzdorf. Hamden, Conn.: Shoe String Press, 1953.

Davis, Richard Beale. "Edward Tyrrel Channing's American Scholar of 1818." *Key Reporter* 26 (Spring, 1961): 1–4.

Delbanco, Andrew. *William Ellery Channing: An Essay on the Liberal Spirit in America.* Cambridge: Harvard University Press, 1981.

Dewey, Orville. *Oration Delivered at Cambridge before the Society of Phi Beta Kappa: August 26, 1830.* Boston: Gray and Bowen, 1830.

DuBois, W.E.B. *The Education of Black People: Ten Critiques 1906–1960*. Edited by Herbert Aptheker. Amherst: University of Massachusetts Press, 1973.

———. *The Souls of Black Folk*. Edited by David W. Blight and Robert Gooding-Williams. Boston: Bedford Books, 1997.

Dwight, William T. *An Address Delivered before the Phi Beta Kappa Society, Alpha of Maine, in Bowdoin College, Brunswick, September 6, 1849*. Portland, Maine: Mirror Office, 1849.

Earhart, Amy E. "Representative Men, Slave Revolt, and Emerson's 'Conversion' to Abolitionism." *American Transcendental Quarterly* 13 (1999): 287–303.

Edgell, David Palmer. "A Note on Channing's Transcendentalism." *New England Quarterly* 22 (1949): 394–397.

———. *William Ellery Channing: An Intellectual Portrait*. Boston: Beacon Press, 1955.

Ellis, George E. *Memoir of Jacob Bigelow, M.D., LL.D.* Cambridge, Mass.: John Wilson and Son, 1880.

Eliot, Charles W. *Harvard Memories*. Cambridge: Harvard University Press, 1923.

Emerson, Edward Waldo. *Emerson's Concord. A Memoir*. Boston: Houghton Mifflin, 1889.

Emerson, Lidian Jackson. *The Selected Letters of Lidian Jackson Emerson*. Edited with an introduction by Delores Bird Carpenter. Columbia: University of Missouri Press, 1987.

Emerson, Mary Moody. *The Selected Letters of Mary Mood Emerson*. Edited by Nancy Craig Simmons. Athens: University of Georgia Press, 1993.

Emerson, Ralph Waldo. *A Historical Discourse, Delivered before the Citizens of Concord, 12th September, 1835*. Boston: I. R. Butts, 1835.

———. "Michael Angelo." *North American Review* 44 (January, 1837): 1–16.

———. "Carlyle's French Revolution." *CE* 23 (1838): 386.

———. *The Complete Works of Ralph Waldo Emerson*. Edited by Edward Waldo Emerson. 12 vols. Boston: Houghton Mifflin, 1903–1904.

———. *The Letters of Ralph Waldo Emerson*. Edited by Ralph L. Rusk and Eleanor M. Tilton. 10 vols. New York: Columbia University Press, 1939–1995.

———. *The Early Lectures of Ralph Waldo Emerson*. Edited by Stephen E. Whicher et al. 3 vols. Cambridge: Harvard University Press, 1959–1972.

———. *The Journals and Miscellaneous Notebooks of Ralph Waldo Emerson*. Edited by William H. Gilman et al. 16 vols. Cambridge: Harvard University Press, 1960–1982.

———. *The Collected Works of Ralph Waldo Emerson*. Edited by Alfred E. Ferguson et al. 5 vols. Cambridge: Harvard University Press, 1971–1994.

———. *Essays and Lectures*. Edited by Joel Porte. New York: Library of America, 1983.

———. *The Complete Sermons of Ralph Waldo Emerson*. Edited by Albert J. von Frank et al. 4 vols. Columbia: University of Missouri Press, 1989–1992.

———. *The Later Lectures of Ralph Waldo Emerson, 1843–1871*. Edited by Ronald A. Bosco and Joel Myerson. 2 vols. Athens: University of Georgia Press, 2001.

Emerson, Ralph Waldo, and Thomas Carlyle. *The Correspondence of Emerson and Carlyle.* Edited by Joseph Slater. New York: Columbia University Press, 1964.

Everett, Edward. *Orations and Speeches on Various Occasions.* 4 vols. Boston: Little Brown and Co., 1850–1868.

Felton, C. C. "Emerson's Essays." *CE* 30 (1841): 253–263.

Finney, Charles Grandison. *Lectures on Revivals of Religions.* 2nd ed. New York: Leavitt, Lord & Co., 1835.

Firkins, Oscar W. *Ralph Waldo Emerson.* Boston: Houghton Mifflin, 1915.

Follen, Charles. *The Works of Charles Follen, with a Memoir of His Life.* Edited by Eliza Lee Follen. 5 vols. Boston: Hilliard, Gray, and Company, 1841–1842.

Frothingham, Octavius Brooks. *Theodore Parker: A Biography.* Boston: J. R. Osgood, 1874.

——. *George Ripley.* Boston: Houghton Mifflin, 1883.

——. *Recollections and Impressions, 1822–1890.* New York: G. P. Putnam's Sons, 1891.

Frothingham, Paul Revere. *Edward Everett: Orator and Statesman.* Boston: Houghton Mifflin, 1925.

Fuess, Claude M. *The Life of Caleb Cushing.* 2 vols. Hamden, Conn.: Archon Books, 1965.

Fuller, Margaret. *The Letters of Margaret Fuller.* Edited by Robert N. Hudspeth. 6 vols. Ithaca: Cornell University Press, 1983–1994.

Garvey, T. Gregory. "Mediating Citizenship: Emerson, the Cherokee Removals, and the Rhetoric of Nationalism." *Centennial Review* 41 (1997), 461–469.

——, ed. *The Emerson "Dilemma": Essays on Emerson and Social Reform.* Athens: University of Georgia Press, 2001.

Gilman, Samuel. "Unitarian Christianity Free from Objectional Extremes." *CE* 8 (1830): 133–146.

Gilmore, Michael T. *American Romanticism and the Marketplace.* Chicago: University of Chicago Press, 1985.

Gohdes, Clarence. "Alcott's 'Conversation' on the Transcendental Club and the *Dial.*" *American Literature* 3 (1931): 14–27.

Gonnaud, Maurice. *An Uneasy Solitude: Individual and Society in the Work of Ralph Waldo Emerson.* Translated by Lawrence Rosenwald. Princeton: Princeton University Press, 1987.

Gougeon, Len. "Ellis Gray Loring and a Journal for the Times." *Studies in the American Renaissance* 1990: 33–48.

——. *Virtue's Hero: Emerson, Antislavery, and Reform.* Athens: University of Georgia Press, 1990.

——. "'Fortune of the Republic': Emerson, Lincoln, and Transcendental Warfare." *ESQ: A Journal of the American Renaissance* 45 (1999): 259–324.

Gougeon, Len, and Joel Myerson, eds. *Emerson's Antislavery Writings.* New Haven: Yale University Press, 1995.

Habich, Robert. "Emerson's Reluctant Foe: Andrews Norton and the Transcendental Controversy." *New England Quarterly* 65 (1992): 212–216.

Hadot, Pierre. *Philosophy as a Way of Life: Spiritual Exercises from Socrates to Foucault.* Edited by Arnold I. Davidson. Malden, England: Blackwell, 1995.

Hale, Edward E., ed. "A Harvard Undergraduate in the Thirties: From the Diary of Edward Everett Hale." *Harper's Monthly Magazine* 132 (1916): 691–702.

Hale, Nathan O. *The Democratization of American Christianity.* New Haven: Yale University Press, 1989.

Hall, Peter Dobkin, "What the Merchants Did with Their Money: Charitable and Testamentary Trusts in Massachusetts, 1780–1880." In *Entrepreneurs: The Boston Business Community, 1700–1850,* edited by Conrad Edick Wright and Kathryn P. Viens. Boston: Massachusetts Historical Society, 1997.

Handlin, Lillian. *George Bancroft: The Intellectual as Democrat.* New York: Harper & Row, 1984.

———. "*Babylon est delenda*: the Young Andrews Norton." In *American Unitarianism: 1805–1865,* edited by Conrad Edick Wright. Boston: Massachusetts Historical Society, 1989.

Hardman, Keith J. *Charles Grandison Finney, 1792–1875: Revivalist and Reformer.* Syracuse: Syracuse University Press, 1987.

Hedge, Frederic Henry. "Coleridge's Literary Character." *CE* 14 (1833): 109–129.

———. "An Address Delivered before the Phi Beta Kappa Society in Yale College, New Haven, August 20, 1833, by Edward Everett." *CE* 16 (1834): 1–21.

———. "Writings of R. W. Emerson." *CE* 38 (1845): 87–106.

———. *Martin Luther and Other Essays.* Boston: Roberts Brothers, 1888.

Hill, William Bancroft. "Emerson's College Days." *Literary World,* 22 May 1880, 180–181; reprinted in *Emerson the Essayist.* Vol. 1. Edited by Kenneth Walter Cameron. Hartford: Transcendental Books, 1945.

"History of Harvard University from Its Foundation, in the Year 1636, to the Period of the American Revolution, A." *CE* 15 (1835): 30.

Hoeltje, Hubert H. *Sheltering Tree: A Story of the Friendship of Ralph Waldo Emerson and Amos Bronson Alcott.* Durham: Duke University Press, 1943.

Hofstadter, Richard. *Academic Freedom in the Age of the College.* New Brunswick, N.J.: Transaction Publishers, 1996.

Hofstadter, Richard, and Wilson Smith, eds. *American Higher Education: A Documentary History.* 2 vols. Chicago: University of Chicago Press, 1961.

Holmes, Oliver Wendell, Sr. *Ralph Waldo Emerson.* Boston: Houghton Mifflin, 1885.

———. *The Autocrat at the Breakfast Table.* New York: E. P. Dutton, 1906.

Hotson, Clarence Paul. "Sampson Reed, A Teacher of Emerson." *New England Quarterly* 2 (1929): 249–277.

Howe, Daniel Walker. *The Unitarian Conscience: Harvard Moral Philosophy, 1805–1861.* 2nd ed. Middletown, Conn.: Wesleyan University Press, 1988.

Howe, Julia Ward. *Reminiscences: 1819–1899.* New York: New American Library, 1969.

Howe, M. A. DeWolfe. *The Life and Letters of George Bancroft.* New York: Charles Scribner's Sons, 1908.

Humphrey, Heman. *Discourse Delivered before the Connecticut Alpha of Phi Beta Kappa at New Haven, August 14, 1838.* New Haven: Hitchcock & Stafford, 1839.

Hunter, Doreen. "Frederic Henry Hedge: What Say You?" *American Quarterly* 32 (1980): 186–201.

Hurth, Elizabeth. "Sowing the Seeds of 'Subservience': Harvard's Early Göttingen Students." *Studies in the American Renaissance* 1992: 91–106.

Hutchinson, William R. *The Transcendentalist Ministers: Church Reform in the New England Renaissance.* New Haven: Yale University Press, 1959.

Jackson, Leon. "The Social Construction of Thomas Carlyle's New England Reputation, 1834–1836." *Proceedings of the American Antiquarian Society* 106 (1996): 165–189.

James, Henry. "Emerson." In *American Transcendentalism: An Anthology of Criticism,* edited by Brian M. Barbour. Notre Dame, Ind.: University of Notre Dame Press, 1973.

Kant, Immanuel. *Critique of Pure Reason.* Edited and translated by Norman Kemp Smith. London: Macmillan & Co., 1933.

Kazin, Alfred. "The Father of Us All." *New York Review of Books* 28 (21 January 1982): 4–6.

———. "Where Would Emerson Find His Scholar Now?" *American Heritage* 38 (1987): 93–96.

Kuehn, Manfred. *Kant: A Biography.* Cambridge: Cambridge University Press, 2001.

[L., A.] Review of Norton's *Evidences of the Genuineness of the Gospels.* CE 22 (1837): 321–343.

Lathrop, George P. "Literary and Social Boston." *Harper's New Monthly Magazine* 62 (February, 1881): 381–398.

Litton, Alfred G. "The Development of the Mind and the Role of the Scholar in the Early Works of Frederic Henry Hedge." *Studies in the American Renaissance* 1989: 95–114.

———. "'Speaking the Truth with Love': A History of the *Christian Examiner* and Its Relation to New England Transcendentalism." Ph.D. diss., University of South Carolina, 1993.

Longfield, Bradley J. "From Evangelicalism to Liberalism: Public Midwestern Universities in Nineteenth Century America." In *The Secularization of the University,* edited by George Marsden and Bradley J. Longfield. New York: Oxford University Press, 1992.

Lowell, James Russell. "Thoreau's Letters." *North American Review* 101 (1865): 597–608.

Malachuk, Daniel S. "The Republican Philosophy of Emerson's Early Lectures." *New England Quarterly* 71 (1998): 404–428.

Martineau, Harriet. "The Claims of Harvard College upon Its Sons." *CE* 17 (1834): 93–127.

———. *Society in America.* 3 vols. London: Saunders and Otley, 1837.

———. *Retrospect of Western Travel.* 2 vols. London: Saunders and Otley, 1838.

Mathews, James W. "Fallen Angel: Emerson and the Apostasy of Edward Everett." *Studies in the American Renaissance* 1990: 23–32.

Matthiessen, F. O. *American Renaissance: Art and Expression in the Age of Emerson and Whitman.* New York: Oxford University Press, 1941.

Maxfield-Miller, Elizabeth. "Elizabeth of Concord: Selected Letters of Elizabeth
    Sherman Hoar (1814–1878) to the Emersons, Family, and the Emerson Circle
    (Part Three)." *Studies in the American Renaissance* 1986: 113–198.
McAleer, John J. *Ralph Waldo Emerson: Days of Encounter*. Boston: Little,
    Brown and Co., 1984.
McCaughey, Robert A. *Josiah Quincy, 1772–1864: The Last Federalist*. Cam-
    bridge: Harvard University Press, 1974.
———. "The Transformation of American Academic Life: Harvard University,
    1821–1892." *Perspectives in American History* 8 (1974): 255–263.
McCuskey, Dorothy. *Bronson Alcott, Teacher*. New York: Macmillan & Co.,
    1940.
McKivigan, John R. *The War against Proslavery Religion: Abolition and the
    Northern Churches, 1830–1865*. Ithaca: Cornell University Press, 1984.
McLachlan, James. "The American College in the Nineteenth Century: Toward a
    Reappraisal." *Teachers College Record* 80 (1978): 287–306.
McLoughlin, William Gerald. *Modern Revivalism: Charles Grandison Finney to
    Billy Graham*. New York: Ronald Press, 1959.
Menand, Louis. *The Metaphysical Club: A Story of Ideas in America*. New York:
    Farrar, Straus and Giroux, 2001.
Milder, Robert. "'The American Scholar' as Cultural Event." *Prospects* 16 (1991):
    119–147.
———. "The Radical Emerson?" In *The Cambridge Guide to Ralph Waldo Emer-
    son*, edited by Joel Porte and Saundra Morris. Cambridge: Cambridge Univer-
    sity Press, 1999.
Perry Miller. "Emersonian Genius and the American Democracy." *New England
    Quarterly* 26 (1953): 27–44.
———. *The Life of the Mind in America from the Revolution to the Civil War*.
    New York: Harcourt, Brace & World, 1965.
———, ed. *The Transcendentalists*. Cambridge: Harvard University Press, 1950;
    reprinted, New York: MJF Books, 1978.
Minter, David. "The Puritan Jeremiad as a Literary Form." In *The American Puri-
    tan Imagination: Essays in Revaluation*, edited by Sacvan Bercovitch. Cam-
    bridge: Cambridge University Press, 1974.
Morison, Samuel Eliot. "The Great Rebellion of Harvard and the Resignation of
    President Kirkland." *Colonial Society of Massachusetts, Transactions* 27
    (1927–1930): 54–112.
———. *Three Centuries of Harvard, 1636–1936*. Cambridge: Harvard University
    Press, 1936.
Mott, Wesley T., ed. *Biographical Dictionary of Transcendentalism*. Westport,
    Conn.: Greenwood Press, 1996.
———. *Encyclopedia of Transcendentalism*. Westport, Conn.: Greenwood Press,
    1996.
Mott, Wesley T., and Robert E. Burkholder, eds. *Emersonian Circles: Essays in
    Honor of Joel Myerson*. Rochester: University of Rochester Press, 1997.
Murray, James O. *Francis Wayland*. Boston: Houghton Mifflin, 1891.
Myerson, Joel. "A Calendar of Transcendental Club Meetings." *American Litera-
    ture* 44 (1972): 197–207.

Myerson, Joel. "'In the Transcendental Emporium': Bronson Alcott's 'Orphic Sayings' in the *Dial*." *English Language Notes* 19 (1972): 31–38.

———. "Practical Editions: Ralph Waldo Emerson's 'The American Scholar.'" *Proof* 3 (1973): 370–394.

———. "Frederic Henry Hedge and the Failure of Transcendentalism." *Harvard Library Bulletin* 23 (1975): 396–410.

———. "Bronson Alcott, 'Journal for 1836.'" *Studies in the American Renaissance* 1978: 17–104.

———. *The New England Transcendentalists and the Dial: A History of the Magazine and Its Contributors*. Rutherford, N.J.: Fairleigh Dickinson University Press, 1980.

———, ed., *Ralph Waldo Emerson: A Descriptive Bibliography*. Pittsburgh: University of Pittsburgh Press, 1982.

———, ed. *The Transcendentalists: A Review of Research and Criticism*. New York: Modern Language Association of America, 1984.

———, ed. *Transcendentalism: A Reader*. New York: Oxford University Press, 2000.

[N., W.] "Andrews Norton." *CE* 55 (1853): 425–452.

Nelson, Adam R. *Education and Democracy: The Meaning of Alexander Meiklejohn, 1872–1964*. Madison: University of Wisconsin Press, 2001.

Neufeldt, Leonard. *The House of Emerson*. Lincoln: University of Nebraska Press, 1982.

Newmyer, R. Kent. *Supreme Court Justice Joseph Story: Statesman of the Old Republic*. Chapel Hill: University of North Carolina Press, 1985.

Norton, Andrews. "Moore's Poems." *Monthly Anthology and Boston Review* 4 (1807): 41–45.

———. "Report on the Inauguration of President Kirkland of Harvard." *Monthly Anthology and Boston Review* 9 (1810): 347–350.

Nye, Russell B. *George Bancroft*. New York: Washington Square Press, 1964.

Packer, Barbara L. *Emerson's Fall: A New Interpretation of the Major Essays*. New York, Continuum, 1982.

———. "Origin and Authority: Emerson and the Higher Criticism." In *Reconstructing American Literature*, edited by Sacvan Bercovitch. Cambridge: Harvard University Press, 1986.

———. "The Transcendentalists." In *The Cambridge History of American Literature*, edited by Sacvan Bercovitch. Cambridge: Cambridge University Press, 1995.

Parker, Theodore. *The Works of Theodore Parker*. Edited by George Willis Cooke. 15 vols. Boston: American Unitarian Association, 1907–1911.

Parsons, Theophilus. *On the Duties of Educated Men in a Republic*. Boston: Russell, Odiorne & Co., 1835.

Peabody, Andrew P. "Unitarianism Vindicated against the Charges of Skeptical and Infidel Tendencies." *CE* 11 (1831): 179–195.

———. *Harvard Reminiscences*. Boston: Ticknor and Company, 1888.

Peabody, Elizabeth Palmer. *The Letters of Elizabeth Palmer Peabody: American Renaissance Woman*. Edited Bruce A. Ronda. Middletown, Conn.: Wesleyan University Press, 1984.

Perkins, Ephriam. "The Oneida and Troy Revivals." *CE* 4 (1827): 243–265.

Perry, Amos. "Old Days at Harvard 2." *Boston Transcript*, 21 June 1899.

Perry, Bliss. "Emerson's Most Famous Speech." In *The Praise of Folly and Other Papers*. Boston: Houghton Mifflin, 1923.

Poirier, Richard. *The Renewal of Literature: Emersonian Reflections*. New York: Random House, 1987.

———. *Poetry and Pragmatism*. Cambridge: Harvard University Press, 1992.

———. *Trying It Out in America*. New York: Farrar, Straus and Giroux, 1997.

Pommer, Henry F. "The Contents and Basis of Emerson's Belief in Compensation." *PMLA: Publications of the Modern Language Association of America* 77 (1962): 248–253.

Porte, Joel. *Representative Man*. New York: Oxford University Press, 1979.

Quincy, Edmund. *Life of Josiah Quincy*. Boston: Ticknor and Fields, 1868.

Quincy, Josiah. *The History of the Boston Athenaeum with Biographical Notices of Its Deceased Founders*. Cambridge: Metcalf and Co., 1851.

Quincy, Maria Sophia. "The Harvard Commencement of 1829." *Harvard Graduates' Magazine* 26 (1918): 580.

Railton, Stephen. *Authorship and Audience: Literary Performance in the American Renaissance*. Princeton: Princeton University Press, 1991.

Reed, Sampson. "Oration on Genius." In *Emerson the Essayist. An Outline of His Philosophical Development through 1836*, edited by Kenneth Walter Cameron. 2 vols. Hartford: Transcendental Books, 1945.

Review of "A Letter to William E. Channing, D.D. on the Subject of Religious Liberty, by Moses Stuart, Professor of Sacred Literature in the Theological Seminary, Andover." *CE* 10 (1831): 87–128.

Review of Orville Dewey's Oration. *CE* 9 (1830): 218–235.

Reynolds, David S. *Beneath the American Renaissance: The Subversive Imagination in the Age of Emerson and Melville*. New York: Alfred Knopf, 1988.

Richards, Leonard L. *"Gentleman of Property and Standing": Anti-Abolition Mobs in Jacksonian America*. New York: Oxford University Press, 1970.

Richardson, Joan. "Emerson's Sound Effects." *Raritan* 16 (1997): 83–101.

Richardson, Robert D., Jr. *Emerson: The Mind on Fire*. Berkeley: University of California Press, 1995.

Ripley, George. "Degerando on Self-Education and Development." *CE* 9 (1830): 70–107.

———. "Inaugural Discourse, Delivered before the University in Cambridge, Massachusetts, September, 1831, by Charles Follen." *CE* 11 (1832): 373–380.

———. "Martineau's Rationale of Religious Enquiry." *CE* 21 (1836): 226–254.

Roberson, Susan L. *Emerson in His Sermons: A Man-Made Self*. Columbia: University of Missouri Press, 1995.

Roberts, Josephine E. "Elizabeth Peabody and the Temple School." *New England Quarterly* 15 (1942): 497–508.

Robinson, David M. *Apostle of Culture: Emerson as Preacher and Lecturer*. Philadelphia: University of Pennsylvania Press, 1982.

———. "William Ellery Channing." In *The Transcendentalists: A Review of Research and Criticism*, edited by Joel Myerson. New York: MLAA, 1984.

Robinson, David M. "The Road Not Taken: From Edwards, through Chauncy, to Emerson." *Arizona Quarterly* 48 (1992): 45–61.

———. *Emerson and the Conduct of Life: Pragmatism and Ethical Purpose in the Later Work*. Cambridge: Cambridge University Press, 1993.

Rorty, Richard. "Genteel Syntheses, Professional Analyses, Transcendentalist Culture." In *Two Centuries of Philosophy in America*, edited by Peter Caws. Oxford: Basil Blackwell, 1980.

———. "Education without Dogma: Truth, Freedom, and Our Universities." *Dissent* 36 (1989): 198–204.

Rose, Anne C. *Transcendentalism as a Social Movement, 1830–1850*. New Haven: Yale University Press, 1981.

Rudolf, Frederick. *The American College and University: A History*. New York: Alfred Knopf, 1962.

Rusk, Ralph L. *The Life of Ralph Waldo Emerson*. New York: Columbia University Press, 1949.

Ryan, Thomas R. *Orestes A. Brownson, a Definitive Biography*. Huntington, Ind.: Our Sunday Visitor, 1976.

Sanborn, Franklin Benjamin. *The Personality of Emerson*. Boston: Charles E. Goodspeed, 1903.

Sanborn, Franklin Benjamin, and William T Harris. *A. Bronson Alcott: His Life and Philosophy*. 2 vols. Boston: Roberts, 1893.

Schlesinger, Arthur M., Jr. *The Age of Jackson*. Boston: Little, Brown and Co., 1945.

Scott, Donald M. "The Popular Lecture and the Creation of a Public in Mid-Nineteenth Century America." *Journal of American History* 66 (1980): 791–809.

Scudder, Townsend. "Emerson's British Lecture Tour, 1847–1848." *American Literature* 7 (1935): 166–180.

Sealts, Merton M., Jr. *Emerson on the Scholar*. Columbia: University of Missouri Press, 1992.

Sealts, Merton M., Jr., and Alfred R. Ferguson. *Emerson's Nature—Origin, Growth, Meaning*. New York: Dodd, Mead & Co., 1969.

Shklar, Judith N. "Emerson and the Inhibitions of Democracy." *Political Theory* 18 (1990): 601–614.

Simmons, Nancy Craig. "A Calendar of the Letters of Mary Moody Emerson." *Studies in the American Renaissance* 1993: 1–41.

Slater, Joseph. "George Ripley and Thomas Carlyle." *PMLA* 67 (1952): 341–349.

Smith, Henry Nash. "Emerson's Problem of Vocation—A Note on 'The American Scholar.'" *New England Quarterly* 12 (1939): 52–67; reprinted in *Emerson: A Collection of Essays* edited by Milton R. Konvitz and Stephen E. Whicher. Englewood Cliffs, N.J.: Prentice-Hall, 1962.

Spencer, Benjamin T. *The Quest for Nationality: An American Literary Campaign*. Syracuse: Syracuse University Press, 1957.

Spooner, William Jones. *The Prospects of American Literature*. Boston: Oliver Everett, 1822.

Sprague, William B. *Annals of the American Pulpit; or Commemorative Notices of Distinguished American Clergymen of the Various Denominations.* 9 vols. New York: Robert Carter & Brothers, 1857–1869.

Steele, Jeffrey. "Transcendental Friendship: Emerson, Fuller, and Thoreau." In *The Cambridge Guide to Ralph Waldo Emerson,* edited by Joel Porte and Saundra Morris. Cambridge: Cambridge University Press, 1999.

Story, Ronald. *The Forging of an Aristocracy: Harvard and the Boston Upper Class, 1800–1870.* Middletown, Conn.: Wesleyan University Press, 1980.

Story, William W., ed. *The Miscellaneous Writings of Joseph Story.* Boston: Charles C. Little and James Brown, 1852.

Strauch, Carl F. "Emerson's Phi Beta Kappa Poem." *New England Quarterly* 23 (1950): 65–90.

———. "Emerson Rejects Reed and Hails Thoreau." *Harvard Library Bulletin* 16 (1968): 257–273.

Strysick, Michael. "Emerson, Slavery, and the Evolution of the Principle of Self-Reliance." In *The Emerson "Dilemma": Essays on Emerson and Society Reform,* edited by T. Gregory Garvey. Athens: University of Georgia Press, 2001.

Sutherland, Arthur E. *The Law at Harvard: A History of Ideas and Men, 1817–1967.* Cambridge, Mass.: Belknap Press, 1967.

Tarbox, Increase N. *An Address on the Origin, Progress and Present Condition of Philosophy: Delivered before the Hamilton Chapter of the Alpha Delta Society on Its Eleventh Anniversary at Clinton, N.Y.* Utica: R. W. Roberts, 1843.

Thomas, John L. *The Liberator: William Lloyd Garrison.* Little, Brown and Co.: Boston, 1963.

Thoreau, Henry David. *The Correspondence of Henry David Thoreau.* Edited by Walter Harding and Carl Bode. New York: New York University Press, 1958.

Ticknor, George. *Life, Letters, and Journals of George Ticknor.* Edited by George Stillman Hillard and Anna Eliot Ticknor. 2 vols. Boston: James R. Osgood and Company, 1876.

Tillinghast, William Hopkins, ed. *The Orators and Poets of Phi Beta Kappa, Alpha of Massachusetts.* Vol. 42 of *Bibliographical Contributions.* Cambridge: Harvard University Library, 1891.

Tilton, Eleanor. "Emerson's Lecture Schedule—1837–1838—Revised." *Harvard Library Bulletin* 21 (1973): 382–399.

Turner, James. "Secularization and Sacralization: Speculations of Some Religious Origins of the Secular Humanities Curriculum, 1850–1900." In *The Secularization of the Academy,* edited by George M. Marsden and Bradley J. Longfield. New York: Oxford University Press, 1992.

———. *The Liberal Education of Charles Eliot Norton.* Baltimore: Johns Hopkins University Press, 1999.

Tyack, David B., *George Ticknor and the Boston Brahmins.* Cambridge: Harvard University Press, 1967.

Updike, John. "Emersonianism." *New Yorker,* 4 June 1984, 115.

Urbanski, Marie Mitchell Olesen. "The Ambivalence of Ralph Waldo Emerson towards Margaret Fuller." *Thoreau Journal Quarterly* 10 (1978): 26–36.

Verplanck, Gulian C. *The Advantages and the Dangers of the American Scholar. A Discourse Delivered on the Day Preceding the Annual Commencement of Union College, July 26, 1836.* New York: Wiley and Long, 1836.

Von Frank, Albert. *An Emerson Chronology.* New York: G. K. Hall & Co., 1994.

Walker, James. "Review of Dr. Codman's Speech in the Board of Overseers of Harvard College, February 3, 1831." *CE* 10 (1831): 137–160.

Ware, William, ed. *American Unitarian Biography. Memoirs of Individuals Who Have Been Distinguished by Their Writings, Character, and Efforts in the Cause of Liberal Christianity.* 2 vols. Boston: James Munroe and Co., 1850–51.

Wells, Ronald Vale. *Three Christian Transcendentalists.* New York: Columbia University Press, 1943.

Whicher, Stephen E. *Freedom and Fate: An Inner Life of Ralph Waldo Emerson.* Philadelphia: University of Pennsylvania Press, 1953.

Wider, Sarah. "What Did the Minister Mean: Emerson's Sermons and Their Audience." *ESQ: A Journal of the American Renaissance* 34 (1988): 1–21.

Williams, David R. "The Wilderness Rapture of Mary Moody Emerson: One Calvinist Link to Transcendentalism." *Studies in the American Renaissance* 1986: 1–16.

Wilson, R. Jackson. "Emerson as Lecturer: Man Thinking, Man Saying." In *The Cambridge Guide to Ralph Waldo Emerson*, edited by Joel Porte and Saundra Morris. Cambridge: Cambridge University Press, 1999.

Woodall, Guy R. "The Journals of Convers Francis." *Studies in the American Renaissance* 1982: 227–284.

———. "The Record of a Friendship: The Letters of Convers Francis to Frederic Henry Hedge in Bangor and Providence, 1835–1850." *Studies in the American Renaissance* 1991: 1–57.

Wright, Conrad. "The Election of Henry Ware: Two Contemporary Accounts Edited with Commentary." *Harvard Library Bulletin* 17 (1969): 245–278.

———. *The Liberal Christians: Essays on American Unitarian History.* Boston: Beacon Press, 1970.

Yacovone, Donald. *Samuel Joseph May and the Dilemmas of the Liberal Persuasion, 1797–1871.* Philadelphia: Temple University Press, 1991.

INDEX

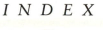

References to Ralph Waldo Emerson and "The American Scholar" in the index have been abbreviated as "RWE" and "AS" respectively.